The Entrepreneur in Focus

The Entrepreneur in Focus

Achieve Your Potential

Bill Bolton and John Thompson

THOMSON

Australia • Canada • Mexico • Singapore • Spain • United Kingdom • United States

The Entrepreneur in Focus – Achieve Your Potential

For more information, contact Thomson Learning, High Holborn House, 50–51 Bedford Row, London, WC1R 4LR or visit us on the World Wide Web at: http://www.thomsonlearning.co.uk

British Library Cataloguing-in-Publication Data
A catalogue record for this book is available from the British Library

ISBN 1-86152-918-X

First edition published 2003 by Thomson Learning

Typeset by Dexter Haven Associates, London

Printed in Great Britain by TJ International, Padstow, Cornwall

Contents

List of figures

Foreword

Dianne Thompson, Chief Executive, Camelot plc

I was very flattered when, on giving a lecture at the University of Huddersfield recently, I was introduced by Professor John Thompson as a good example of a corporate entrepreneur. He was not referring to my very high profile fight against Sir Richard Branson to win the second licence to operate the National Lottery for Camelot. Rather, he was reflecting on the massive changes I have had to put in place since that time to shake up and develop a company that had become battle-scarred, weary and risk averse. It was a company in which creativity and innovation had been stifled by a flawed bid process – and one which suffered a 31 percent attrition rate after the bid had been won.

Being described as a corporate entrepreneur prompted me to think about what makes someone an entrepreneur. We can all think of businessmen and women who we admire, but are they all entrepreneurs? I think not.

I came to the conclusion that, for me, a true entrepreneur is someone who does things that make a significant difference. He or she is invariably creative and innovative, at the heart of change, and always optimistic. Entrepreneurs are determined in face of adversity. They see opportunities and seize them. They are good networkers and for me, perhaps most importantly, they are passionate about what they do.

Entrepreneurs sometimes are not the best educated or the most well trained – they operate by gut instinct.

An entrepreneur is not afraid of change – in fact, they embrace change. 'If it ain't broke, don't fix it' is certainly not a tenet that entrepreneurs subscribe to!

Entrepreneurs come in all shapes and sizes. There are individuals who start with a dream and create vast empires. My erstwhile adversary, Sir Richard Branson, is an excellent example of this at Virgin. I truly admire what he has achieved. Who would have ever believed that a single brand could encompass such a diverse range of products, from a music business and radio station, to an airline, to cosmetics, bridal wear and even a cola drink? – but it has. Anita Roddick at The Body Shop is another great example.

There are corporate entrepreneurs who, like me on a small scale and my great idol, Jack Welch, on a grand scale at General Electric (GE), came into existing businesses and turned them upside down.

Jack had a great vision – he wanted GE to become the most competitive enterprise on earth. He took an already successful business and during a 20-year stint as head of the US's largest company, developed it into a business full of entrepreneurs. GE's market value rose from $13 billion to $550 billion in the process.

Then, there are the social entrepreneurs who really make a difference to society and the environment in which we live. Dame Cicely Saunders, the founder of the Hospice Movement, is a true social entrepreneur, as is the Rev. Andrew Mawson at the Community Action Network. Visit his project in Bow and see what a real difference an entrepreneur can make.

The Entrepreneur in Focus talks about these three groups of entrepreneurs, the general business, the corporate and the social, and looks in great detail at the character sets that make them who they are. Six themes are identified – Focus, Advantage, Creativity, Ego, Team and Social (a handy mnemonic – 'facets'!) – and these are used to paint a full picture of the entrepreneur. As a reader, throughout this book you are encouraged to measure yourself against these facets to assess your own entrepreneurial potential. The book is full of examples of great entrepreneurs, with fascinating looks at both the retail and airline sectors. It is peppered with wonderful quotations, including one of my favourites from Anita Roddick – which, when you realise that I am only 5 foot in height, will make you see why it is so apposite: 'If you think you are too small to have an impact, try going to bed with a mosquito!'

Bill Bolton and John Thompson have written a book which analyses all types of entrepreneurship and the characteristics or facets that make us what we are. The reader is made to think and to evaluate his or her own potential as an entrepreneur.

The book importantly acknowledges that not everyone does have the potential to be an entrepreneur – some of us may just be enterprising – and there is nothing wrong with that! However, by understanding the characteristics of the true entrepreneur, one can recognise them and give them a helping hand because, as the authors say, 'Entrepreneurs are prosperity in the making'.

This is a fascinating and comprehensive study of entrepreneurs. It is an easy read; it makes you think: go on and enjoy it!

About the authors

Dr Bill Bolton is an international consultant in enterprise development and entrepreneurship. He has held a personal UNITWIN (UNESCO) chair in Innovation and Technology Transfer. Dr Bolton was the founding director of the St John's Innovation Centre in Cambridge and taught engineering at Cambridge University. He has more than 25 years' experience in business and industry and is currently a non-executive director of a number of companies. Dr Bolton is a Visiting Professor at the University of Huddersfield.

John Thompson is Roger M Bale Professor of Entrepreneurship at the University of Huddersfield and a Visiting Professor in Finland and New Zealand. Prior to this post he was head of the department of Management at the same university, and he has held management posts in retailing and the steel industry. He has written a number of books and papers on strategy and entrepreneurship, including his textbook *Strategic Management*, which is now in its fourth edition. He has raised money to open a business generator for embryo creative businesses and he advises organisations in the private, public and non-profit sectors.

Bill Bolton and John Thompson's first book together was *Entrepreneurs – Talent, Temperament, Technique*, which was published in 2000. They are currently working on a new project which looks at the entrepreneur and the leader.

The Entrepreneur in Focus **builds upon** *Entrepreneurs – Talent, Temperament, Technique*. This book provided fresh ideas on who entrepreneurs are, what they do and what people say about them. Their new book takes the next step. It is about identifying and releasing entrepreneurial potential. It introduces a unique and original framework for identifying the entrepreneur, based on six key character themes, the 'facets' of the entrepreneur – namely Focus, Advantage, Creativity, Ego,

Team and Social. These facets enable us to understand and explain the entrepreneurs at large in the world, whatever their fields of activity – but most importantly they help us to identify the person with entrepreneurial potential. When you have read this book you will have a much clearer idea if that person could be you. The authors hope that it will give you the confidence to take your first steps towards achieving your potential.

Introduction

The Entrepreneur in Focus – Achieve Your Potential

Welcome to this book. One of the greatest challenges of this generation is to release the entrepreneurial talent in its midst. Identifying, releasing and applying that talent is the theme of this book.

We hope you will see the entrepreneur in a new and clearer light – that you will discover what makes entrepreneurs tick, that you will find out for yourself if you are or could be one. We want you to achieve your potential!

Entrepreneurs do things that make a difference.

They are the people who create economic and social prosperity within societies.

They are the agents of change, who see opportunities and bring them to fruition.

But where are they?

Entrepreneurs do things that make a difference

Entrepreneurs have shed their 'fast-buck' image and are now seen in a more respectable light, as those who bring jobs and create something of value – people like Bill Gates and Richard Branson.

The sad thing is that there are not more of them around.

The message of this book is that they are around but that they have yet to surface – they remain hidden in the woodwork, waiting for their talent to be released.

Entrepreneurs are ordinary people with a particular set of talents and a temperament to match.

In fact, there is something of the entrepreneur in most of us.

This book looks at what it takes to be an entrepreneur – whether alone, in a team, as part of a large company or in the local community.

You are given the opportunity to rate your own entrepreneurial potential.

Even if you find you are not an entrepreneur we hope that at least you will begin to recognise those who are and give them a helping hand.

Entrepreneurs are prosperity in the making

Remember also that we can all be more innovative and more enterprising in most of the things we do.

We hope that this book will help you to release the entrepreneur within – that it will change the way you see the world and those who are trying to make it a better place.

Entrepreneurs are prosperity in the making.

Chapter 1

The Entrepreneur in Focus

Entrepreneurs are all around us. We can see the results of their endeavours but they seldom grab the headlines. In this book we seek to bring the entrepreneur into focus. We want you to be able to recognise the entrepreneur, to spot those with entrepreneurial potential – we want you to consider seriously if you might have what it takes to be an entrepreneur.

Entrepreneurs are at the heart of change in every field of activity. They are the people who spot opportunities and do something about them. They have particular talents which they use to create things that others perceive to be valuable. They make a difference. Sometimes they see things that others can only appreciate with hindsight.

Entrepreneurs are everywhere – in businesses and other organisations, large as well as small. They can be found in communities and countries around the world. Entrepreneurs can be men or women, young or old.

Today's world of uncertainty and change is a world in which the entrepreneur is at home. It is the entrepreneur's natural habitat. What brings anxiety and even fear to some creates opportunity for the entrepreneur.

Their significance and their contribution is increasingly being recognised. Richard Branson is highly visible and much admired around the world – to many people he is an entrepreneurial hero who has started a string of successful businesses. But this image does not describe all entrepreneurs. Jack Welch, recently retired as chief executive of General Electric (GE), is an entrepreneur with a different style and in a different context.

For some people, the word 'entrepreneur' continues to conjure up an image of a hard-nosed deal-maker looking for the fast buck. Television has given us entrepreneurial characters like Arthur Daley, Derek Trotter and J.R. Ewing. Entrepreneurs certainly are advantage-oriented, as we shall see, but this is a distorted image. The truth is that entrepreneurs make a contribution to society far in excess of their number. On job creation alone the figures are impressive.

Even if we are not entrepreneurs who create jobs or transform leading companies, we can always be more creative and innovative – more enterprising – in our actions and activities.

This matters because we live in a world where nothing is predictable or certain any more. Where the big successful companies of today are the sick and dying of tomorrow. Where the time for this to happen is now just three or four years and not thirty or forty.

Entrepreneurs make a difference

The renowned economist Joseph Schumpeter (1883 – 1950) argued that the world is turbulent, and that current balances can be disrupted in unpredictable and sometimes violent ways.

Entrepreneurs trigger innovation, both intentionally and by accident. Sometimes they stumble on something radically new – Schumpeter called this 'alpha innovation'. This in turn has secondary – 'beta' – effects on a wide range of businesses and industries as new entrepreneurial opportunities are opened up. More entrepreneurs are drawn in. Many new businesses are started. Fresh improvements trigger further activity.

Steam engines, petrol engines and microprocessors are examples of alpha innovations. Schumpeter argues that 'heroic entrepreneurs' can bring about a 'gale of creative destruction' which allows some sectors of the economy to grow at the expense of others.

One hundred years earlier, the French economist Jean Baptiste Say (1767–1832) commented that 'the man who conceives or takes charge of an enterprise, sees and exploits opportunity is the motive force for economic change and improvement'.

Both of these economists were saying the same thing – entrepreneurs make a positive difference. But they were also saying that entrepreneurs build the future.

Entrepreneurs build the future

Today more than ever the status quo is not an option, and we need entrepreneurs who can see and exploit opportunities to the benefit of all. In this we include social entrepreneurs as much as economic entrepreneurs – without these people, the quality of the world the economic entrepreneurs help to build would be diminished.

Their three worlds

Entrepreneurs are found broadly in three worlds.

- » general business – new ventures as they start and grow
- » corporate sector – established, often large, organisations
- » the community – including the voluntary sector.

The word 'entrepreneur' was first applied in the general business world. It was derived from the French *'entreprendre'*, meaning to 'undertake or start a venture' – the emphasis being on the start-up and growth of a business.

As the corporate sector recognised its need for constant innovation and renewal, many established businesses found the answer lay in entrepreneurship. The terms 'corporate entrepreneurship' and 'intrapreneurship' were coined to describe this new approach.

Jack Welch, described as 'perhaps the greatest corporate leader of the twentieth century' was 'perhaps the greatest corporate entrepreneur'.

Profile Jack Welch

When Jack Welch took over as CEO of GE in 1981, he commented that he intended to make GE the most competitive company in the world. He would do this by creating a business where people were not afraid to use their initiative and try out new ideas, and where only their own personal abilities and standards would be a ceiling for their endeavours.

More recently, he commented that he always wanted to create a fast, flexible and adaptable small business culture inside a large, established industrial corporation.

Crainer, Business The Jack Welch Way, *2001*

The third 'world' in which we find the entrepreneur is the community, where there is a great dependency on voluntary contributions. This sector includes a wide mixture of charitable projects and businesses with an underlying social purpose. Businesses that serve the community are generally small and they often struggle to keep their head above water. From time to time this pattern is broken and significant enterprises are established. It has only recently been recognised that these were examples of entrepreneurs at work. They are described by the new term 'social entrepreneur' – presumably to distance them from the ordinary entrepreneur, whose motive is perceived to be profit. The term 'social enterprise' has also come into use to describe businesses that are set up to create social as well as financial capital.

Social entrepreneurs have of course been around for many years. Included in this category are people like Dr Barnardo, who founded the orphanages that still bear his name, and William and Catherine Booth, the founders of the Salvation Army, which has become an international organisation working amongst the deprived and disadvantaged in society.

Each of these three worlds present the same kinds of barriers to the emerging entrepreneur. We suggest three questions against which to check the world that you are familiar with.

>> How much does the culture welcome and recognise the entrepreneur?
>> Do rules and regulations discourage and stifle the emergence of the entrepreneur?
>> Are the barriers of funding, facilities and resources insurmountable?

The most common answers to these questions in order is 'It doesn't', 'Yes' and 'Yes'. In short, life is difficult for the entrepreneur. Some would say this is a good thing because it ensures that only the strongest survive. We think this 'macho' approach is naive and fails to recognise the real potential there is out there, if only people had 'half a chance'. We hope this book will help towards providing that 'half chance'.

Mr, Mrs, Ms, Miss Entrepreneur

Entrepreneurs are the people who seek, seize and exploit the opportunities they spot. But they come in all shapes and sizes.

The talents and temperament of the entrepreneur are no respecter of persons.

Entrepreneurs are the driving force that creates entrepreneurial activity and makes the difference, and it doesn't matter where they start from. They may be the sons and daughters of millionaires – J. Arthur Rank, who founded the British film industry, was the son of Joseph Rank, once the wealthiest man in England – or they may be penniless refugees in a foreign country, like the Cuban refugees who transformed the economy of Miami in the 1960s and 1970s.

Motivation and ability are what counts, but they are still only a partial explanation of the person. They certainly don't tell us much about entrepreneurs and what makes them tick. Nor do they help us to identify the person with the talent and the potential to be an entrepreneur.

Most of this book is devoted to the person of the entrepreneur. A new insight is offered, using the idea of the facets of the entrepreneur's character – 'facets' also forms a convenient acronym to identify an entrepreneur's key attributes, or 'character themes' as we prefer to call them.

From this you will be able to look at yourself and make an evaluation of the extent to which you are – or could be – an entrepreneur, a corporate entrepreneur or a social entrepreneur – or, in fact, all of them at different times.

The measuring 'pole'

All large businesses were micro-sized once. They grew and prospered from small beginnings because they got four things right: we can use a measuring 'pole' to check these factors – to explain or assess success and failure.

The four key factors are:

»» P: the person – his or her character, talents and temperament
»» O: the opportunity – its nature and growth potential
»» L: leadership and championing of the opportunity in order to exploit its potential to the full
»» E: exploitation and control – how resources are acquired, deployed, managed and controlled.

This book is about the P factor and how it affects the O, L and E factors. In the right person the other factors flourish.

Profile Philip Green

In 1999 Philip Green was interested in acquiring the then faltering Marks & Spencer (M&S) retail chain. City institutions stood in his way. In the end he switched his target and acquired Bhs, previously known as British Home Stores, investing some £50 million and borrowing some more. The business was then valued at £220 million.

In under two years he had transformed the business and increased its value to £1.2 billion. He had made the fastest ever £1 billion in retailing.

The *Times*, 16 January 2002, commented that entrepreneurs need a gambling streak in their make-up – and Green had exactly that.

The entrepreneurial process

To put the entrepreneur in context, we consider how they do things and how we can help them along.

Entrepreneurs operate within a process of which they are the key element, but they take with them into that process an opportunity that they exploit and turn into something of recognised value as they go along.

They meet many hurdles on the way and have to draw upon their inner entrepreneurial resources to win through. Often they are the believers who strive for their goal when others think they are wasting their time.

The output of the process is a vibrant economy, as entrepreneurs create wealth and provide jobs. In a few places around the world an entrepreneur culture has developed and entrepreneurs have emerged, as if from nowhere.

In this book we consider some of these issues, believing that it is possible for a region to work towards the creation of an entrepreneur culture. Because entrepreneurship is talent-based, we see it as a natural process which will 'just happen' once the conditions are right.

The creation of wealth can have serious downsides, as some people exploit people and situations for their own ends. This is part of human nature, but there is also another side. More entrepreneurs than we might think are driven by a social cause and use their entrepreneurial talents to create social capital. The Social facet to the entrepreneur's character that is responsible for this will be discussed.

●———●

We hope that you will enjoy this book and be challenged by it to think differently about the entrepreneur and to seriously consider whether there is an entrepreneur within you trying to escape – if so, let it out: achieve your potential!

Chapter 2 The Potential Entrepreneur

It could be you! In this chapter we introduce you to eight potential entrepreneurs. They all exist, but their names have been changed. We hope that you will relate to some of these stories – you may have felt the same yourself. If so, then there could be an entrepreneur inside you trying to get out.

The would-be entrepreneurs are:

> » John – the managing director
> » Charles – the technical director
> » Jim – the international consultant
> » Liz – the MBA student
> » Helen – the NHS occupational therapist
> » David – the academic
> » Bob – the delinquent
> » Adam – the gardener.

John worked in the private sector. He was the managing director of a major distributor of electronic and electrical components covering the east of England. He had a good reputation in the industry and had been head-hunted to his present position. John's results had been impressive. He had doubled turnover and profit in two years. Things were going well, and several of his innovative ideas had been copied by his colleagues in the other regions. There was talk that he was next in line for the national job.

Overnight his fortunes changed. His company was bought out by a competitor and John was out of a job. It was a real shock to his system, and John sat around at home for the first week unable to concentrate on anything. He decided he needed a holiday and so took his family off to the west coast of the US for a couple of weeks. As he relaxed, John began to see his predicament in a different light. He sensed the opportunity around him: the childish wonder of Disneyland, the sheer luck of Las Vegas, the skill of those who had built the Hoover Dam and the awesomeness of the Grand Canyon.

There was more to life than working for somebody else. 'Why don't I take my destiny into my own hands?' he thought. 'I'm always full of ideas and I do know how to run a business.' He shared his thoughts with his wife. 'You sound like an entrepreneur, John,' she said.

John wasn't sure he knew what an entrepreneur was, but he thought it would be fun finding out.

'Why don't I take my destiny into my own hands?' he thought

Charles was the technical director of a large multinational responsible for new products. He knew that time was running out on their existing product range but wasn't sure what to do about it. He had tried brain-storming techniques and encouraged his people to think differently, but after the initial enthusiasm life had settled back to normal.

Charles's managing director called an unexpected board meeting one day and tabled an article he had just read: 'In the 1960s it took 20 years to displace the top 35% of the top American companies – now it takes 4 or 5 years'. The MD wanted a response before the end of the day and he meant it. 'If we sit here and do nothing we'll join them,' he said. 'Can I ask who wrote the article?' ventured Charles. 'Some American professor of entrepreneurship,' the MD snapped, but that was the clue Charles needed.

'I'm not sure what an entrepreneur is,' Charles told his fellow directors, when the MD had left the room, 'but let's put the most enterprising, innovative and driven person in each department together and see what happens.' They worked on the idea and put a proposal to the MD. To their surprise he jumped at it, and gave the team three months to come up with something.

Charles had discovered the role that entrepreneurs can play in the big company

The strategy worked, and over the years a new dynamic entered the company. Charles had discovered the role that entrepreneurs can play in the big company – the secret was to release their potential. Create the right conditions and give them their head, that was the trick.

Charles learned that others had made the same discovery and had invented the term intrapreneur to describe entrepreneurs within the large organisation.

Jim was upwardly mobile, jetting all over the world with an international consultancy company. He was their expert in digital systems and knew he could jump into any job he wanted. He had already been approached by IBM and had turned them down. Two things bothered him about his job. He knew it was a young man's profession with a high burn-out rate and that not many people made it to partner – when the time came he would be dispensable.

Jim liked to read management books as he flew around the world. He particularly liked stories of people who had started from scratch and built an empire. Michael Dell, Bill Gates, Jim Clark, Steve Jobs (Jim was an Apple enthusiast), Richard Branson – he'd read them all.

As he sat in the first-class lounge at Singapore Airport sipping champagne, his eyes caught a headline in a newspaper on the coffee table 'Singapore entrepreneurs do it again'. He picked up the paper and read the article – it claimed that there were more entrepreneurs per head of population in Singapore than in Silicon Valley. Some claim, Jim thought, but as he read on he began to realise that Michael Dell et al. were the visible entrepreneurs and that there were many more out there. Singapore, like Silicon Valley, was an environment where entrepreneurs seemed to be everywhere.

There are more entrepreneurs per head in Singapore than in Silicon Valley

On his flight back to the UK, Jim decided to leave his burn-out job as a 24-hour consultant and try his hand at being an entrepreneur. He would read those books again and see what he could learn from them.

Liz was on the final leg of her MBA. She had a first degree in engineering and had worked for a large company in their marketing department. She thought the MBA would equip her for a senior post in another large company. 'Your stepping stone to the future,' as her father had put it.

To her surprise, the MBA had turned her off big business. Multinationals were dull and boring and had none of the excitement of the entrepreneurs she had heard speak on her course. She'd also realised that even the best of jobs could disappear at a moment's notice. Big business comprised one takeover after another.

It was the monthly 'entrepreneur evenings' that had got her thinking this way. These people had really made it happen, she thought, and wondered if she could do it. Liz took all the entrepreneur options that were on offer. She found that she responded to entrepreneur case studies and got excited about them, but the stuff on entrepreneurship and the theory of it all sent her to sleep.

True entrepreneurs just get on with it and leave the theory to others

Concerned about how this might affect her final marks – she always strove for excellence – she spoke to her tutor. 'Maybe it's because you have an entrepreneur inside you trying to get out. True entrepreneurs just get on with it and leave the theory to others,' she was told.

'Why don't you just go for it, when you finish here?' she suggested. 'I think I will,' she replied, thrilled at the idea.

Helen had had a bad morning in her NHS job. Yet another organisational change had been decreed by the management. She was a professional occupational therapist, and had seen managers come and go. It wasn't that she didn't like change – in fact she felt very much at home with it – but not this kind of change for change's sake.

She had had to tell her team about the changes and had found it hard to put over something she didn't believe in or think was necessary. Helen always had plenty of ideas on how to improve things. She had introduced the integrated service that her team now delivered. Care in the hospital and afterwards in the patient's home had become a seamless procedure. These new arrangements worked well. Everybody was pleased with the result – except of course the management, which measured success by the number of discharges from the hospital and not their quality.

It was a throwaway remark by one of her team that got her thinking. The idea of spinning-off their occupational therapy service and operating it as a separate business was not new and it had come up again in the discussion. 'What we need is an entrepreneur who can make it happen,' Sarah had said as she left the room and the meeting broke up.

It was a throwaway remark that got her thinking...

'I wonder if that could be me?' thought Helen.

David rode his bike in to the university's engineering department. He had done this every day for some years but he had never seen a brand-new, red Porsche in one of the staff parking slots before. He wondered whose it was. Academics didn't earn that sort of money.

The answer came during the mid-morning break. The red Porsche was the only topic of conversation in the common room. It belonged to Professor Digby-Smith. David knew that he ran a small company in his spare time and it turned out that this was why the red car had appeared. Digby-Smith's accountants had apparently told him that he had had a very good year, and that if he didn't spend some of the profits the taxman would have them. So out he had gone and bought the car of his dreams.

Most of the academics argued that the whole thing was immoral. 'This university is about research excellence, not about spending your time running businesses and making money for yourself.' 'He uses his research students to do all the work.' 'He's never around because he spends all his time on his business. It was a real problem getting his exam questions off him last year.' Things were not going well for Digby-Smith, until a new staff member who had recently come from the business world asked what all the fuss was about. 'This place is full of ideas going nowhere. We should be pleased that we have an entrepreneur in our midst.'

'We should be pleased that we have an entrepreneur in our midst'

That was when Digby-Smith entered the room and the conversation stopped.

As David pedalled his way home that day he wondered if he might be an entrepreneur. 'Surely if Digby-Smith can do it so can I.'

Bob was out of control. At least that's what his parents thought, and so did the police. The young offenders place hadn't done much for him. He was on his way down a too-familiar path when he was given a new probation officer. This man was different from anybody he had ever met. He was always talking about bettering yourself like they all did, but he kept on about undiscovered talent. His pet phrase was 'There's something you can do better than 10,000 other people' – yes, breaking into cars, Bob thought, but then it dawned that he was talking about talent and not skills. Something you were born with.

'I think you'd make a good salesman,' his probation officer told Bob, and introduced him to a business friend, Joe. They talked things over together and Joe suggested they go to a toy warehouse and buy some small talking-robot toys and sell them in the local market. Bob was not sure, but off they went. The warehouse manager encouraged Bob and offered the goods on sale or return. Bob thought the man obviously didn't know his background. No one had ever trusted him like that before.

Bob set his wares out on the market stall, and he soon had a crowd around him. He was loving it, and within two hours had sold everything. 'You're a natural, Bob,' Joe told him. 'I think you could find that you are an entrepreneur.'

'What's an entrepreneur?' asked Bob.

'What's an entrepreneur?' asked Bob

Adam had an administrative job at the university where he had studied and where he had been president of the Student Union. He enjoyed the fact that it brought him extensive contact with students, but he didn't feel he was being stretched.

In his spare time Adam was a passionate gardener. With his allotments he provided his family with all the vegetables they needed. He also exhibited some of his flowers occasionally. He believed in organic methods, and would talk passionately about this with anyone.

After a lengthy discussion with a wealthy businessman and local landowner about an idea he had, Adam found himself being offered the land to develop his project.

His idea was to use students who were keen to do voluntary work to help him establish an organic garden – with poly-tunnels – to grow flowers and vegetables. Student projects – linked to their degrees – could then support a range of possible activities and developments.

The businessman told Adam he was an entrepreneur-in-waiting

With appropriate supervision, young people who were too disruptive for mainstream schooling might find it an attractive experience. Disabled youngsters could also be brought in to smell and touch the flowers and learn about the project. The produce would be sold, but any surpluses reinvested in the activity.

During one of their discussions, the businessman told Adam that he was an entrepreneur-in-waiting.

Adam had heard the term 'social entrepreneur' and wondered if he might be one of those.

●——————●

Now you have heard these stories we hope that as you read on you will continue to ask yourself – could it be me?

You will meet these potential entrepreneurs again in chapter 6.

Chapter 3

The Proven Entrepreneur

Entrepreneurs are already out there, making the difference.

The general business entrepreneur

In the area of general business three levels of proven entrepreneur can be identified.

- » the growth entrepreneur – who creates a sustained high-growth business
- » the entrepreneur – who creates a significant business
- » the enterprising person – who creates a small or micro-business.

The relation between these three levels is set out in the triangle below.

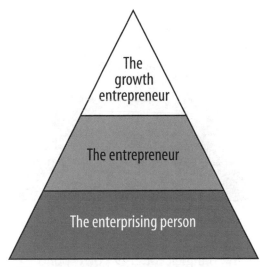

The
growth
entrepreneur

The entrepreneur

The enterprising person

The general business entrepreneur

We have chosen a triangle to indicate that there are more enterprising people than there are entrepreneurs, and more entrepreneurs than growth entrepreneurs.

As people discover their talents and develop them they move up the triangle. Unless the entrepreneur also possesses important leadership talents, it is unlikely he or she can continue to run successful growth businesses as they inevitably become more formalised. The link between the entrepreneur and the leader is taken up in chapter 14.

We most commonly associate entrepreneurs with the general business sector but as has been said in chapter 1, they are also found in the corporate sector and in the community and voluntary sector.

The corporate entrepreneur

The proven entrepreneur in the corporate sector operates at similar levels to the general business entrepreneur. The corresponding triangle is shown below.

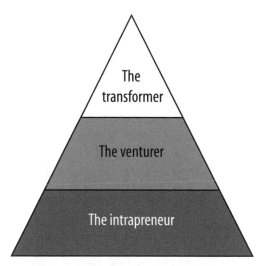

The corporate entrepreneur

The levels in both triangles roughly correspond, so that the intrapreneur is the enterprising person in the big company. The venturer is the equivalent of the entrepreneur and the transformer is the growth entrepreneur of the corporate sector.

These three levels of proven entrepreneur will now be looked at, first in the general business sector and then in the corporate sector.

The chapter concludes with some comments on the social entrepreneur, who operates in the community and voluntary sector.

As you read these examples think of people that you know and see if you are able to identify the level they are operating at and whether they might be able to progress further up the triangle.

In later chapters, the various character themes that define the entrepreneur, what we call the facets of the entrepreneur, are examined. Some entrepreneurs possess more of the themes than others. In addition, the relative strength of a particular theme varies from individual to individual. We will see that as we move from the enterprising person to the entrepreneur to the growth entrepreneur, and from the intrapreneur to the venturer to the transformer, the number and strength of the character themes increases.

The general business sector

Enterprising people

We prefer to call people who run small and micro-businesses 'enterprising people' rather than entrepreneurs. Micro-businesses would typically employ five people at the most. Small businesses are the next stage up.

In terms of sheer numbers such businesses represent the majority in every economy. A figure in excess of 90 percent would not be unusual. In advanced economies this group, whilst essential, is not packed with entrepreneurs, although we sometimes use the term to describe them. They are not strictly entrepreneurs because their small businesses are not different in any material way – they are like lots of other similar small businesses. They have little potential to grow beyond a handful of employees and a largely local market, simply because they are not significantly different.

But they remain vitally important, and, in reality, the majority of us could start and run a micro-business. We might not become rich as a result, and our survival and success would depend upon our ability to find and retain customers and to control the business.

The borderline between the enterprising person and the entrepreneur is not clear-cut. Some enterprising people possess a particular entrepreneurial trait that makes them stand out. Others see this one feature and conclude they have met an entrepreneur.

People like Roy spot opportunity after opportunity and start a string of different micro-businesses. This strong entrepreneurial trait of being an habitual opportunity spotter does not alone make Roy an entrepreneur – he remains an enterprising person.

Other borderline people who are difficult to classify are those who operate in a harsh business environment. People who successfully grow small businesses in third-world economies have to be more than just enterprising. In many cases it is only the entrepreneurs who have any real chance of survival.

We visited the Central African Republic in the late 1990s, shortly after a revolution. The blue berets of the UN were being worn by the soldiers at the roadblocks. Much of the infrastructure of the country had been destroyed. In this difficult climate we found a remarkable entrepreneur. His first business had been signwriting. He then added to that carpentry and made the sign boards. His third business was in metal work and welding as the sign boards became larger.

We asked him how he had coped with all the problems the country was having. He gave the typical entrepreneur's answer: that he liked challenges and thrived on turning problems into opportunities. He clearly took revolutions in his stride.

Of course, when the enterprising person sets out, he or she has no idea whether they might turn out to be true entrepreneurs. The stories of three people follow, all farmers' wives, who set off on the same journey to find new forms of income as their farm income declined.

Ann thought she could earn some extra money if she sold cut flowers from her garden. She began selling in a lay-by close to the M1 motorway. Initially she sat on a chair with a garden umbrella for shade and shelter.

She cut her flowers fresh every day for part of the summer. The following year her husband grew more flowers and made sure that she had ones that bloomed at different times. Potatoes and then other fresh vegetables were added to the product list. All were home-grown. Ann next graduated to a proper wooden stall, which she took home every night in a van. Now she has a lockable, green container permanently situated in the lay-by. The business has developed but it still employs just one person.

Ann was certainly an enterprising person but probably not an entrepreneur.

Joan, from Sussex, saw an opportunity unrelated to her farming background. She has developed a major IT estate agency. Her husband travels around properties when he is not active on the farm, photographing them with a digital camera and putting up the ubiquitous 'For Sale' boards; Joan masterminds the IT side of the business. Because the business has been able to secure a number of properties in the high-price south east and London areas, the business is lucrative.

Joan's business has potential and is something that could probably be franchised. Maybe she will make the transition from enterprising person to entrepreneur.

Sally Robinson is someone who is already making that transition. Ample Bosom, is an online company which sells bras for the fuller figure from a farm in North Yorkshire. Sally was able to secure a £7500 diversification grant, and she had access to a disused farm building. Her Internet site was getting some 15,000 hits a week by the year 2000, from buyers as far away as Singapore and New Zealand. The aim of the business is to supply a wide range of styles in less common sizes, not readily available in high-street shops but using products supplied by leading manufacturers.

Entrepreneurs

We now move up the triangle to consider the entrepreneur – the company founder who establishes a viable recognised business. These are successful medium-sized enterprises which have grown to a good size without having joined the corporate league.

The entrepreneur behind Flying Flowers saw the opportunity of delivering flowers to the end customer by post. The company was set up in Jersey in the Channel Islands in the early 1980s around a struggling glasshouse business. By 1996 turnover had grown to £35 million, with pre-tax profits of £4 million.

Success was based on specific strategies adopted by the entrepreneur. Firstly, the company holds only low stocks of the actual flowers, many of which it buys in cheaply from countries such as Colombia. (Flowers from Jersey does not have to mean flowers grown in Jersey!) Demand fluctuates markedly, peaking twice, at Christmas and Mother's Day, when the company typically receives 15,000 postal and 5000 telephone orders per day for a short period. Therefore, and secondly, Flying Flowers makes careful and extensive use of casual hotel and restaurant staff, who are relatively plentiful on an island of scarce labour resources, and who conveniently are often laid off temporarily over Christmas and Mother's Day when tourism declines.

Thirdly, the company employs a disused glasshouse to house a noisy, steam-breathing machine which produces polystyrene boxes every working day of the year. These are then piled high to ensure that any demand peak can be catered for. Fourthly, and very critically, Flying Flowers has invested in IT to support both control and marketing. It holds a one-million-person database and carefully targets its direct mail, analysing all responses and orders in detail. It has opened a telephone call centre in Witham, Essex.

The skills and competencies developed in Flying Flowers have been further exploited with the acquisition of other businesses. Later in the 1990s, Flying Flowers bought Gardening Direct (mail-order bedding plants), Stanley Gibbons (publisher and stamp supplier) and another supplier of first-day stamp covers.

Continued growth into a large corporation would require further diversification, with its inherent risks. Sometimes such risks are taken; sometimes they are not.

We believe that these risks are often not taken for at least three reasons.

1. Some entrepreneurs hold back the growth of their businesses by choice. They know that they could grow a sizeable business but they see their business as a means of providing them with a particular lifestyle. Actually owning and running their own show is important for them because they crave independence, but beyond that it is lifestyle that matters. They fear that higher growth implies more time pressure, more strain on the family and greater risks.

   There can of course be a downside to this approach, as many lifestyle family businesses have found out. Excessive drawings and underinvestment in a business can make it vulnerable. It can also seriously undermine the value of the business so that the founders will not have the retirement nest egg they thought they had.

Profile Alan and Steve

Alan and Steve were made redundant from the same printing company. This prompted them to start their own printing business, specialising in packaging. They invested their savings and borrowed more money. After a few years hard work the business was successful. The founders began to increase their drawings to each buy a much bigger house – and their families ran expensive, new cars through the business. Each year they took longer and longer holidays.

Investment in the business all but stopped. Employees began to wonder what would happen when the founding partners retired.

2. Other entrepreneurs are happy for their business to grow, but only to a level at which they can retain control. At the outset the entrepreneur makes all the key decisions. Their ability to do this becomes stretched as the business grows and more and more decisions have to be made. If they are reluctant or unwilling to employ other managers and delegate real responsibility to them, then growth may be held below the potential that is there. Again the business can become vulnerable as a consequence.

Roy, Ann, Joan, Sally, Alan, Steve, Nigel and Arthur are all real people. The stories we have told about them are also real. For obvious reasons we have changed some of their names.

3. Some entrepreneurs do not progress to become high-growth entrepreneurs because they simply do not have the ability to do so.

They may be very good at the start-up and early stages of the business but lose interest when consolidation is required as a prelude to further growth. It is at this stage that they need some of the attributes of the leader such as strategic thinking and the ability to envision others.

Growth entrepreneurs

These people are at the top of the entrepreneur triangle – they are the star performers that we all recognise. This book features numerous stories of successful entrepreneurs and sustainable high-growth businesses – chapter 15, for example, explores a number of them, including Richard Branson, Alan Sugar and Ken Morrison. Branson continues to head Virgin, which has exploited its highly visible brand to diversify into a wide range of activities. Sugar is still firmly in charge of Amstrad, the consumer electronics company he founded in 1968. Morrison is 70 years old and a billionaire – and still running his supermarket empire.

They are able to do this because they possess leadership talents to complement their entrepreneur character themes. They are leader entrepreneurs.

Where the successful entrepreneur does not possess leader qualities, or does not wish to act as the strategic leader of a large corporation, he or she will often make a timely exit and move on to a fresh challenge.

Profile Jim Clark

Jim Clark is unique in having created three separate and distinctive billion-dollar corporations, leaving each one after it had become successful. Clark is a Texan from a relatively poor background and a curtailed high-school education. He obtained a PhD and became an academic before starting Silicon Graphics, which gave us 3D imaging for CAD and CAM systems. His next business was Netscape, the first Internet browser. Finally came Healtheon, software for streamlining administration in the US healthcare system.

Jeff Bezos is a highly successful growth entrepreneur who has been able to 'change the rules of competition' in an industry.

Amazon.com, the 'Earth's largest bookstore', pioneered book-selling via the Internet, and in the process changed consumer buying habits and forced the existing major booksellers to react and also offer Internet sales and postal deliveries. Paradoxically, this has happened in an environment where – and in parallel – 'good bookstores have become the community centres of the late twentieth century' by providing comfortable seats, staying open late and incorporating good coffee bars.

Amazon.com was founded in 1994 by Bezos, the son of a Cuban immigrant. He had once dreamt of being an astronaut. As a consequence he went on to graduate in electrical engineering and computer science from Princeton. But after Princeton he became a successful investment banker on Wall Street. Intrigued by the speed of growth of the Internet in the early 1990s, he decided to 'seize the moment'. He had experienced his trigger and he left the bank with the straightforward intention of starting an e-commerce business.

At this stage he had no specific product or service in mind, and so he began by drawing up a list of possible activities. He narrowed down his first list of 20 to two – music and books – before choosing books. In both cases, the range of titles available was far in excess of the number any physical store could realistically stock.

The secret of Bezos's success lay in his ability to establish an effective supply chain. Warehouses are strategically located and Amazon makes sure it can deliver either from stock or from publishers within days of receiving an order electronically. Music, computer games, toys and pharmaceuticals are just some of the products Amazon now supplies as well as books. In addition, Bezos has formed alliances with numerous other businesses which could sell books as an adjunct to their own goods – for a sales-revenue percentage their sites are hyperlinked to the Amazon site.

Amazon.com continues to grow, and to be able to do this has received extensive funding. The business has yet to declare an annual profit, but recorded its first quarterly profit at the end of 2001.

This section concludes by looking at those who at first sight appear to be growth entrepreneurs, but that history proves are not. They are people who clearly possess entrepreneur character themes, but who are perhaps entrepreneurs without leadership talents, or entrepreneurs who try to grow too quickly, or entrepreneurs who fail to put in place the necessary control systems.

For a short period the 'world of dot.com businesses' was full of stories of entrepreneurs who have been successful in raising substantial funding but have failed to build successful businesses. Sometimes they failed to build a robust organisation; sometimes they failed to generate sufficient demand. As a result the businesses have gone bust and the investors have lost their money. Bezos has been able to keep Amazon.com going and growing but, as was said earlier, he has yet to declare a full year's profits.

We all like to identify the growth entrepreneur and 'Entrepreneur of the Year' awards are testimony to this, but in reality the only way to identify high-growth entrepreneurs is to see how they perform over the long haul. When people have been successful at the entrepreneur level there is always pressure from investors – and often their own ego – to try and cross a 'bridge too far'. The complexities of running and growing a large organisation can be beyond the entrepreneur or simply be something he or she is just not interested in.

Below are two stories of entrepreneurs which time has shown were not growth entrepreneurs though once they appeared to be.

The first Pierre Victoire restaurant was opened in Edinburgh in 1988 by French chef, Pierre Levicky. It was his first new venture. Within eight years he would own 18 restaurants and another 83 franchised outlets.

His successful idea was based on quality French food and wine at reasonable prices with a simple decor (originally this was by necessity) of whitewashed walls, wooden floors and sometimes second-hand furniture. Levicky produced a cookbook of 500 recipes to guide the other chefs in the chain.

"I didn't envisage this success. It has happened because it is a charming concept" – Levicky

In the early days Levicky was very hands on, doing most of the cooking himself. When he opened a second restaurant he did not worry himself with management controls. He was soon in debt, but his bank helped him to set up the necessary structure and controls. On a firmer financial footing, he set up two new restaurant concepts, one a vegetarian restaurant, and grew rapidly through franchising. With hindsight, his selection of franchisees was inadequately robust. 'Some business experience and acumen' mattered more than direct experience in the restaurant business. Levicky helped the franchisees recruit continental chefs, and in a number of cases this resulted in personality conflicts.

The corporate team initially comprised loyal employees. Levicky promoted from within, although later he did recruit external specialists. It was 1996 before the chain benefited from a centralised information system. In that year there was a planned flotation, but it never happened, and 10 percent of the business was sold to an investment trust. Undercapitalised, Pierre Victoire went into voluntary receivership in 1998 with undisclosed debts.

As the early novelty of Levicky's French restaurants had worn off and he had failed to develop the concept as competition had grown, and as quality across the chain was inconsistent because of the variations in skills and experience, there wasn't a business to rescue.

Freddie Laker was the creator of Skytrain, an early low-price, no-frills transatlantic airline which flew from Stansted to Newark – outer London to the outskirts of New York. At that time the connections to Stansted from central London were relatively undeveloped. Passengers queued to buy tickets – there was no advance booking – and they had to take their own sandwiches on board. But the prices were very low and early demand soon outstripped the number of seats available. Laker became tempted to expand his fleet, even though he had once said 'If we get any bigger than 6 planes you can kick my arse'. In 1979 he ordered 15 new aircraft, a mixture of McDonnell Douglas DC10s and Airbuses.

Two events conspired to bring the business down. Laker had no distinct competitive advantage other than his low prices. When British Airways (BA) and Pan American lowered theirs and maintained their higher level of service, Laker suddenly looked relatively unattractive and uncompetitive. Losing revenue, he sold his Airbuses. Then, after a fatal crash – nothing to do with Laker himself – all DC10s around the world were grounded temporarily. With huge loans and unable to fly his planes, Laker was unable to service his debts.

The corporate sector

The intrapreneur

We now consider the corporate entrepreneur, starting with the intrapreneur – the first level on the corporate entrepreneur triangle.

Intrapreneurs are the innovators behind:

»» new products
»» new services
»» new processes
»» new market opportunities
»» new distribution channels and opportunities.

They are the champions of change inside larger organisations. Their success lies partly in their entrepreneurial talent and potential and partly in the culture of the organisation in which they work.

»» **The Minnesota Mining and Manufacturing Company, better known as 3M,** based in St Paul, Minnesota, has developed a leading reputation for being innovative and creative. The story of 3M's Post-It Notes is really the stuff of legends. The internal entrepreneur in this case was an employee called Arthur Fry, who had become annoyed that pieces of paper he placed inside his church hymn book as markers kept falling out when he was singing. Fry was a 3M chemical engineer who knew about an invention by a scientist colleague called Spencer Silver. Silver had developed a new glue which possessed only a very low sticking power, and for this reason was perceived as a failure! Fry saw the new glue as the answer to his problem – when he applied it to his paper markers they stayed put, but they were easily removed. Realising that many others also shared the same problem, Fry sought approval to com-mercialise his idea – but initially he was met with scepticism. The idea took hold when he passed samples around to secretaries within 3M and other organisations. The rest, as they say, is history!

Over the years 3M has developed more than 60,000 new products, including masking tape and everything that bears the Scotch brand name, including sellotape and video cassettes. The company also manufactures heart-lung machines. Employees are actively encouraged to work on developing new ideas and products. They can legitimately spend 15 percent of their working time on new projects that they initiate, and they can apply for internal company development grants of up to $50,000. When ideas are taken forward they also have the option of championing the new business in its later development stages. There is an understood tolerance of both opt-out and failure, but employee bonuses depend on new product development. A supportive management accounting system is used to advise on the cost implications of bringing new ideas to market, assessing the impact on existing businesses and establishing realistic targets and milestones. This enables effective prioritisation.

This is one organisation that has long realised the entrepreneurial potential that many employees have and has created an environment in which it can flourish. Sometimes the talent is released with a completely different trigger – the following story only serves to highlight how it can be a mistake to ignore the latent entrepreneur-ship in many employees.

After it was announced that Dutch fashion retailer C&A was in trouble and would close all its branches in the UK in 2000, individual store managers no longer had to follow stock, display and staffing instructions from their head office. They were given the freedom to choose the goods they felt would best meet the needs of local customers. The freedom also extended to the numbers of people they employed and the hours they worked. In most stores both sales and profits increased.

Although it would be easy to argue that once-loyal customers were taking advantage whilst the stores were still open, this might just be an example of empowered management succeeding. Local managers were being allowed to act as internal entrepreneurs – intrapreneurs. They were improving existing practices – there was no 'blue sky' invention involved. But most things can be improved if we ask the right questions and tease out fresh opportunities.

The venturer

The venturer is the next level up from the intrapreneur. These are the people who spin off businesses from existing ones. There are two types.

In the first case, entrepreneurs leave an established business to start a completely new one. There is some transfer of intellectual capital because of the personal learning experiences involved, but the original business has little, if any, involvement in the new one.

The story of Silicon Valley features numerous examples of people who have left growing companies to start up their own entrepreneurial business. Perhaps the most famous example is Intel, which began when a number of employees left Fairchild Semiconductor. Intel was, in fact, one of several spin-offs from Fairchild.

In the second case, venturers seize an opportunity when companies either develop new ideas which, for whatever reason, do not fit into their existing portfolio but still have growth potential, or they conclude that certain businesses they own no longer fit their existing strategic portfolio and would be better divested.

Sometimes the large companies participate by retaining a financial stake in the venture or encouraging the relevant managers to buy out the business they wish to divest – forms of corporate venturing in which all parties should benefit.

University spin-offs or campus companies, as some call them, are a variant of this second case. The venturers use ideas from university research and turn them into businesses, with the university often retaining a stake in the business. Although a university may not be part of the corporate sector it is similar in being a large organisation in which the activities of entrepreneurs are not seen as mainstream. The university venturer has to overcome institutional barriers just as the corporate venturer does.

Profile **Premier Brands**

Premier Brands was formed in 1986 as a result of a management buy-out from Cadbury's. Cadbury's drinking chocolate, biscuits, Smash instant mashed potato, Marvel and Coffee Complement, Chivers and Hartley's products and Typhoo tea were the main brands involved. Cadbury's had decided to focus on its main chocolate products and, through its merger with Schweppes, soft drinks.

The new chief executive of Premier Brands was Paul Judge. Within a few years the spin-off company was floated on the Stock Exchange. Judge, who was now a rich man, opted to retire. He funded the Judge Institute of Management at Cambridge University with some of his newly acquired wealth.

Profile **Filtronic**

In contrast, Filtronic is an entrepreneurial business which has been spun off by a venturer from university research.

David Rhodes, at the time a lecturer at the University of Leeds and aged in his thirties, established Filtronic as a campus spin-off company in 1977. Rhodes had a research background in microwave engineering and he had worked at universities in both the US and the UK. His intention was to develop a series of electronic and mechanical devices for separating and processing microwaves and which had a commercial potential. In the early days Filtronic secured a contract from the US military to develop products which would jam enemy radar. The company also worked on the stealth bomber project. Filtronic's products could identify aircraft by their radar signatures and communicate with space probes. Real growth, however, came in the late 1980s and early 1990s when Rhodes was able to capitalise on the fast-growing market for mobile phones. Filtronic could supply products which separate signals to and from mobile phones, increasingly useful as the radio-wave space available to the various system providers becomes ever more congested.

By the end of the 1990s, Filtronic employed 2500 people in the UK, US and Australia. Annual sales exceeded £220 million, with 20 percent of the revenues being generated in the UK and 50 percent in the US. Rhodes remained as chairman and chief executive of the company he had started, retaining a 10 percent shareholding in the business. To this day he still lectures part-time for the University of Leeds; students on an MSc programme in Microwave Engineering have several of their lectures at Filtronic, whose headquarters are just a few miles away.

Transformers

Transformers are at the top of the corporate entrepreneur's triangle. As was the case with growth entrepreneurs in the general business environment, we again see a need for the person to possess a number of key leadership characteristics. This time we might describe the person concerned as an entrepreneurial leader.

Three types of transformer can be distinguished.

The first type is the person who rises through the ranks, becomes head of the corporate empire and then transforms it. Such people are rare because the corporate structure does not generally allow them to get to the top. In the process they often leave the corporate sector and found their own businesses.

To succeed in the corporate world the transformer needs more than exceptional entrepreneurial talents. He or she has to be politically sensitive and know how to climb up the hierarchy. Jack Welch of GE possessed all these attributes and was an outstanding transformer. He made an already successful business even more successful, but it was a 20-year journey. Welch is quoted throughout this book, and his story is told in chapter 15.

The second type is the strategic transformer, who turns around companies in difficulty. It is frequently the case that these transformers are recruited specially to replace a strategic leader who is seen, at least in part, to be responsible for the declining fortunes. It is possible for turnaround transformers to be recruited from within an organisation, but the actions they need to take will always be more difficult for an insider.

They typically start by refocusing a business around a core of key activities, equivalent to the 'company doctor' role. But they go further – they take the entrepreneurial step. Having rationalised the business, often with fewer employees, they find new opportunities, new means of adding value for customers, new ways to leverage the resources of the business. [see PROFILE, KIM WINSER, opposite]

The third type of corporate transformer is the entrepreneur who succeeds in 'rewriting the rules of competition' in an industry, as Jeff Bezos was able to do with Amazon.com. Rival organisations are forced to take note and to respond. It remains the case that these entrepreneurs are more likely to be found breaking into an industry with a new venture. Such was the case with Herb Kelleher and

Southwest Air, and Sam Walton and Wal-Mart, stories told in chapters 19 and 20. However, Ted Turner inherited a $1 million media business from his late father. He expanded and diversified, introducing CNN, the 24-hour Cable News Network, which clearly transformed television news presenting. Turner was a corporate transformer.

Again drawing parallels with the general business sector, there are corporate transformers who succeed at first but then make strategic errors. Their controls are inadequate or their speed of growth outstrips the resources they have available and can acquire.

George Davies and his time at Next is the story of a corporate transformation that stalled, but his subsequent successes illustrate an entrepreneur who has created two significant businesses.

Employed by the long-established menswear retailer J Hepworth, Davies was promoted to be the strategic leader and he successfully transformed a dowdy chain into the high-street giant, Next, in the 1980s. Buoyed by rapid growth and success, more and more outlets were opened in towns and cities up and down the country. New brands and lines were added, sometimes with the acquisition of other existing chains. Jewellery, luggage and leather goods were added to men's and women's fashion. Later Next would start its own direct mail catalogue and acquire Grattan plc, a leading multi-product direct mail business.

Davies was innovative, but he had not developed a strong enough organisation. Direct mail and high-street retailing demanded different competencies and capabilities. Later in the 1980s, inflation meant shop rents and rates increased dramatically. Next's finances were stretched, and Davies left to make way for a successor with a strong financial background. The business was saved but Davies had had to move on.

A serial entrepreneur, Davies went on to develop the very successful George clothing range for Asda, now part of Wal-Mart. More recently he has designed the Per Una range for M&S. Davies designs the clothes, commissions and monitors their manufacture and controls the in-store merchandising. The initiative is a joint venture; he is not an employee of M&S.

We have considered the different levels of entrepreneur to be found in the general business and corporate sectors. This chapter on the proven entrepreneur concludes by giving examples of social entrepreneurs.

Social entrepreneurs

Whilst many businesses donate both cash and employee time to social and environmental projects, social entrepreneurship is truly present in the organisation when the mission and strategies embrace social and environmental causes.

We describe examples which correspond in some ways to the three levels of entrepreneur that we identified for the general business sector and the corporate sector:

>>> A local community entrepreneur who started a unique initiative which would be hard to replicate.

>>> A community entrepreneur who grew a more substantial organisation which has received national recognition and which could be copied with the right team of people.

>>> A pioneer social entrepreneur who founded a major organisation and a business entrepreneur who found she was also a social entrepreneur.

The Get Sorted Academy of Music in Rotherham, South Yorkshire, makes an important social contribution on a small, local scale. Its founder, Genya Johnson, was a full-time special needs teacher whose Russian father had moved to England after the Second World War and opened a chain of small shops. She inherited his entrepreneurial talent, but chose to use it for helping others in her spare time.

Originally called the Get Sorted Crew, the academy occupies the upper floors of what was a motorcycle shop and it began by providing soundproof rehearsal rooms for teenage bands. This was initially supplemented by access to recording facilities, the organising of gigs for the bands in order to raise funds and a management agency for those bands good enough to secure independent bookings. Johnson first appreciated the gap and the opportunity when she was recruited by the local police force to help with a drugs awareness campaign. She listened to what the youngsters said when asked what they needed. She helped the first band by allowing them to practise in her own home, before setting out to find appropriate premises.

Initially she had to rely more on free handouts (such as spare tins of paint) and volunteers' time than on any financial assistance. She herself took no reward for her part-time commitment, which amounted to every evening and weekends, and in fact she bought things, such as a small van, out of her own savings. Over 100 bands and 500 young people, from a range of social backgrounds, some from several miles away, were soon making use of the facilities, for which they have always had to pay just a token rental. Friends of the musicians use the centre and help with promotional material, and all the renovation work has been completed by those engaged in the venture.

Johnson is now committed full-time at Get Sorted, which has expanded into one-to-one special needs teaching and guitar, keyboard, singing and music composition classes. There are eight other full-time helpers, funded by a variety of grants. In one important respect, Get Sorted is a social centre which keeps young people off the streets and often out of trouble. Whilst it would be easy to make a case for a similar initiative in many more towns and cities, it would be much less easy to find a plethora of Genya Johnsons willing to devote the time and energy such ventures require.

The Castleford Community Learning Centre in West Yorkshire provides an excellent example of a need drawing in a social entrepreneur. Margaret Handforth, miner's wife, ex-secretary and mother of three sons, had demonstrated her latent talent by founding a local playgroup but had never thought of herself as an entrepreneur before the 1984 miners' strike. Forming a small group, she set up a soup kitchen to help people survive the traumas of the time. Invited to speak to students at local universities in exchange for a collection, the women set foot on university campuses for the first time in their lives. They began to realise that education can broaden horizons, and Handforth had a vision of a better life through self-improvement. She had 'no idea how to do it, just a determination to start something off'. Although the venture has grown remarkably, most of the founding team have no current involvement. Margaret has recruited a new team to help her.

Originally called the Castleford Women's Centre, the venture started gradually in humble premises that the team were able to restore with the help of a small grant. Support and counselling was supplemented with tea dances and craft classes, 'really anything that would bring people in'. Additional contacts led to additional grants, and the venture took off. It was really growth out of necessity – the need had found the right person to fill the gap. Known locally as the University of Life, the Women's Centre has moved into new premises with a new name. A wide raft of courses up to degree level, validated by local colleges and universities, is now available, usually at low or no cost to women in this economically deprived area. It has succeeded because it has always been flexible, opportunistic and close to its customers. A serial entrepreneur, Margaret next began to plan for the development of a residential college in a nearby old mansion and a leisure and diving centre on the site of a flooded quarry.

Michael Young, more formally Lord Young of Dartington, was a remarkable social entrepreneur. His obituary in the *Times* said that he 'recognised unmet needs and, with tireless energy and unflagging imagination, demonstrated an extraordinary ability to turn ideas into action'.

Young founded more than 30 social and community ventures mostly concerned with education, health and consumer affairs. One of these was the School for Social Entrepreneurs he set up in 1997. Better known is the Consumer's Association and its magazine, *Which*, that he founded in 1957.

The Open University (OU) was perhaps his greatest achievement. He started the National Extension College in 1962, the first open learning institution in Britain, as a pilot project for the OU that he founded six years later. Since then it has provided higher education to more than two million students in the UK, Europe and across the world. It currently has over 200,000 students enrolled on its courses.

Michael Young was clearly a remarkable social entrepreneur. Now follows the example of Anita Roddick, who, after starting as a business entrepreneur, moved increasingly to the position of a social entrepreneur.

The Body Shop was started in England in 1976 by Anita Roddick and her husband Gordon, who used their savings of £12,000 to open the first shop, partially to help provide an income for Anita and her two daughters. Stores have subsequently been opened in over 40 countries, and The Body Shop was floated on the UK Stock Exchange in 1984. Well-renowned for its environmental and ethical stance and strategies, The Body Shop has made an impact around the world.

Anita's motivation for starting her business was always influenced by her personal commitment to the environment and to education and social change. In her case, her talent for business was channelled into a cause. The business and its financial success have been a vehicle to achieve other, more important, objectives. The Body Shop's declared 'Reason for Being' 'dedicated the business to the pursuit of social and environmental change'.

Roddick was concerned to do something which was 'economically sustainable, meeting the needs of the present without compromising the future'. Her ideas were the outcome of her world travels. She had visited many third-world countries, 'living native', and had seen how women used natural products efficaciously and effectively. From these observations and experiences she conceptualised – and realised – her opportunity. She would use natural products from around the world to produce a range of new products. People in third-world villages were asked to supply her with the natural ingredients she needed – a form of 'trade not aid'.

The business grew rapidly as stores were franchised. The Body Shop opened a new market segment and naturally attracted

"If you think you are too small to have an impact, try going to bed with a mosquito"
– Anita Roddick

competition. As a consequence, the growth in revenue and profits has not been consistent and sustainable but the commitment to the environment has never been compromised in favour of profits. Initially, The Body Shop manufactured many of its own products but more recently it has opted to outsource them. Employees are given time off, and franchisees encouraged to take time off, during working hours, to do voluntary work for the community.

The Body Shop is an idiosyncratic and unusual business; Roddick is an entrepreneur who has made a very individual contribution. She has shown how financial and social capital can be created in harmony – at the same time helping, rather than destroying, the environment, or having no impact on it. It has not been easy and has required courage in the face of criticism, hostility and setback.

Chapter 4 Conventional Wisdom

A conventional wisdom has built up around the entrepreneur. In this chapter we challenge some of that wisdom. Although not wholly wrong it is often based on a narrow view of what an entrepreneur is and on assumptions which are not quite right.

In our view it would be unusual, but not inaccurate, to describe Mozart as an entrepreneur. In his own way, and in the context of the world in which he lived – his environment – Mozart did things entrepreneurs do. He created and innovated. He made things happen. He made a difference to the world and to other people's lives. He continues to do so. He left his 'footprints' on the world. Something which successful entrepreneurs always do.

Carry on and ask about where entrepreneurs and entrepreneurship is most likely to be found in the world. Silicon Valley should feature – after all, Silicon Valley creates more millionaires per square mile or per day than anywhere else on the globe. And yet there is just as much entrepreneurship – albeit of a radically different kind – in the world's poorest countries.

Unfortunately we often fail to appreciate the extent and the value of the entrepreneurship that is around us, because we fail to appreciate the true meaning of the word. And this is a lost opportunity – because, as we have said already, we need more entrepreneurs and entrepreneurship to deal with the unpredictability and the rapid speed of change in our world.

>» we must challenge the conventional wisdom that conditions our thinking
>» we must realise that we do live in a world full of entrepreneurs and potential entrepreneurs
>» we must learn to recognise and value the entrepreneurs who can drive improvements and bring new benefits.

So: what does conventional wisdom say about the entrepreneur and why is it so often wrong? Conventional wisdom tells us that:

>>> age, family background, education and experience are deciding factors
>>> anyone can be an entrepreneur
>>> entrepreneurs are only found in the world of business
>>> inventors are entrepreneurs
>>> entrepreneurs are individuals who work alone
>>> entrepreneurship is about start-up businesses
>>> entrepreneurship and small business management are one and the same
>>> entrepreneurship is about ideas.

Like all conventional wisdom, it does possess an element of truth – indeed, there are research studies to back some of the assertions. But you can have the right entrepreneur profile in terms of age, family background and education and still not be an entrepreneur. Conversely, you can have a poor entrepreneur profile in those terms and yet still be an entrepreneur. Just because you were not the first-born male in your family and your father was not in business it does not mean that you may not be an entrepreneur.

We now review each of these assertions in turn.

Assertion 1: Age, family background, education and experience are deciding factors

Age can sometimes be important, but really only because of other factors. Many entrepreneurs begin when they are very young, with some venture or another that boosts their pocket money. If they are encouraged and succeed they are likely to continue. Such people are keen and determined to 'do their own thing' at the earliest opportunity.

As young people settle down, buy houses and start families, the personal risk of setting up a new business may be enough to dissuade them for some years. Hence the incidence of start-ups when people are in their late twenties, thirties and early forties will often decline. But when people are financially secure in middle age, the opportunity is there again, and many do take it up. Ray Kroc was in his early fifties when he met and bought out the McDonald brothers. Colonel

Harlan Sanders was in his sixties when he started Kentucky Fried Chicken – and he experienced several rejections before his tasty new coating became popular. As they say, is it ever too late?

Family background is not an accurate pointer either. Entrepreneurs emerge from rich and poor backgrounds and from both solid and broken homes. Parental careers are not a determinant.

It is sometimes argued that the first-born child is likely to develop entrepreneurial characteristics as, being the eldest, he or she has a strong chance of developing self-confidence. But what about the youngest child in a large family? Some parents will allow their youngest greater freedom than the elder siblings because they have learned more about parenting, are more relaxed and are willing to let the child pursue those things it finds most stimulating.

Of course, children often do succeed their parents in family businesses. Clearly there are examples where later generations have built substantial businesses upon foundations laid previously. On other occasions, children from wealthy or comfortable backgrounds may not possess the hunger that the founders had. Instead of growing, the business declines when they take over. Hence the expression: 'rags to riches and back again in three generations'.

Education is an interesting issue. Successful entrepreneurs in the high technology and biotechnology fields are often highly educated, sometimes to PhD level. It is their research that has provided the idea and the opportunity. These fields are also prime candidates for academic spin-off companies. Dot.com entrepreneurs are often people with high academic attainment, in part because their time at university or business school will have introduced them to colleagues who have joined banks and venture capitalists, where they need to go for the substantial funding they require.

But education can be restrictive for the most creative people who are required to conform and are not allowed freely to pursue those things that stimulate them.

Profile Paul Sykes

Lifelong and serial entrepreneur and multi-millionaire, Paul Sykes, whose main wealth has come from property development, was once asked if he regretted leaving school at 15, with no formal qualifications. He confirmed that he did. He had, in fact, wanted to leave at 11. 'Those four years cost me a lot of money.'

We find many successful entrepreneurs who have become frustrated in school or college and walked away from qualifications. This issue reinforces that entrepreneurship must contain an element of fun for those involved. Without enjoyment and satisfaction, entrepreneurs may not be able to weather the inevitable setbacks they will face and the mistakes or misjudgements they will make.

Entrepreneurship must contain an element of fun for those involved

Things are happening in education, with encouragement from governments, but fostering greater creativity and innovation in the education system requires a culture change. However, a greater challenge is one of identifying those with true entrepreneurial potential and giving them special attention.

Related to – but not the same as – education, is experience. Many people who start new businesses choose activities and industries with which they are familiar. They will have gleaned valuable knowledge which they can use. However, others will enter industries or undertake activities which are unfamiliar to them. They may well have an instinct for the customers and the market, and their approach will be fresh, uninhibited by perceptions from the past.

Assertion 2: Anyone can be an entrepreneur

This is simply not true.

Many of us can – and should – be more enterprising, but that is not the same thing.

We should all consider that we might be entrepreneurs, but that does not mean that we all are.

Many of us could start up something new and valuable, whether it be a small and localised profit-seeking business, a scout group or a project to raise money for a new community hall. None of these is likely to be really different – they mimic what someone else has done somewhere else. This does not diminish their worth and value, but it does mean that those concerned should be described as 'enterprising' rather than 'entrepreneurs'. True entrepreneurship happens when the people move onto further initiatives and projects, and keep building new things, or when their idea is new and becomes a model that others replicate.

This has important implications for the way we teach entrepreneurship in schools and universities. Youngsters who want to play football or the piano should not be discouraged, nor should the entrepreneur. Everyone should have an opportunity. Educators have a duty to foster talent but they also have a duty to identify the different talents their students possess.

It is appropriate and desirable to teach everyone about entrepreneurship and encourage them to be creative, innovative and enterprising – but those with exceptional entrepreneurial talent also need to be identified and prepared for entrepreneurship, which is a separate and different challenge. Their talent needs to be identified and nurtured.

Of course, this task is not made easy by the reality that many potential entrepreneurs are restless in the education system, which they find inhibiting and constraining.

Assertion 3: Entrepreneurs are only found in the world of business

Entrepreneurship is most commonly associated with business, but entrepreneurs are found in several other places as well!

We have just identified Dame Cicely Saunders as a social entrepreneur who built something truly valuable and made a difference. We do not have to look far to also find people who have enjoyed – and continue to enjoy – a successful career in business who are also championing an important community project. Similarly, we will find people who champion one initiative and then another and another. The serial, habitual element is apparent.

One important feature of the community sector is the number of people with entrepreneurial potential who lack awareness and confidence and only discover their true talents once they are drawn in by a cause.

At the same time, some people with entrepreneurial talent succeed in one area of endeavour and then switch to the world of business. Sport is an excellent example:

- » Footballer David Whelan is the founder of leading sports goods retailer, JJB Sports.
- » Tennis player David Lloyd opened a string of leisure centres, sold them to Whitbread to become a multi-millionaire, and then started another chain of fitness centres.
- » Motor racing champion Jackie Stewart has established (and sold) a Formula One team.

Paradoxically, a number of British-based entrepreneurs are keeping the UK at the forefront of Formula One whilst the British car industry falls increasingly under foreign ownership. One might say that one is driven by entrepreneurs, the other is not!

Few people would deny that Andrew Lloyd Webber and Terence Conran are successful entrepreneurs and businessmen – they are multi-millionaires. But asked to describe themselves, would they choose 'businessman' or 'entrepreneur' – or 'composer' and 'designer' respectively?

Profile Terence Conran

Conran is a serial entrepreneur: he has succeeded as a designer, restaurateur and retailer.

'I have always seen myself as a designer first, rather than a businessman, although I've made things happen, and enjoyed making them happen. The businesses are a way of putting my ideas and products in front of the public.'

Sir Terence Conran

The important point behind this is that entrepreneurs do not simply create financial capital. They also create social and aesthetic capital.

Social capital is manifested in community services that the over-stretched welfare system cannot or has not thought of providing.

Aesthetic capital is reflected in music, art, design and architecture – things which make the world a more enjoyable place in which to live and which give us a 'feel-good' factor. Although neither Mozart nor Michelangelo acquired fabulous wealth, they were the entre-preneurs of their era because they were able to seize the opportunities that were available to them at the time and create legacies that have changed the world. Alive with their talent in today's world, they would be fabulously wealthy!

Petty criminals in business and elsewhere are sometimes enterprising – and the perpetrators of major crimes can be entrepreneurs. Their pursuit of financial wealth is often creative, innovative and daring – and, unfortunately, causes suffering for individuals and investors and occasionally for society. Significantly, it is often claimed that regulations and red tape inhibit entrepreneurship – and, undoubtedly, they do. Whilst relaxing rules and restrictions smoothes the path for the honest entrepreneur, it also makes life easier for the dishonest one.

This assertion simply fails to recognise that the actions and behaviours that characterise the successful business entrepreneur will be found in others who choose to use their talents in different endeavours. We will also find enterprising military leaders who change the nature of warfare. Heinz Guderian, creator of *blitzkrieg* tactics, was undoubtedly entrepreneurial. Amundsen, who beat Scott to the South Pole, was better prepared and organised – an entrepreneur as well as an adventurer.

Assertion 4: Inventors are entrepreneurs

Sometimes they are – but not always.

James Dyson was persistent in his endeavour to design a new dual-cyclone vacuum cleaner and build a successful business. He is both an inventor and an entrepreneur – but this is a rare combination.

Trevor Baylis, inventor of the clockwork radio, was happy to allow others to build the business that exploited the idea and the opportunity – with the support of the Red Cross and others – to sell the product in developing countries where the cost of batteries is prohibitive. Baylis receives a percentage of revenues and can focus on inventing, which is where his talents lie.

In general, inventors are too focused on inventing to be really concerned with the commercial exploitation of their idea. They may grumble about the way entrepreneurs steal their ideas but at heart they love coming up with new things. They often get to the prototype stage and then lose interest.

We believe there is a great opportunity for linking inventors with entrepreneurs, and planning things so that the 'baton' is handed from inventor to entrepreneur in a fair way, allowing the inventor to continue inventing and the entrepreneur to commercially exploit the idea.

Patenting is an important part of this equation, in that it legally captures the ownership of the idea.

Edison of course was one of those special people, like Dyson, who combined the talents of an inventor with those of an entrepreneur. In reality the link between the inventor and the entrepreneur is one of the weak points in the entrepreneurial process.

Assertion 5: Entrepreneurs are individuals who work alone

Again, some do. But many don't.

The founders of Ben and Jerry's Ice Cream and Nantucket Nectars, two hugely successful businesses, were partners from day one. In fact, it has been estimated that two-thirds of all new businesses are started by more than one person.

For any organisation to grow, an effective team of people must be set up, moulded and managed. Successful entrepreneurs must possess team skills – they can operate alone for only so long.

Assertion 6: Entrepreneurship is about start-up businesses

As we saw in chapter 3, sometimes it is – but not always. Corporate entrepreneurs can be found making a difference in many large organisations.

In reality, an innovative manager in a large organisation may well be more of an entrepreneur than the second or third generation owner-manager of a family business. The issue concerns the person and his or her talents and behaviours, rather than where that person might be found.

Entrepreneurship is, however, a process that always has a start. All large businesses were once small. Virgin and Microsoft grew from humble beginnings.

For a business to be started up someone has to have an idea and be minded to do something about it. Some ideas for a new business, however creative they might be, will not succeed. Those involved fail to find willing customers; there is no real opportunity. When such a business is started, its life will be short. There is no growth and no entrepreneurship.

On other occasions, the people with potentially winning ideas cannot find the resources required to exploit their idea. Finance is the most likely problem. Backers often prefer an idea to have been developed into a prototype and initial customers found before they are willing to commit. So who has the faith to provide the funding for the unproven idea?

The next assertion follows automatically…

Assertion 7: Entrepreneurship and small business management are one-and-the-same

All too often this is an assertion accepted by politicians and educationalists. They assume that if they encourage more small businesses to start up they are spawning entrepreneurs.

Profile Pret à Manger

Another sandwich shop in the local high street represents a new small business; the product and service may be very similar to the other local sandwich shops. If the new venture involves some innovative and different way of marketing sandwiches, then the venture is entrepreneurial.

Julian Metcalfe was able to build the Pret à Manger chain of shops in London based on a different ambience and a new range of sandwich fillings.

Significantly, many small businesses do not survive for very long, and a large proportion of those that do stay small. They never develop beyond a handful of employees who all earn a living; they never grow anything that makes a real difference. They were never intended to be anything else. Their contribution to their customers and to economies is vitally important, and they should be encouraged – but that does not mean these owner-managers are true entrepreneurs.

Many simply do not have a product or service idea that is really different from competing products and services and so the growth potential is automatically limited. Because they are not entrepreneurs, they don't realise the importance of being different and creating a competitive advantage.

Possibly those concerned have chosen to start a business because it is the best option open to them if paid employment is hard to come by – they are not setting out with the desire to make a difference, but with the intention of earning a living.

Assertion 8: Entrepreneurship is about ideas

Certainly entrepreneurship requires ideas.

But ideas have to be crafted into opportunities.

Successful entrepreneurship begins with an idea that is crafted into a market opportunity (the strategy) and then exploited with effective project championing. Inventors are strong on ideas – their natural abilities may not stretch into the project championing skills required to pursue and capture the opportunity.

It is a mistake to assume that people with ideas can automatically develop an entrepreneurial business from these ideas. Academic researchers continually come up with new and original ideas in a variety of disciplines. Students on design courses are required to produce new ideas and designs for known markets and problems.

But that does not mean they have identified an opportunity. It is more correct to say that entrepreneurship is about opportunities than to say it is about ideas.

Another part of this assertion is that a person with a good idea is an 'entrepreneur-in-waiting'. Many 'business start' programmes fall into this trap and confuse the quality of the idea with the person's ability to deliver. In reality the person involved may simply not possess the required entrepreneurial talents.

If we rely on the ideas person, who is not an entrepreneur, to identify and exploit an opportunity individually and build a successful venture, we are likely to be sadly disappointed. Instead we need to identify and foster mechanisms for exploiting an idea, including the blending of ideas people with others who have the talent to exploit those ideas commercially.

There are many definitions out there – ours, first aired in Bolton and Thompson, *Entrepreneurs – Talent, Temperament, Technique,* 2000, is based on what entrepreneurs do: 'An entrepreneur is a person who habitually creates and innovates to build something of recognised value around perceived opportunities'

Let's look at these six important elements:

>> 'a person' who
>> 'habitually'
>> 'creates and innovates'
>> 'to build' something of
>> 'recognised value' around
>> 'perceived opportunities'.

'A person'

We are using the word 'person' to represent an individual, whoever they might be and wherever they might be found, or a team of people who work together on a venture. There is no single type of person who is likely to become a successful entrepreneur. What matters is the way they act and behave. Often the demands of creating and building something successful requires skills and abilities, not all of which are possessed by the person who has the idea in the first place. When this happens others, with complementary skills, abilities and behaviours, need to become engaged in the venture.

It is always important to have a balanced team with an appropriate set of skills but we are saying something more than that. To grow a successful business there has to be an entrepreneur or an entrepreneur team. The character themes that we describe in chapters 7–13 under the acronym 'facets' must be present either in the one individual or across the team as a whole.

'Habitually'

The idea of serial behaviour is often what separates the entrepreneur from the small business owner. The entrepreneur is rarely satisfied with one opportunity, one venture. He or she continues to spot new opportunities – indeed entrepreneurs are always questioning why things are as they are and looking for ways in which they might be changed and improved. They are perpetually curious.

Ironically, this behaviour in children is often frowned upon.

Once entrepreneurs have an idea, they are not content until they have turned it into an opportunity and followed it through in some way.

'Following through' could imply a growing business which diversifies into new activities, or the entrepreneur selling one business to create the time and capital to start something different.

People whom we would describe as successful entrepreneurs throughout their lives do not get it right every time. There are failures as well as successes. Either the number or the scale of the successes dwarfs the failures. Indeed, one leading US venture-capital provider prefers entrepreneurs who have a failed venture behind them – they have had the opportunity to learn from their mistakes.

Entrepreneurs are restless and active people

Some successful businessmen with entrepreneurial talent will use their abilities in alternative activities. They may become the champion of a community project, breed racehorses or take over a football club.

Entrepreneurs are restless and active people.

It is not unusual for a successful small business person to start one business and then another and another in a serial way. These people are entrepreneurs because there is something habitual in their behaviour. They keep doing new and different things.

Many successful entrepreneurs continue 'entrepreneuring' long after they can afford to retire or might be expected to retire on age grounds.

However rich some entrepreneurs become, they find retirement unattractive. [see PROFILE, SIR TOM FARMER, opposite]

'Creates and innovates'

The word 'create' demands the creation of something, and it also implies creativity. It emphasises that entrepreneurs start something from scratch, conceptualising something new – and ideally different – and then bring it into being.

It requires curiosity.

Innovation happens when an idea is transformed into something of value. To accomplish this, an opportunity has to be identified and then realised.

Innovation can be at either of two levels. First, it can represent the improvement of something which already exists – something a person or a company already does, or something which is currently done by others. Both options provide opportunities. Second, it can be 'blue sky' or something completely new, which metaphorically rewrites the rules of competition in an industry. In chapter 19 we see how Herb Kelleher's competitive model for Southwest Air did exactly that.

Arguably, today we are limited only by our imagination. If we can throw off the gravitational pull of the past, there is almost nothing that cannot be imagined – and then made to happen by the entrepreneurs in our world. Organisations and their managers should never become complacent – 'out there' are imaginative competitors, some of them unrecognisable at the moment, who can and may, render any company's products, services and strategies obsolete.

◆——————●

In this context, you might well ask yourself:

»» *Are you looking outside your current organisation to find new ways of adding value and competing – which will render the strategies of your rivals obsolete?*

- »» *Are you working inside your organisation to make sure you stay ahead of your rivals?*
- »» *Do you create, dream and imagine?*
- »» *Do you explore and experiment?*
- »» *Or are you standing back, letting the world pass by?*
- »» *Are you doing nothing but still waiting anxiously for the inevitable?*

'Builds'

Using the word 'build' takes us on to the output. Resources have to be acquired and deployed in an effective, efficient and timely manner if something of value is to be built. The resources include people as well as finance, facilities and raw materials – the land, labour and capital of economists. One of the remarkable things about entrepreneurs is that they never complain about lack of resources – they seem to be able to find what they need.

The New Zealand term 'number eight wire' captures this idea well. Its origins are in the isolated farmsteads where resources were scarce and people had to 'make do with what was available'. It suggests using anything that comes to hand and will fix a problem situation – something entrepreneurs do naturally.

Entrepreneurs build because they have to – it is in their blood. They are hands-on people who often find delegation difficult, but because of their astonishing work rate they accomplish far more than most people.

'Building' is a useful word, as it also implies overcoming obstacles. Change invariably incurs resistance of some form and rarely do things progress smoothly. The entrepreneur requires courage and perseverance to deal with all the setbacks he encounters on his journey.

'Recognised value'

Entrepreneurs start a business or new venture because they want to. There will always be an element of personal motivation and achievement involved. They will want to do things their way, and they will care passionately about the outcomes. Their aim will be to build something of which they can be proud. Depending upon the strength of their Ego, a key character theme, they may also crave wider recognition by society for their achievements.

It is actually essential that others also believe the outcomes are important. Entrepreneurs want to be noticed. Of course the value of the product or service must be recognised by customers as well as by the entrepreneur or it will not be commercially successful. The same is true for social projects. Unless it is seen as valuable by those it targets it will not be used.

Successful entrepreneurs are customer-focused – some are even customer-obsessed. They have an uncanny 'gut feeling' for customers and what they will buy. Rigorous market research is not the source of the idea or the opportunity. The customers are the first to recognise the value of what the entrepreneur has to offer, and entrepreneurs know this.

> **Successful entrepreneurs are customer-focused – some are even customer-obsessed**

So how do we measure success? By what do we measure the achievements of the entrepreneur?

Business entrepreneurs are generally ranked by their personal wealth, even if it is all tied up in the business. Their business success is measured in such terms as growth in sales revenue, the value of the business and numbers of people employed. These days the same measures apply to the corporate entrepreneur, because of share options, as much as they do to the owner entrepreneur.

In contrast, the ultimate test of a social entrepreneur's venture is the extent to which the community would be worse off if it no longer existed.

Building and value recognition are factors which separate the inventor from the entrepreneur. Inventors who remain unrecognised may be not be happy about it but their primary motive is to invent. Entrepreneurs, on the other hand, build things in order to be recognised. Recognition is what drives them – they often feel they have something to prove.

'Perceived opportunities'

An idea is not the same as an opportunity. An opportunity always has advantage attached.

Entrepreneurs see opportunities clearly. They keep things simple and somehow know what needs to be done. With this broad strategy comes their direction, focus and source of advantage.

Ray Kroc did not invent the business model for McDonald's, but when he saw it being practised by the two McDonald brothers in a single unit in California, he realised the potential and bought them out.

Howard Schultz built Starbucks around opportunities he saw when he went in coffee bars in Italy. Initially he attempted to interest his current employer – Starbucks Coffee Importers and Merchants – but it dismissed his idea. He left, set up on his own and eventually bought out his previous employers and adopted their name.

Jeff Bezos recognised the potential of the Internet for selling certain consumer products and began Amazon.com.

But not every 'opportunity' becomes a successful business.

Boo.com was established to sell designer sports clothes and shoes over the Internet. The idea appeared to be a winner – after all, people do buy designer sportswear, and few outlets can afford the stock to provide a wide range of products and sizes. But establishing the supply chain ate up cash and the website required computer memory in excess of that many people had. The business failed as quickly as it began.

We use the term 'perceived opportunity' because it is an opportunity in the mind of the entrepreneur. Others either do not see the opportunity at all, or if they do they dismiss it as impractical or unrealistic. Many an entrepreneur has been told they are wasting their time – but they generally have the last laugh.

Here are a few examples.

This 'telephone' has too many shortcomings to be seriously considered as a means of communication. The device is inherently of no value to us.

Western Union internal memo, 1876

I think there is a world market for maybe five computers.

Thomas Watson, chairman of IBM, 1943

There is no reason anyone would want a computer in their home.

Ken Olson, president, chairman and founder of Digital Equipment Corp., 1977

A cookie store is a bad idea. Besides, the market research reports say America likes crispy cookies, not soft and chewy cookies like you make.

Response to Debbi Fields' idea of starting Mrs. Fields Cookies

We don't like their sound, and guitar music is on the way out.

Decca Recording Company rejecting the Beatles, 1962

Now – how about you?

Having read our first five chapters what are you thinking?

» *Are you underutilised and undervalued?*
» *Do you think your boss is stupid and holding you back?*
» *Are you questioning any perceptions you hold or assumptions you make about yourself?*
» *Maybe for the first time, are you beginning to think of yourself as possibly something of an entrepreneur?*
» *Are you already characterised by others as an entrepreneur, but interested in understanding more about what this means and implies?*
» *Do you think you might have entrepreneurial potential that has yet to be exploited?*
» *Do you believe you are creative and innovative, and could achieve more?*

If so, read on ... and as the German poet and philosopher, Goethe, urged 'whatever you can do, or dream you can, begin it'.

In the next few chapters we begin to home in on what makes an entrepreneur. We consider the spirit of the entrepreneur – that intangible but essential essence that has to be given its freedom. Then we introduce the character themes that describe the successful entrepreneur – the behaviours and actions that come naturally to them. Successful entrepreneurs possess a number of these important character themes and to a high degree. You might surprise yourself!

Those of you who possess the entrepreneur character themes, but with a lower intensity, will find opportunities to be creative and innovative in a variety of important ways without necessarily changing the world – as long as you are minded to do so.

Others of you will have fewer of the entrepreneur character themes – possibly none, although this would be rare. When people without the appropriate character themes of the entrepreneur start off down the route of self-employment and owner-management, their chances of survival and prosperity are relatively low. This is why it is important to check yourself against the entrepreneur character themes before you start out.

But if you are not strong on the entrepreneur character themes you will have other character themes – we all do – which will allow you to make your best contribution in some other activity. It is simply a case of 'horses for courses'.

And remember, the Gallup Organisation has suggested that we can all do something better than 10,000 other people. Behind this assertion is the reality that we can all achieve excellence at something. For some of us, this could be entrepreneurship.

Chapter 6 The Spirit of the Entrepreneur

What makes the entrepreneur tick?

We introduced you to John, Charles, Jim, Liz, Helen, David, Bob and Adam in chapter 2. These are all people we can recognise. We now return to the situations in which they found themselves.

For different reasons each asked the question 'Am I or could I become an entrepreneur?' Maybe you have done the same thing at some time in your life.

The answer is already inside you, but because it lies somewhere between the heart and the head, you can't be sure.

In this chapter we look at the 'heart questions'.

Michael Dell, the founder of Dell Computers, is one of the richest men in the world. He started with $627 in 1984 and is now worth $12.5 billion.

Michael says you can't learn to be an entrepreneur. 'It comes from somewhere deep inside'.

Heart questions are about

>» instinct
>» finding if the cap fits
>» fun
>» doing something about it.

Profile Anita Roddick

Anita Roddick, founder of The Body Shop, commented that as her business grew and became a global enterprise she had to constantly re-invent her role.

She had to do this without route maps or manuals. Her passion was her guide; and her instinct was vital for dealing with the various challenges she had to face.

Roddick, Business as Unusual, *2000*

Instinct

Instinct is what we do naturally without really thinking about it. If we have an entrepreneur's instinct then we will have done entrepreneurial things at sometime in our lives, most probably in childhood.

David became an academic, but he remembers the time he hired out his Gameboy to his schoolfriends and made himself some pocket money. Charles sold conkers from the tree in his garden, with one price for untreated conkers and another for those he had hardened by his secret method. David and Charles both got into trouble for this display of enterprise. Soon this entrepreneurial instinct dried up as they followed careers that were open to them because of their intellectual ability.

Small wonder that educational attainment does not correlate with entrepreneurial achievement. The system closes off the opportunity.

Can you think of any examples from your childhood when you did something that might be considered as entrepreneurial?

To make the point, here are two examples of those who started young:

Bernie Ecclestone, of Formula One fame, believes that 'you have an instinct. You can't learn business.'

He first showed his entrepreneurial instincts when, at the age of 9, he exploited wartime shortages. Seeing a market opportunity he bought Chelsea buns in bulk and sold them to his school friends (Steiner, *My First Break,* 1998).

At the age of 9, Michael Dell sold his stamp collection to make some money and by the age of 14 had worked out a clever way to sell newspapers. This netted him almost $20,000 a year. More than some of his teachers earned (Dell and Fredman, 1999).

Finding 'if the cap fits'

Helen, frustrated with the NHS and Bob, frustrated with life, both began to wonder if they might be entrepreneurs in their own way. Helen was straining at the leash in the NHS and longed to be able to do things her way. She had surprised herself in her immediate reaction to Sarah's comment that they needed an entrepreneur to make it happen. Bob had suddenly found he could do something and he had found it surprisingly easy. He took to selling like a duck to water. Joe had told him he was a natural and that he might discover he was an entrepreneur.

Adam did not feel stretched in his job at the university, but then he was invited to set off on a new adventure. He was offered the land he needed to start the project he had been talking about. At this point he could have backed away and stayed in his relatively secure environment. He chose to see whether the cap fitted.

Aptitude and the speed with which skills are acquired is a sure sign of talent in sport. Coaches have to be careful that technique does not overshadow basic talent and cramp the style of the athlete. Many sportsmen and women have lost their edge when they began to think about things too much.

> **If the cap fits and feels comfortable it is a sign of talent**

If the cap fits and feels comfortable it is a sign of talent.

If you are not already doing so, why not begin to take your first steps as an entrepreneur? Talk about it to friends, think it through, talk with any entrepreneurs that you know and see what happens. If you begin to worry about the whole idea then forget it, but if the idea grows on you and you find you pick things up quickly then it could be a sign that the cap fits.

Fun

John wasn't having fun. His company had been sold and he'd lost his job. Liz was the odd one out on her MBA course. All the others were after highly paid jobs with the corporates, but she had felt a buzz when she read the case studies of entrepreneurs and had met some. John and Liz were both excited by the possibility of new opportunities.

Adam was in exactly the same position.

Emotional response is not a sure sign of anything but it is an important indicator. John thought it would be fun to find out if he was an entrepreneur and Liz was thrilled with the idea.

People enjoy doing what they are good at. There is a special thrill in exercising your talent. Athletes have often described their best performances as 'going with the flow'. They say that it is easier to run a lifetime best than it is to underperform.

Doing what we do best should be fun and a great source of personal satisfaction.

Think of those times when you have found real satisfaction in what you have done. When you have thought to yourself 'This is fun and they even pay me for it'?

Fun is one of life's barometers. If your present job is great then fine, but if you are not having fun then maybe you should do something else. Perhaps that something is being an entrepreneur.

Profile Silicon Valley

The west coast of the US has developed a culture of fun and irreverence. In her presentations to corporate America, author and academic Rosabeth Moss Kanter has often used elephant stories to explain this.

Silicon Valley companies have hired elephants – and sometimes other animals – when they wanted to demonstrate some new product or special achievement.

An elephant with a sign on its back being paraded outside the company would not be an unusual sight.

Doing something about it

Jim had read the books but not applied them to himself. It was when he realised that other people's stories could become his story that he decided to take action.

People like John who have been made redundant often say it was the best thing that ever happened to them. They became entrepreneurs and found a new lease of life.

Entrepreneurial behaviour is often triggered by an event or situation. For some the event is fairly straightforward, as it was for Jim and Adam, but for others like John it can be traumatic.

Perhaps we all need a jolt of some kind for us to take the first step.

Many entrepreneurs often speak of an apprenticeship when they learned how not to run a business by observing others making a mess of it! It is the feeling that 'I can do better than my boss' which often makes people branch out on their own.

Jim had served his apprenticeship with one of the best consultancy firms in the business and had seen inside some big-name companies. He knew that though products and markets are important it was the person at the helm that made the difference. He had observed that the companies that thrived in today's world were those run by entrepreneurs or to be more precise venturers and corporate entrepreneurs.

• — •

As you read this chapter you may have sensed an entrepreneur's instinct within and felt that the entrepreneurial cap could fit. You will have thought about work being fun. Perhaps you have decided it is time for action.

The next chapters will help you to put that decision on a firmer basis. They will take you through some of the entrepreneurial attributes you should look for in yourself – but they will make more sense if there is an intention to do something about it. It is important to decide one way or the other. There is no such thing as a half-hearted entrepreneur.

• — •

Some people leave things a bit late and wish they had started earlier.

'Britain's entrepreneurs go grey in 20 years': this headline in the *Sunday Times* was saying that over the past 20 years the number of businesses started up by those over 45 years of age had increased by a third whilst the number started by those in their 20s was at its lowest for 20 years.

There are clearly a significant number of late starters – but there needn't be!

Chapter 7 The 'Facets' of the Entrepreneur

What makes an entrepreneur?

In the next few chapters we describe what it takes to be an entrepreneur and give you the opportunity to assess your own entrepreneurial potential.

But we begin with the personal view of a successful entrepreneur – Anita Roddick. These are important observations from an entrepreneur who has made it.

Anita Roddick proclaims that she 'never set out to be an entrepreneur. I'd never heard of the word and wasn't interested in its definition.' But after 25 years of experience she came up with a list of 10 qualities that 'you need to be a natural entrepreneur'.

Some of her qualities may 'ring bells' with you.

Make a note of those that do and those that don't.

You never know, you might be an Anita Roddick of the future.

We hope that the next few chapters will help you answer that question.

【see PROFILE, ANITA RODDICK, opposite】

Why the 'facets' approach works

Much has been written about the entrepreneur. Many writers – including academics and journalists as well as entrepreneurs like Anita Roddick – have described the entrepreneur. Some of the conclusions are anecdotal; some are the result of academic research. If we put these ideas together, we find the entrepreneur described in terms of personality and behaviour.

Anita Roddick's 'entrepreneur top ten'

1. A *vision* for something different, coupled with a belief that turns it into a reality.
2. An element of *crazy* behaviour.
3. Acting *instinctively*, based upon one's personal perceptions, to stand out as being different.
4. Having *ideas* bubbling inside with such a force that they pop out all the time.
5. *Optimism*, believing nothing is impossible.
6. An appreciation that you don't have to know *how* to do everything when you set out.
7. Being '*streetwise*'.
8. Acting *creatively*.
9. The ability to *blend* together these first eight factors. Entrepreneurs learn by experience – they ask questions, but they make up their own minds and then act upon their decisions.
10. Telling a good *story* – which ultimately defines the extent of the difference an entrepreneur makes.

Adapted from *Roddick*, Business as Unusual, *2000*

In terms of personality our entrepreneur will often be

>>> confident
>>> optimistic
>>> compulsive
>>> courageous
>>> persistent
>>> extroverted.

He or she will exhibit

>>> high energy and drive
>>> urgency
>>> imagination
>>> initiative.

He or she will be someone who can

>>> persuade and maybe even inspire
>>> focus on outcomes and results
>>> engage the support of others
>>> build support for new initiatives.

The reason we see these things in entrepreneurs is because they possess the 'facets' character themes that are described in this and subsequent chapters. It is these themes that underpin and explain their personality and behaviour. They are the causes behind the effects. Once we understand them we are then in a position to identify the person with entrepreneurial potential – and as we have said, that could be you!

Discovering the entrepreneur within

We believe that the key to identifying the entrepreneur is to look at a person's character, specifically at those things that are habitual, come naturally and are done well. Each of us has a particular character set that makes us the way we are – that means we excel in some roles but not in others.

In this chapter and the following six the character set for the entrepreneur is described and you are given the chance to measure yourself against it.

We use the words 'character theme' to describe the elements that make up the character set. We add the word 'theme' to capture the idea that we are dealing with habitual behaviour – rather as a 'theme tune' is used by a band or a television soap – it describes a recurring pattern.

Thus a character theme is 'a personality attribute or characteristic that defines our normal expected behaviour'. We each possess a set of character themes that form our inner psychological core. They define the things we do most readily and instinctively.

In the workplace, in our social activities, in our hobbies, at home and even on holiday – wherever we are – we demonstrate our particular set of character themes: we can't help it.

To check this approach out, think what your character theme set might look like. Think about what you do best, what you enjoy doing, what you have an aptitude for.

Think through the jobs that you have had. Which were the most fun? Which did you excel at? Was this because you were part of a great team or was it because you made things happen?

What do you think are your greatest strengths? For example you might be a very focused person who concentrates on the job in hand until it is completed.

We shall continue with these type of questions as we home in on the character themes of the entrepreneur so keep a note of your answers for future reference.

Where we begin

A person's character themes are the starting point. They are the core, and like the centre of the snowball that gathers more snow as it rolls down the hill, so the core gathers knowledge and experience as it proceeds. But this particular snowball is selective in what it picks up. The character themes build knowledge and experience in areas that they can relate to. A person with a strong character theme of Creativity will get more out of a situation that calls for adaptation and change than a person low on Creativity.

Life's experiences can develop and strengthen character themes, but they can also diminish them. A culture that serves the status quo and is locked into tradition is unlikely to help the development of entrepreneurial character themes.

Our education and training also adds to the shape and size of our snowball. When it is in line with our character themes we have a balanced whole that can achieve excellence. But when it is not we have a distortion and are ineffective and probably unhappy.

The importance of knowing our character themes cannot be overemphasised – and the earlier in life we know them the better. Howard Gardner of the Harvard Graduate School of Education was close to the mark when he commented:

> The time has come to broaden our notion of the spectrum of talents. The single most important contribution education can make to a child's development is to help him toward a field where his talents best suit him, where he will be satisfied and competent.
>
> We should spend less time ranking children and more time helping them to identify their natural competencies and gifts, and cultivate those. There are hundreds and hundreds of ways to succeed and many, many different abilities that will get you there.

Goleman, *Emotional Intelligence*, 1996

The entrepreneur's character themes

The entrepreneur has six main character themes – and they conveniently form the acronym 'facets'.

>>> F for Focus
>>> A for Advantage
>>> C for Creativity
>>> E for Ego
>>> T for Team
>>> S for Social

They constitute the facets of the entrepreneur. They are the reason why entrepreneurs are what they are and do what they do. We can measure ourselves against these facets and assess our entrepreneurial potential.

The number, the mix and the relative strength of the entrepreneur character themes determine whether our talent lies in business or social entrepreneurship, where we fit on the entrepreneur triangles described in chapter 3 and how far up them we are likely to climb.

Crystals and facets

All crystals have their own particular geometry. The formation and number of facets define the crystal.

Quartz is an interesting example. Its six-sided columnar structure is easily recognised, but there are many different kinds of quartz. Depending on small amounts of trace elements they can be pink, yellow or green. Amethyst is a purple quartz and is valued as a semi-precious gemstone.

Like the quartz crystal we can recognise entrepreneurs by their six facets. But they too have their trace elements and some facets are more distinct than others, with the result that there are many different types of entrepreneur out there. Some are household names – they are famous – others are relatively ordinary and many are so buried in the rock that they have yet to be discovered.

Steve Jobs, who founded Apple Computers and recently returned to lift its fortunes, is a celebrity as an entrepreneur – he is in the 'gemstone' category.

Entrepreneurs in the gemstone category are recognised and acclaimed – but each has a different hue.

>>> Alan Sugar, of Amstrad fame, was 'king of the personal computer market' in the UK for several years. He began as a trader in electronics products before venturing into manufacturing, and he is allegedly proud of his 'barrow boy' image, although he never was one. The street trader or merchant entrepreneur is probably the oldest type of entrepreneur in the world.

>>> Richard Branson, founder of the Virgin Group, is the tycoon type of entrepreneur, with his finger in many pies and a larger-than-life personality.

>>> The Body Shop, founded by Anita Roddick, is a vehicle for her crusading spirit. At heart she is a social entrepreneur with a passion for the world's environment.

>>> Bill Gates has grown the Microsoft empire from nothing but still loves computer programming. He is a 'techy' entrepreneur.

>>> Jack Welch is a classic example of a corporate entrepreneur. He took an already successful General Electric from a market value of $13 billion to $550 billion in 20 years. He proved that a strategy of diversification could succeed when many 'experts' were proclaiming that focus strategies were superior.

>>> In Stagecoach Brian Souter has created a £1 billion business by cashing in on the deregulation of the bus industry. He is an opportunist entrepreneur.

If you read the biographies of these people it is clear that they possess the facets of the entrepreneur and yet at the same time they are all different.

The working-class roots of Alan Sugar and Brian Souter – who are from London and Scotland respectively – provide the trace elements that give them a distinctive style. Roddick's mother taught her to challenge everything. This gave the courage part of her 'E' facet, Ego, a special hue.

But it isn't just the trace elements that produce this difference. Some of the facets are more perfectly formed than others.

Richard Branson and Anita Roddick are both strong on the 'T' facet, Team. Their employees think they are great.

In her autobiography *Business as Unusual*, Roddick has a chapter headed 'We were searching for employees but people turned up'.

Jack Welch also believes in people. He has said that 'getting the right people in the right jobs is a lot more important than developing a strategy'. But he was talking about people who could 'kick ass and break glass'. He once slimmed down the GE workforce so much that he was known a 'Neutron Jack' – he kept the buildings but not the people. But he knew about teams and how to reward people. Welch is second only to Bill Gates in the number of people he has made millionaires.

Entrepreneurs, then, come in all shapes and sizes because:

» They have their own trace elements, often related to their upbringing.

» Their entrepreneur facets are differently formed – some are clearer and stronger than others.

» Some have additional facets that supplement their entrepreneurial facets.

As we noted in chapter 3, the corporate entrepreneur needs some of the facets of the leader.

Aesthetic entrepreneurs like Andrew Lloyd Webber have their special talents. Although a multi-millionaire businessman and a composer, he would wish to be remembered more for his music than his business acumen.

These factors explain their differences, but what about their similarities?

The entrepreneur's crystal formation

With the entrepreneur it is often a case of 'we know one when we see one'.

The facet analogy explains why. It is the 'crystal formation' of the entrepreneur that we are seeing.

If we cut across the crystal we can see the facets laid out.

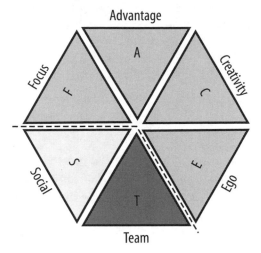

The entrepreneur's crystal formation

The 'colours' or shading show three important combination sets.

The Focus, Advantage, Creativity and Ego facets are found in all entrepreneurs. Conveniently, their acronym provides another metaphor – they are the 'face' of the entrepreneur. It is what we see when we look at any entrepreneur – it is his or her character theme set. A successful entrepreneur needs strength in these four facets.

Strength in either the Team or the Social facet adds to the basic profile of the entrepreneur and creates some important differences.

The presence or absence of the Team facet affects the growth potential and progress of the business or initiative.

The presence and relative strength of the Social facet affects the nature of the business.

In the next few chapters we describe the six facets of the entrepreneur.

As you read them through it will become clear that they overlap in various ways and combine to form a stronger whole. Thus a person who is strong on the Focus and Team facets will be able to build a very focused high-achieving team.

The serial entrepreneur Tim Waterstone understands the need for a number of facets – he calls them gifts – and the importance of their interaction.

As the description of each facet proceeds, you are encouraged to make your own assessment of how strongly you possess that facet. This will be subjective but at the end you may surprised at its accuracy.

This DIY approach to evaluation gives it a personal validity. It is not a case of us telling you about yourself but of you finding out. So be as honest and open with yourself as possible and go back over your evaluations if you are unsure.

A first evaluation

We now give a quick run through each of the facets. As you read, think how you measure up against them and give yourself a score.

Later when you have read through the chapters on each facet you can give yourself a more considered score but it will be useful to compare your initial response.

Focus

The person with a strong Focus facet is able to lock on to a target, to concentrate, never losing sight of critical issues – to discriminate between the important and the trivial and to set goals and targets daily.

Focus can include a desire to act with urgency and not waste time, a desire to make things happen, to get things done, to persevere.

>» *Are you a focused person, not easily distracted?*
>» *Does concentration and perseverance come to you easily?*
>» *Can you discriminate between tasks?*

or

>» *Do you put things off and procrastinate?*
>» *Do you try to do too many things at once, always juggling things around and never quite completing anything?*

Give yourself a score out of 10: **my Focus facet score is** _____

Note: There is no right or wrong about these scores. You are simply trying to find out if you have the character themes of an entrepreneur.

If you have, then perhaps you should be doing something about it, but if not there will be another role that your character theme set will match. It may be manager or leader, or something quite different.

Advantage

The Advantage facet is based around the ability to identify opportunities, to know which of a number of options will give the greatest benefit.

Some people enjoy detail and like to measure things, but the entrepreneur does this to serve the one purpose of gaining advantage, of winning the race.

The ability to find resources and the vision to see things ahead of the pack are important elements of this Advantage facet.

The Advantage facet is one of the easiest to spot. It often shows itself at an early age so think back to any examples of when you saw an opportunity and took advantage of it.

My Advantage facet score is _____

Creativity

Creativity is about buzzing with ideas, about seeing opportunities all around. The Advantage facet gives the ability to know which opportunity to go for, but without the Creativity facet there would be none to choose from.

Coming up with solutions and enjoying the challenge of a problem are all part of this Creativity facet.

Do you consider yourself a creative person, with a willingness to think 'outside the box' and challenge convention.

Are you an ideas person and can you tell the difference between an idea and an opportunity.

My Creativity facet score is _____

Ego

People strong in this facet want to be in charge of their own destiny, to make a difference, to leave their 'footprints'.

They are responsible, accountable people with the courage to face setbacks and overcome resistance.

They have an inner drive that motivates them. They are self-starters with confidence and a dedication that marks them out.

You will know if you are like this! But think of some difficult situations you have had to face:

» *Have you done so with courage and been able carry the 'burden of the day'?*
» *Do others look up to you at times of crisis?*
» *Do you take life as it comes or do you take the initiative and live with the consequences?*
» *Are you a competitive person?*

My Ego facet score is _____

Team

The Team facet constitutes the ability to find the right people and get them working as a team. This means acknowledging your limitations and knowing when you need help. But it also means having the ability to pick good people and develop their potential.

The ability to network effectively and make useful contacts is part of the Team facet.

Not all entrepreneurs are strong on the Team facet, but when they are it makes a significant difference in what they can achieve.

» *Are you a people person or are you a loner?*
» *Can you motivate and inspire others?*

Think of times when you have been in teams or leading teams that have really worked. Did you play a key role in making the team a success? If so, you are probably strong in this facet.

My Team facet score is _____

Social

People strong in this facet orient their lives around a cause. They take belief and values seriously but they also take the important steps to action. They have a mission in life, their cause is their passion.

The desire to serve others often involves great personal sacrifice but that doesn't matter. They are 'called to serve'.

This is the key facet of the social entrepreneur.

You will already know if this facet is strong in you. It will dominate your life and influence all areas of your thinking. You will already be serving others in some capacity or looking for the opportunity to do so.

My Social facet score is _____

Now you have completed a first evaluation of your entrepreneurial potential you can work through the next six chapters for a more thorough assessment.

In the meantime, begin to think in terms of the six entrepreneur facets. When you read newspaper articles about entrepreneurs or even their obituaries, see if you can spot these facets – they will be there.

After a while the facets will become familiar and they will leap out from the page. The more you learn to look for them, the more you can see them.

Entrepreneurs, managers, leaders

The crystal analogy can be applied to a wide range of different roles. The manager, the leader and the entrepreneur each have their own crystal formation.

But some facets are shared.

The F facet, Focus, of the entrepreneur is shared with the manager, and both Focus and the T facet, Team, with the leader.

When a manager or leader is particularly strong in one or more of the entrepreneur facets, such as the A facet, Advantage or the E facet, Ego, then we have an entrepreneurial manager or an entrepreneurial leader.

A list of what entrepreneurs, managers and leaders do shows that there are some overlaps and some distinguishing differences.

The entrepreneur	The manager	The leader
has fun	manages	leads
innovates	administers	innovates
creates	maintains	develops
focuses on the business	focuses on systems	focuses on people
builds a team	relies on control	inspires trust
sees opportunities	sees problems	sees the future
asks how and when	asks how and when	asks what and why
acts short term	acts short term	thinks long term
does the right things	does things right	uses influence

Entrepreneurs, managers and leaders excel at what they do when they are strong in the facets that define their crystal formation. Excellence is achieved by developing these facet strengths and their interaction.

Talent, temperament, technique

Crystals form naturally and grow their particular shape when conditions are right. Craftsmen take this raw material and produce excellence.

Talent and temperament are part of the natural formation of the crystal. They make it what it is. We can think of talents as natural abilities, things we are born with. People can learn to use their time more productively or be more creative, but unless they have a natural talent they will never achieve excellence.

Temperament is our needs and drives. Temperament is something that we have to learn to manage if we are to make the most of our talents.

Technique is equivalent to the work of the craftsman that adds value to the crystal – that turns a rough diamond into one of great worth.

If we want true entrepreneurs, we have first to look for them

This analogy teaches us one important lesson. If we want true entrepreneurs, we have first to look for them.

Technique alone, whether in the form of education and training, structured and unstructured learning, cannot make entrepreneurs.

In the worst case, entrepreneur programmes produce 'replicas' – like the sculptor who carves the shape of a particular crystal in a replica material so that it looks like the real thing – but of course it isn't. Other than looks, it has none of the properties.

In the next to worse case they produce 'artificial' entrepreneurs – like the synthetic or artificial diamond that has some of the properties of the natural diamond but is just not the real thing.

Talent and temperament are interesting bed-fellows. You can have all the talent in the world, but if it is not matched by the right temperament it will never reach its full potential.

Sport is full of examples of great talent destroyed by temperament.

Profile George Best

Legendary footballer, George Best, described as 'the fifth Beatle' at the height of his fame, was extraordinarily gifted. He had a unique beauty and grace on a football field. He was football's first 'pop star'.

George Best, Blessed, *2001*

With a ball at his feet he could beat most defenders – but he struggled to beat his addiction to alcohol.

When he was still rich and famous, one cartoonist showed him sat at a bar. His girlfriend at the time, a Miss World winner, had her arm around him. The punchline: 'Oh George! Where did it all go wrong?'

It is the same with some entrepreneurs. Their talent can take them to dizzy heights quickly, but their temperament fails them and they become the also-rans.

The right temperament, on the other hand, can compensate for lesser talents. The 'will to win' can be a greater contributor to success than the 'ability to win'.

Technique has an important role to play in the link between talent and temperament. In sport, the coach imparts technique that develops talent and helps the athlete to manage temperament. Often it is this work of the coach that lifts an athlete from national to international level – that is how important technique can be.

The entrepreneur has to pick up business know-how from some-where and gain experience. This is often done through some form of informal 'apprenticeship', during which the potential entrepreneur learns the basics of business – the tricks of the trade. The experience of watching someone else trying to run a company is often a spur to the entrepreneur to make a better job of it.

But it is always important that talent and temperament are enhanced and not diminished. Too much emphasis on technique can mean that the potential entrepreneur begins to think too much about things and stops relying on instinct – like the golfer with the natural but unorthodox swing whose game suddenly deteriorates because he tries to follow the book.

Entrepreneurs have to learn to trust their own judgement – a temperament issue. This can be very difficult for the entrepreneur who is just starting out and who tends to either listen to nobody and make silly mistakes, or else listens to everybody and becomes very confused. The best thing is to accept that mistakes will be made and learn from them.

We once asked one of Silicon Valley's most successful venture capitalists what sort of people he invested in.

He said 'I only invest in people who have failed once or twice. These people have learnt the hard way. Successful people generally have no idea why they have been successful.'

The three 'T's triangle

Talent, temperament and technique link together in various ways. The triangle opposite shows one configuration.

Technique is set alongside talent, which it can enhance and bring to maturity. In some people the talent element will be large and the need for technique less – in others it will be the opposite. What is clear is that each cannot stand alone.

Temperament is then the element that makes the talent and technique deliverable. Without the right temperament to carry it off, real talent and sound technique will not realise their full potential.

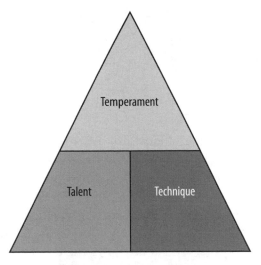

The three 'T's triangle

The talent facets

Four of the facets of the entrepreneur are talents.
They are

>>> Focus
>>> Advantage
>>> Creativity
>>> Team

– another convenient acronym!
These are inborn, we either have them or we don't.
But there are techniques to help us improve in these areas:

>>> Focus can be improved by time-management and project-planning techniques
>>> Advantage may be helped by decision analysis and financial skills
>>> Creativity can be enhanced by a wide range of techniques – from brain-storming to problem solving
>>> Team leadership and motivation are always popular course topics.

The technique support for the entrepreneur is actually in good shape, though entrepreneurs rarely sit still long enough to take advantage of it. This is because entrepreneurship is basically a talent issue and they know it. They prefer doing to listening. Entrepreneurs don't like classrooms!

The temperament facets

The Ego facet and the Social facet link with temperament.

Some aspects of these facets are inborn and some are a function of our environment. It is a case of both nature and nurture.

Self-confidence and self-assurance, part of the Ego facet, are affected by our upbringing and can be built up or squashed and diminished.

Entrepreneurs as different as J. Arthur Rank, Richard Branson, Anita Roddick and Jack Welch attribute their self-confidence to the influence of their mother.

Profile Jack Welch

Jack Welch believes the greatest gift his mother gave him was self-confidence. He was born with a stutter, but she always told him it was an indication that he was extra smart. His tongue could not keep up with his brain.

It was only in later years that he realised how influential and valuable this had been to him.

Lowe, Jack Welch Speaks, *1998*

The Ego facet components of motivation, courage and responsibility are all issues of temperament. They gain in strength as we build on them.

The Social facet is built around belief, mission and service. For some people this is their nature. They have always had a sense of caring and found pleasure in helping others. They are the born social entrepreneurs. Other people have an experience that changes their outlook on life and gives them a new perspective and dynamic. Their Social facet comes alive and their entrepreneurial talent has a new direction. They would have probably been successful entrepreneurs anyway, but because of their new motivation they become social entrepreneurs.

Techniques and the facets

All six facets can be enhanced and developed by the learning and application of techniques.

We agree with Tim Waterstone who, when chairman of HMV Media, commented that unless an entrepreneur understands both the flow of cash and the cash requirements of a business they have no right to even start a business, let alone take on the responsibilities of borrowing money and employing other people.

Business planning and cashflow management do have their place. They are essential techniques for the would-be entrepreneur in every field of activity. But we need to remember that technique alone is not enough. The right talents and temperament, the right entrepreneurial facets must be there.

The ability to write a business plan and manage cashflow does not define the entrepreneur

The ability to write a business plan and manage cashflow does not, and never will, define the entrepreneur.

Achieving excellence

Talent and temperament are the raw materials. By structured and unstructured learning and experience we can develop talent, manage temperament and impart technique to enhance and develop skills. The outcome will be a seamless excellence.

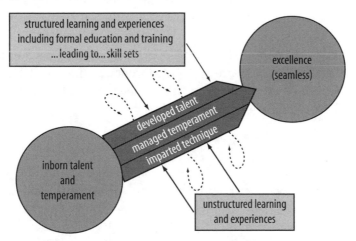

structured learning and experiences including formal education and training ...leading to...skill sets

excellence (seamless)

developed talent
managed temperament
imparted technique

inborn talent and temperament

unstructured learning and experiences

The nature–nurture model

But excellence is not achieved in a vacuum. There has to be the opportunity that releases the entrepreneurial potential.

Opportunity

We all start life with a talent and temperament package. If that includes the entrepreneur facets, then given half a chance we will become successful entrepreneurs.

But people don't always get that half chance. Their circumstances and their culture block off opportunity – as Benjamin Franklin once put it they are like 'sundials in the shade'.

To some, the light of opportunity is a harsh one. It isn't fun being a Cuban refugee fleeing to Miami or an Asian kicked out of East Africa, and yet that experience of serious dislocation brought the entrepreneurs in those groups to the fore and transformed the economic and social situation of the refugees and the communities they built.

In the developed world of today, the light of opportunity is shining for the entrepreneur more than it has ever done. Places like Silicon Valley have set the pace and shown what is possible. Given the right environment the entrepreneurs simply come out of the woodwork.

The release of entrepreneurial talent is one of the pressing needs of our time. For this to happen we need a climate of opportunity where people are more positive about the role of the entrepreneur as a generator of economic and social capital. We need to see the word 'entrepreneur' in a wider context, and give the entrepreneur a new level of respect. Why should it not be a serious job option for the fresh graduate, the redundant worker, the long-term unemployed or even the asylum seeker?

We need a culture that supports entrepreneurship and enterprise so that even if people are not entrepreneurs they will encourage those who are. They will celebrate the achievements of the entrepreneur rather than be jealous of them.

Profile Linus Torvalds

Linus Torvalds, the Finn who literally gave the world the Linux operating system, moved his base to Silicon Valley because 'Here, if you're successful, people tend to respect you. In Europe, if you're successful, people tend to envy you. Here it's easier to be rich and successful.'

San Jose Mercury News, *1999*

Chapter 8 Focus

Focus is not exclusive to the entrepreneur – we all need it, whatever we do – but it is not possible to be an entrepreneur if Focus is not one of your strengths.

The entrepreneur needs to be able to concentrate for long periods of time and be dedicated to the task in hand. There may even be a degree of obsession about it. The entrepreneurial task can come before family and friends. Entrepreneurs are consumed by their enterprise, it is their passion.

For some, Focus comes naturally – they get on with the job and complete it. They do this task after task, and get through an amazing workload.

For entrepreneurs like this there is often a downside – they find delegation to lesser mortals difficult. 'If I want a job done well I have to do it myself' is a frequent comment. People with this attitude find it difficult to grow a business of any size.

A businessman in the West Midlands supplied components to large engineering companies. He had grown his business from scratch and over the years had delegated everything except pricing. When we spoke to him he said 'I can't trust anybody else to get it right – if you don't get your pricing right you soon don't have a business'.

This person was a businessman but not an entrepreneur, and his business never grew beyond his ability to cope with the number of quotations that he could handle.

For some, Focus needs an external impetus before it will kick in to action. This may be pressure from our peers or a time deadline but once we get going we can really focus and the results sometimes even surprise us. Our disposition may be to be laid back and relaxed, but we discover that we can focus and work hard when we have to.

Focus is an important feature of the entrepreneur and when combined with the Team facet the result can be remarkable. At such times a team of five can do the work of twenty.

> The work ethic, intensity, hard drive, creativity, youthfulness and informality were woven into the very fabric of Microsoft from the start. 'We were just having fun and working really hard' said Steve Wood who took over as general manager in 1977. 'When I think about it, I'm amazed. You look back then and we were just five or six people. Now Microsoft is nearly a two-billion-dollar-a-year company.'

> Wallace and Erickson, *Hard Drive*, 1993

The Focus shades

The Focus facet comes in three different shades. It is good to have something of each but most of us are stronger in one of them.

There can be a focus on

>>> target
>>> time
>>> action.

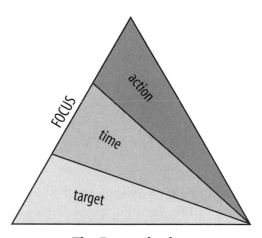

The Focus shades

This diagram is the Focus element of the crystal hexagon diagram introduced in chapter 7.

These three shades or strands are the what, the when and the how of the Focus facet.

They answer the questions

>>> What target?
>>> When?
>>> How?

Target focus

Target focus is what we generally understand by Focus: the ability to concentrate on what is important and not be deflected despite pressure from many quarters.

Perseverance and single-mindedness have been identified by many researchers as characteristics of the entrepreneur. These are part of target focus and are linked with this ability to concentrate and stay with a task until it is completed.

People without Focus jump from opportunity to opportunity rather like butterflies that flit from place to place. They cannot concentrate on one thing for any length of time – for them the grass is always greener. Entrepreneurs are not like this. They pick a target and go for it.

A few exceptional people are multi-focused. They are able to focus effectively on more than one target at a time.

J. Arthur Rank, who founded the British film industry, was such a man.

J. Arthur Rank had such an ability to concentrate intently on everything he did that it allowed him to happily switch activities whenever he needed to without losing track of anything he was involved in. As a consequence, he was a high business achiever who was also able to enjoy a happy marriage and an active leisure life.

Wakelin, *J. Arthur Rank*, 1997

There is an important element of discrimination within the Focus facet. It allows priorities to be identified and gives the ability to know what to concentrate upon, in what is often a busy and hectic life. The project champion is also strong on target focus and discriminates on a daily basis between what is trivial and what is important. Project planning aids are fine and they help us to identify tasks and bottle-necks, but people strong on target focus will have a real feel of what is going on, balancing choices and discriminating as they go along.

The entrepreneur has an additional ability. It comes when the Focus facet links with the Advantage facet (discussed in the next chapter). This identifies the target in terms of advantage – he or she then discriminates with the purpose of gaining advantage. This involves broader considerations than just getting the job done on time and to specification. The entrepreneur sees round corners that the project manager does not realise are there. This gives the entrepreneur a remarkable edge.

Entrepreneurs are often good at detail and this helps them target. They know how to gather the information that matters and then act upon it.

Profile Brian Souter

Brian Souter, the entrepreneur who built Stagecoach, the transport empire, has a phenomenal ability to master detail. He can discern the key information in any document very quickly. He concentrates on major issues, typically no more than three in any situation.

Woolmar, Stagecoach, *1999*

The entrepreneur always targets something practical. The leader might focus on an idea or a concept but the entrepreneur focuses on a tangible target. He or she is a person who gets things done and is impatient with debate and discussion.

For this reason entrepreneurs tend not to be interested in the big picture and are more concerned with today than tomorrow. This can be a serious drawback, but they are often saved by their ability to make decisions quickly and take prompt action.

Entrepreneurs strong on target focus are good finishers. They never leave a job half done, they always see it through to the end. They complete things.

》》 *How strong are you on target focus?*
》》 *Can you concentrate and persevere on a single target or are you easily distracted?*
》》 *Are you a good project champion?*
》》 *Are you able to discriminate and know which jobs are the most important?*

- *Can you see 'the wood for the trees'?*
- *Do you recognise this link with the Advantage facet that adds something special to the way you make your choices of what to focus on?*
- *Are you a person who thinks in concrete terms and gets impatient with too much discussion?*
- *Are you a finisher or do you leave others to tidy up after you?*

Think through a few examples from your own experience and give yourself a score out of 10: **my target focus score is** _____

Time focus

Time focus is about getting things done now. People strong in this aspect enjoy deadlines. Meeting them provides an adrenaline rush that makes them hungry for more. Once the target has been identified there is no time to waste, every moment counts. This urgency is a characteristic of some entrepreneurs and is why they win through – they run faster and harder than anyone else.

Entrepreneurs are people in a hurry. They often sleep less than the rest of us and are impatient for the day to start. This characteristic comes from the Ego facet but it shows itself in the way in which the entrepreneur focuses on things. They are urgent and passionate about what they are doing.

In the extreme, time focus can become a kind of mania where time becomes more important than target. Some entrepreneurs live on this knife-edge.

> **One manic-depressive is on record as believing that many successful businessmen who have taken risks** and almost lost all their money would be able to describe experiences that were similar to his own in early mania. But they would also have an ability to edit them out, putting them aside on the grounds that they have no relevance to anything other than competition and risk.
>
> Whybrow, *A Mood Apart*, 1999

An undue focus on time can also be a case of 'more haste, less speed'. Urgency can take priority over importance, creating a 'busy fool'. Unless time is spent on the right target that time will be wasted.

Of course, not all entrepreneurs are time-focused in an obsessive way. They appear to be laid back and they are – but this masks a determination to get things done. Richard Branson has taken time out to fly his balloon across the Atlantic and has attempted to fly around the world. He dresses informally and appears relaxed. Yet there is no doubt that he gets things done and sometimes very quickly. He is always 'on the ball'.

People who are weak on this time aspect of Focus will procrastinate. They would rather wait and see what happens than take the initiative to make things happen in their favour. Waiting can sometimes be the prudent thing to do, but entrepreneurs find this difficult. They want to get in there and sort the problem out. Delay in business can be fatal and the entrepreneur knows this by instinct.

We once visited an entrepreneur on a consultancy assignment and were surprised to be told that the meeting would have to take place in his car because he had to go to a customer to collect a cheque that had been promised but had not arrived.

For this entrepreneur there was no time to waste.

●———●

>>> *How are you on time? Are you driven by it?*
>>> *Do you find it hard to focus on deadlines, are you always late and rushing around?*
>>> *Are you laid back and prefer to wait and see?*
>>> *Or are deadlines what you enjoy and do you get a buzz from meeting them?*
>>> *Do you take things in your stride and just get on with what has to be done, and find that time looks after itself?*

Think of how you deal with time. Are you able to handle the 'when' question without too much of a problem or do you find it difficult to prioritise because so many things are demanding your attention?

Give yourself a score out of 10 on how much you think you have the entrepreneur's approach to time: **my time focus score is** _____

Action focus

Action focus is typified by the term 'action man' – this person is tense, always ready to spring into action. He is happy as long as he is doing something and gets great satisfaction from completing a task. The entrepreneur is often a person with amazing energy and is seen by others as hyperactive. The downside is impatience with others who do not go at the same pace.

Profile Andy Grove

Andy Grove, who led Intel to greatness, had a strong action focus. Grove had to write things down, decide objectives, prepare plans and monitor performance. When targets were not met he would deliver a broadside. In one widely circulated memo, he wrote, 'Against the specific milestones we set for ourselves our overall performance rates a "not done". Basically we have not achieved any of the key results that we set in April. Because of that we have again decided to adopt "Getting Organised" as our top corporate objective for the third quarter, with an updated set of specific key results.' Grove may have been more of a manager than an entrepreneur, but he certainly was strong on Focus.

Entrepreneurs are workaholics, and where an entrepreneur culture develops – as in Silicon Valley – everyone follows suit. Entrepreneurs 'eat and sleep' their enterprise, even though this puts pressures on their personal and family life.

Entrepreneurs are doers rather than thinkers; there is no such thing as a lazy entrepreneur.

Those strong on action focus can find completing things difficult if they are not also strong on target focus, because they are always wanting to do the next job. This is not a serious problem if there is a team that can pick up the loose ends, but without that support the entrepreneur leaves a trail of debris behind.

» *How do you measure up against action focus?*
» *Do you enjoy doing things and getting on with the job?*
» *Are you the first in a group to respond when something needs to be done?*
» *Are you a workaholic?*

» Or are you a thinker who prefers to get others to do the work?

» Do you find completing things difficult?

» Does your hunger for action mean that you neglect to finish one job before moving on to the next?

Give yourself a score out of 10: **my action focus score is** ____

Now go back over your other scores and review them. There will clearly be some overlap as we are talking about aspects of the same Focus facet. Review your scores and make any changes you wish. Don't simply take an average because a high score on one of the aspects of Focus can carry the others.

We suggest that you enter your highest score, but move it down a little if you are low on target focus as this is the most important of the three.

My final Focus score is _____

Chapter 9 **Advantage**

The Advantage facet is the distinguishing mark of the entrepreneur – but it is the reason why entrepreneurs have sometimes got a bad name. They are seen to take advantage of others and sell them short.

But most entrepreneurs are not like this – in reality it is the entrepreneur who is responsible for all the prosperity we see around us. It was entrepreneurs in the US in the nineteenth and twentieth centuries who created the largest economy the world has ever known.

> [The entrepreneur] is not chiefly a tool of markets but a maker of markets; not a scout of opportunity but a developer of opportunity; not an optimiser of resources but an inventor of them; not a respondent to existing demands but an innovator who evokes demand; not chiefly a user of technology but a producer of it.
>
> Society is always in deep debt to the entrepreneurs who sustain it and rarely consume by themselves more than the smallest share of what they give to society.

Gilder, *The Spirit of Enterprise,* 1986

Entrepreneurs create economic, social and aesthetic capital that benefits all of us and they are able to do this precisely because they are advantage-oriented. They see the advantage in a course of action that the rest of us miss and, drawing on their Focus facet, they make it happen.

We have seen that the Focus facet is about the ability to concentrate on what is important and not be deflected, but that alone is not enough. The entrepreneur requires another critical element – the ability to spot opportunities and to select the right one. The Advantage facet does all this and then provides the target for the Focus facet to lock on to.

Without a strong Advantage facet the entrepreneur will find it difficult to focus. Instead he or she is likely to try one thing and then another, hoping rather than knowing they are on the right track. It is the Advantage facet that enables the entrepreneur to identify the right target.

Target selection can also be a strategic issue. Strategy is not generally part of the make-up of the entrepreneur, but he or she compensates by having a nose for the opportunity. Entrepreneurs have a knack for being in the right place at the right time and seeing the right opportunity.

But when the entrepreneur is blessed with a talent for strategy it feeds directly in to the Advantage facet. Brian Souter is an entrepreneur with this extra talent.

> **Stagecoach would never have grown beyond a small, regional, coach and bus company** had it not been for Brian Souter's talents. But Souter was always interested in growth. He had a vision; he was forward-looking and always searching for growth opportunities. His greatest attribute – for he was always able to read the market – is strategic thinking.
>
> Woolmar, *Stagecoach*, 1999

When the Advantage facet is strong, entrepreneurs not only know what to do – they know what not to do. They can see disadvantage as well as advantage in a course of action. However, when this facet is weak and Ego is strong, their natural optimism may mean that they fail to see the pitfalls. This links in with the entrepreneur's approach to risk which is considered in chapter 14.

The Advantage facet is one of the easiest to identify. It often shows itself at an early age and is behind the childhood stories of many entrepreneurs. They saw opportunities and they took them.

Profile Sir Tom Farmer

Sir Tom Farmer, the founder of Kwik-Fit, the exhaust, tyre and brake company, started his first business when he was fifteen. He started Kookers Kleaned and went from house to house cleaning ovens.

Steiner, My First Break, *1998*

> **The Sunday Times ran a regular feature on how entrepreneurs got started, under the title 'My First Break'** – headings included 'Age when first in business' and 'Early entrepreneurial ventures'.

Here are some examples:

>>> age 10 years – sold pet food door-to-door, working markets, selling caravans
>>> age 12 years and out-of-pocket – buying run down bicycles, renovating them and selling them on
>>> age 10 years – bait digging for ragworms on the local beach
>>> age 14 years – made dolls and sold them to parents' friends.

Steiner, *My First Break*, 1998

The Advantage fan

The Advantage facet fans out into four elements from a central theme of opportunity selection which links with

>>> benefit orientation
>>> performance orientation
>>> resourcing
>>> vision.

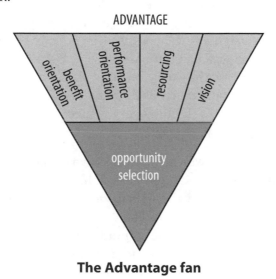

The Advantage fan

Opportunity selection

The Advantage facet helps the entrepreneur to spot, select and target opportunities. The ability to spot opportunities comes when the Creativity facet and the Advantage facet work together, turning ideas into opportunities. The next step is to select the best opportunity from the many. Opportunity selection is the main task of the Advantage facet. Targeting, the final step, comes from combining the Advantage facet with the Focus facet.

Entrepreneurs have a knack or instinct for selecting the right opportunity. They are able to 'pick out of the air' the one opportunity among the many that they can turn into something of recognised value.

Some use their Creativity facet to make connections. They put two and two together and make five. They see things converging and make linkages that create the new opportunity. Rather than spot a host of opportunities they see one now and again. Opportunity spotting and opportunity selection becomes one step.

Akio Morita, joint founder of The Sony Corporation, was the person who spotted and selected the opportunity that became the legendary Sony Walkman.

He has commented that sometimes ideas strike him as being natural. In this particular case he instructed Sony's engineers to take an existing Sony miniature cassette recorder and replace the recording circuit and speaker with a stereo amplifier. He also specified lightweight headphones. At first nobody seemed to like his ideas and he was met with scepticism. He persisted and he also insisted the price had to be one that was affordable to young people. Sony's accountants resisted but he would not back down.

In hindsight he was right in every respect.

Morita, *Made in Japan*, 1994

An important part of Morita's success was that his opportunity selection was customer-led. He knew of his daughter's love of her stereo cassette player and thought it would be a good idea if she could carry it around in her pocket.

Opportunity selection is not just about great ideas – it is also about timing. Entrepreneurs know when to do things as well as what to do. Opportunists can't wait, but the entrepreneur knows exactly when it is time to act. [see PROFILE, JOSEPH RANK, opposite]

Selecting the right opportunity and acting at the right time is the heart of the Advantage facet.

>>> *How do you rate yourself on opportunity selection?*
>>> *Can you think of any opportunities you have spotted that others have selected and picked up?*

>> *If so, think why you missed the opportunity: was it a matter of opportunity or did you not think it worth selecting?*

>> *Are you more of an opportunity spotter than an opportunity selector: can you see lots of opportunities but are never sure which one to go for?*

>> *What is your first reaction to an opportunity?*

>> *Do you think deeply about it and seek more information?*

>> *Do you analyse the opportunity to death?*

>> *– or do you select and go for it?*

The important thing in this assessment is whether you have an instinct for selecting the best opportunity. Whether you see many or few opportunities is less important.

Give yourself a score out of 10 on how close you come to the entrepreneur's talent of opportunity selection: **my opportunity selection score is _____**

The four elements of the Advantage facet that link in with the talent of opportunity selection will now be discussed.

Benefit orientation

For most entrepreneurs, benefit orientation means profit orientation. They know what falls to the bottom line. Some seem to be able to 'smell profit', and find making money very easy. They cannot understand why the rest of us have such a problem.

The benefit orientation of the entrepreneur is often seen in terms of gold.

Entrepreneurs are said to have the 'Midas touch'. Like Midas in the Greek legend, they have been given the power to turn all they touch to gold.

Entrepreneurs are said to have the 'Midas touch'

Early scientists were enthralled at the notion of turning base metals into gold. These alchemists even included Sir Isaac Newton among their number. Entrepreneurs have been seen as 'The New Alchemists' in books by Dick Hanson in 1982 and Charles Handy in 2000.

Silicon Valley has been described as the second Californian goldrush, and Jack Welch, the corporate entrepreneur, saw GE as a goldmine.

Profile Jack Welch

On his journey to the top post in GE, Jack Welch took over as head of GE Credit, now renamed GE Capital. Begun in the 1930s to provide credit for GE's appliance dealers, under Welch the business grew and diversified. In 1977, earnings were $67 million with 7000 employees. In 2000, earnings had grown to $5.2 billion – and there were 89,000 employees.

Welch claims that GE Capital always looked an easy way to make money, 'a goldmine', when lined up alongside an industrial operation. There was no investment in R&D, no factories to be built, and no 'metal to bend'. Competitiveness and success did not depend upon scale and critical mass. The business was based on intellectual capital. GE needed to find smart, creative people and use GE's strong balance sheet to back them.

J. Welch, Jack, 2001

Another aspect of benefit orientation is the ability to get the right deal. While the other party is trying to work out the issues and evaluate the best response, the entrepreneur knows what he or she is after and will get it. If they don't they will simply walk away and not try to do half a deal.

An entrepreneur of our acquaintance had been negotiating with a French company and the time came to finalise the deal. He went to their offices in Paris and met the person he had been negotiating with, who was the son of the owner of the business. Our entrepreneur friend thought it was just a matter of a few minor issues and the contract would be signed and they would have a celebratory dinner together. He was surprised when the father walked in, overruled his son and changed some important details. The father expected that our friend, who was the same age as his son, would just cave in and sign. To his surprise our friend said nothing. He packed his papers away, picked up his coat and walked out. Father and son came running after him and agreed to stay with the original deal.

Brian Souter had this same 'deal-making' talent.

Brian Souter is a deal-maker who enjoys a personal involvement.
In 1997, a study by Merrill Lynch concluded that the so-called 'Souter-factor' contributed 10 percent to Stagecoach's profits. He had a proven record in spotting opportunities, concluding deals and successfully integrating new acquisitions into the existing Stagecoach business.

Woolmar, *Stagecoach*, 1999

Performance orientation

This is the Advantage side of action focus. Excellence in this area generally requires the ability to handle numbers and understand them. Some 'technique' and know-how is required here but there still has to be the ability to pick out the key issues. Entrepreneurs who are strong in this area are also good at detail. They know what really drives performance and they measure and monitor it.

Again, Brian Souter provides a good example. He gained his 'technique' and financial know-how from his accountancy training – when combined with his natural talents it produced an excellence that amazed the City professionals.

Souter had previously worked as an accountant for Arthur Andersen, and valued the discipline this experience had instilled in him. He had realised the importance of recording details and developing a structured approach to decision-making.

As a result he was never overawed by City professionals. It was said of him by one broker that he would never be picked out in a selection parade as a person worth millions, and yet his grip on detailed issues is 'unbelievable'. He knows exactly what matters and can focus on it very quickly.

Woolmar, *Stagecoach*, 1999

Performance orientation is an important requirement for the corporate entrepreneur because big business is often obsessed by performance indicators. The entrepreneur will outshine his management colleagues because he will bring his Advantage facet to bear on the performance issue. This gives the entrepreneur an all-important edge. It is why Jack Welch rose through the ranks of GE to become its CEO at the age of 46.

On his way to the top, the head of GE's human resources (HR) filed this assessment of Welch's potential for heading up the chemical and metallurgical division with sales of $400 million.

Jack Welch has many strengths. He is a natural entrepreneur and driven to grow a business; he is creative, positive and dynamic. He is also a natural leader, with considerable technical and organisational abilities.

But, inevitably, there are some limitations. He does not welcome criticism and he has a tendency on occasions to get too involved in the details. Relying on his quick mind and intuition he can sometimes shun the assistance of others. He can be very protective of his part of GE and take an 'anti-establishment view' of other GE activities.

J. Welch, *Jack*, 2001

Perhaps surprisingly from this review, Welch got the job – but he did so because the business performance of every division he took over became outstanding. His attention to detail, his measurement of what mattered most and his ability to keep his finger on the pulse were what made him able to deliver. It was the ability to perform beyond expectation that enabled this young outsider to enter and eventually win the race for CEO spot. Welch then 'led GE to one revenue-earning record after another' – his behaviour was habitual.

In Welch's case, what was an advantage to the company was also an advantage to himself. Like many successful corporate entrepreneurs, Welch had to threaten to leave in order to get the promotion he knew he deserved. When the crunch comes, the entrepreneur goes for personal advantage rather than advantage to the company.

Resourcing

Entrepreneurs never see lack of resources as a barrier. They just get on with things and find the resources they need as they go along. The resourcing component of their Advantage facet sees to that. They 'beg, steal or borrow', or do whatever it takes to get what they need.

Starting up and then growing an enterprise certainly does require resources – particularly financial. Research has shown that 'under-capitalisation' is one of the most frequent causes of business failure – the business simply runs out of cash.

True entrepreneurs find ways around resourcing problems, as they do with all problems. Most times they turn them into opportunities – an example of their Creativity facet combining with their Advantage facet. Some entrepreneurs have started second businesses providing goods or services that they themselves found were in short supply.

When Anita Roddick opened the first Body Shop in 1976 she had no resources.

Profile **The Body Shop**

The Body Shop's early success was dependent upon Anita Roddick not having any money. She ran the business as people ran their homes in World War II – relying on refilling, re-using and recycling. And those practices were never lost.

A designer produced The Body Shop logo for £25. Friends helped her to fill bottles. Every label was hand-written. She painted everything dark green because that was the best colour for covering the damp patches on the walls.

She discovered that the plastic bottles used by hospitals for urine samples were the cheapest around. She refilled because that saved her having to keep buying new bottles.

Roddick, Business as Unusual, *2000*

Vision

Leaders have their own vision facet that enables them to see the future in new ways. Entrepreneurs have something of this but it is set within their Advantage facet – they see the future in new ways that are advantageous to them and their enterprise.

Entrepreneurs use these insights into the future to gain advantage. Brian Souter could see the way deregulation of the bus industry was going and he took advantage of it. Akio Morita could see that young people wanted a portable stereo recorder. Anita Roddick believes that entrepreneurs have a 'vision of something new and a belief in it that's so strong that it becomes reality'. In Roddick's case it was 'natural cosmetics in different sizes and in cheap, refillable containers' – and that was visionary in the 1970s.

For the entrepreneur, vision may not be quite on the grand scale of the visionary leader but it is an important element of opportunity selection. They see things before other people do and are prepared to have a go.

The vision horizon of the entrepreneur is much shorter than it is for the leader. Entrepreneurs have a vision for things that are close enough to realisation for them to work – they have to be within their reach or only slightly beyond.

Some entrepreneurs feel that 'vision' is too grandiose a word to describe what to them seems obvious, but there is certainly an element of vision in any insight that picks out tomorrow's opportunities.

●———●

Think through the four aspects of the Advantage facet that support the opportunity selection talent.

How do you rate yourself on

> »   *benefit orientation*
> »   *performance orientation*
> »   *resourcing*
> »   *vision?*

Think whether you are much stronger in one of these or whether you have a similar strength across them all.

If you have a particular strength then give yourself a score out of 10 on that – otherwise give yourself an average score: **my score on the elements of opportunity selection is** _____

Compare the opportunity selection score you gave yourself on page 93 with the one you have just given for the four elements. There should be some correlation between the two. It is unlikely that you will be good at opportunity selection if you are not also good at one or more of the elements that feed the selection talent.

Consider the Advantage facet as a whole. Give yourself a final score out of 10: **my final score is** _____

Chapter 10 Creativity

Creativity has a long history and is still going strong.

'When the idea flashed across his mind the philosopher jumped out of his bath exclaiming, "Heureka! Heureka!" And, without waiting to dress himself, ran home to try the experiment.'

Vitruvius Pollio, *De Architectum*, 1st century BC

Archimedes was a Greek philosopher, he was a thinker. He lived in an environment where he was expected to have the answers. So when King Heiro suspected that his new gold crown might have been alloyed with a lesser metal, he went to Archimedes.

Archimedes solved the problem in a moment of insight, a 'Eureka moment', in the public baths. Inventors and scientists are still having their Eureka moments.

Inventors and scientists are still having their Eureka moments

Stephen Hawking, the Lucasian Professor at Cambridge – a position once held by Isaac Newton – had what he has himself called a Eureka moment.

One of Professor Hawking's greatest achievements was in the realm of black holes. His work on black holes began with a 'Eureka moment' in 1970, a few days after the birth of his daughter, Lucy. 'While getting into bed, I realised that I could apply to black holes the causal theory I had developed for singularity theorems.'

The *Independent*, 12 January 2002

These Eureka stories tell us several things about creativity:

>> it can be *triggered* by a problem to solve
>> the answer can come in a *moment* of insight
>> there is *delight* and excitement in finding an answer
>> creativity needs the right *environment*.

Entrepreneurs experience Eureka moments too – an expression of their Creativity facet.

The following story traces Jerry Kaplan's great idea – the pen computer or PDA (Personal Digital Assistant) as we call it today. We look at Jerry's experience under the four Eureka headings.

The trigger

The trigger may be a known problem, as with Archimedes' body density problem or Hawking's black holes. Other times it is the recognition of a problem, as in Jerry Kaplan's case – it's whatever starts you thinking.

> **Jerry Kaplan had a PhD in Artificial Intelligence from the University of Pennsylvania** and had spent time on the research staff of Stanford University. He had been doing some work for Lotus and at the time of this story was visiting their offices in Boston and needed to get home to San Francisco.
>
> Mitchell Kapor was making the same trip in his private jet and Jerry hitched a lift. Kapor, the founder of Lotus, the world's largest independent software company at the time, was 36 years old and a millionaire: a US entrepreneur superstar.
>
> Once they were properly airborne, Kapor showed Kaplan his latest gadget, the lightest and most powerful computer available in the world at that time. He then dug various bits of paper, including a used chewing gum wrapper, out of his pockets. They were the notes he had jotted down that day. Ideas, phone numbers, everything. He began to input the details into his Lotus Agenda.
>
> He complained bitterly about the time it took him to get himself organised every day, moaning most about the need to write something down on scraps of paper before he could enter it into his computer.
>
> Kaplan, *Start Up*, 1997

Mitchell had identified the need and defined the problem. It was this trigger that started them both thinking.

The Eureka moment

The moment of insight – coming up with ideas and solving problems – involves a range of thinking processes: deduction by logic or association, synthesis and analysis, imagination and visualisation, conscious and subconscious thought.

There are also specific abilities that help. Some people are able to pick out patterns from a mass of information. They can spot trends and identify opportunities this way. Others work with incomplete data and jump to the answer. They have a nose for the solution. Perhaps because of their technical backgrounds, Kaplan and Kapor began by logical reasoning.

The two continued to talk about the future of computers, about how small and how light they could be made. They discussed problems in miniaturising components – disk drives, the power supply, the screen and the keyboard.

Were it not for the keyboard, commented Kaplan, it would be possible to make a flat computer which looked like a book.

Animated, they continued to talk about a whole range of possibilities. But they kept returning to the problem of the keyboard.

Their Creativity facet was doing well on the logical reasoning front. The foundation for the Eureka moment had been laid, but it was yet to arrive. They still did not have a solution.

They took a light lunch and Kaplan settled down for a brief nap, thinking 'I get my best ideas in my sleep'.

Kaplan had a doze, but woke up with a start. He had been dreaming about the keyboard problem.

He challenged Kapor with the idea of a pen instead of a traditional keyboard. Instead of typing in the information, design some sort of stylus alternative.

The debate continued and words such as 'notebook' began to seem more appropriate than 'laptop' for what they were imagining.

They suddenly realised their vision of a notebook pointed the way to the future. This was their 'Eureka moment'. The idea was novel, but, at the same time, obvious. They had combined familiar elements into something radically new.

Kaplan, *Start Up*, 1997

Reason and logic had got Kaplan and Kapor to the real question – it required a Eureka moment to give them the answer.

The joy

Wherever Kaplan's creativity came from, it produced the same euphoria that Archimedes had experienced some 2000 years earlier and Stephen Hawking had felt in 1970. He commented that the powerful emotion he felt at the time was one he had experienced a couple of times before – and always at some unexpected moment after he had been struggling with a seemingly intractable problem. This time it left him and Mitchell Kapor momentarily speechless.

Creativity brings joy. Einstein had the same experience as Jerry Kaplan: 'The idea that the gravitational field has only relative existence was the happiest thought of my life' (Pais, *Subtle is the Lord, The Science and Life of Albert Einstein*, 1982).

Joy in creativity is a powerful motivation to continuing creativity – to experience that special moment again and again urges creative people forward. It can also bring great anxiety as they wonder if their creative moments might leave them.

The creative environment

There is a mystery about creativity. We don't really know where it comes from but we can observe that it is strongly influenced by the environment. Artists often know the place or the time when they do their best work. There is a similar environmental influence for the entrepreneur. Silicon Valley has an entrepreneurial culture in which creativity flourishes. It is an environment of encouragement that allows the unthinkable, that permits the wackiest idea to go forward. It is an environment that says 'yes' rather than 'no'.

It is also an environment that attracts creative entrepreneurial people, who spark each other. Being creative in that environment is not difficult.

When Kaplan came up with his great idea it was on the edge – too revolutionary to be put over by reason alone. People had to buy into the idea with their hearts. When he took the idea to a venture-capital group he went without business plan, slide show, financial projections or prototype.

The meeting was not going smoothly. There was scepticism. Kaplan decided to take a risk and tossed his leather document case into the centre of the table, declaring that people ought to realise that this maroon case contained a model of the future of computing. He succeeded in gaining people's attention. The atmosphere changed.

Soon a deal was secured, and the idea was valued at $3 million. Without a business plan and without any proper financial projections, it was clear that it was the idea that was being backed.

Kaplan, *Start Up*, 1997

Six years on and $75 million later, Kaplan's Go Corporation was gone. It was before its time but despite such setbacks Silicon Valley continues to say 'yes' to wacky ideas – its creative entrepreneurial environment lives on.

* * *

»» *Does the story of Jerry Kaplan ring any bells for you?*
»» *Can you recall times when you have had a similar experience?*
»» *Have you had ideas come to you and were they triggered by something?*
»» *Did you then work on the idea and develop it into an opportunity?*
»» *Did that come as a Eureka moment, or was it simply a logical and rather obvious conclusion?*
»» *What about the delight and excitement?*
»» *Have you experienced pleasure when you suddenly see a solution to a problem you have been wrestling with?*
»» *Can you think of places and times that have been particularly creative?*
»» *Have there been situations in which you found it difficult to think creatively?*

Put a tick against the four elements that you recognise from your own experience:

»» *creativity triggers*
»» *moments of insight*
»» *delight and excitement*
»» *a creative environment.*

Creativity: the servant facet

Creativity is a 'servant talent'. It expresses itself through other talents. The scientist, the gifted footballer, the concert pianist and the chess player achieve excellence when they are at their most creative. These people may have outstanding competence in their field, but it is their creativity that makes them different. They do things in new ways that set them apart.

>>> Creativity serves and fuels the other entrepreneurial facets.
>>> Creativity provides the opportunities, Advantage selects, Focus delivers.
>>> It is the first link in the chain.

There is constant feedback in this process as situations change with new barriers to be overcome and new opportunities to be taken. The Creativity facet never sleeps.

Creativity is about ideas and opportunity spotting; Advantage and Focus are about opportunity selecting and taking.

Without Creativity, Advantage has nothing to feed off. Without Advantage, Creativity produces little more than an ideas database. Some inventors are like this and are very unhappy when others exploit their ideas – but the truth is that they are often not able to do this themselves because they are not strong on Advantage.

Creativity and Focus work together

In a newspaper interview, Thomas Edison, one of the world's greatest inventors, made a remark that has become famous: 'Genius is one per cent inspiration and ninety-nine per cent perspiration'.

In our terms Edison was saying that genius is one percent Creativity and 99 percent Focus. This may be true if time is the measure, but in value Creativity must come first – without it there would be no idea to bring to fruition.

The combination of Creativity and Focus points up the difference between invention and innovation. Invention is the Creativity part. Innovation includes that, but employs Focus to take the idea to a successful conclusion – which is where the perspiration comes in.

Creativity serves the Ego facet

The ability to overcome barriers is an important characteristic of the entrepreneur. To achieve this the entrepreneur needs to be strong in the self-confidence and courage elements of the Ego facet. Strength in the Creativity facet feeds directly in to these elements. The entrepreneur knows that there are always solutions to problems. An entrepreneur's creativity brings the ability to see angles on a problem that others miss. Entrepreneurs can think 'outside the box' and come up with novel solutions – often creating an opportunity out of a crisis. This gives the entrepreneur a particular approach to risk that is discussed in chapter 14.

A trinity of outputs

The Creativity facet provides the entrepreneur with three important outputs:

>>> ideas
>>> opportunities
>>> solutions.

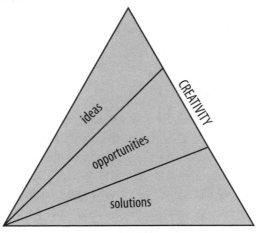

The Creativity facet

Entrepreneurs are people who deliver – they don't just talk. These three outputs are their starting points, but they may not be good at all three.

Those strong on ideas will have some of the characteristics of the inventor. They will need to be careful not to become too fascinated with ideas for their own sake. They must see ideas as a means to an end.

Entrepreneurs thrive on opportunities. They see them everywhere but they need the other facets so as not to waste the opportunities that their Creativity facet has revealed.

Solutions are the output of the creative ability we generally call 'problem solving'. The solutions may produce opportunities but mostly they enable barriers to be overcome or circumvented. Many never complete the entrepreneurial journey because they fail to find solutions to the obstacles along the way. They are weak on this aspect of Creativity.

Ideas

For the entrepreneur there are two difficulties with ideas.

>>> Many ideas are not new: an organisation that helps inventors has found that 40 percent of so-called 'new ideas' are not new at all.

>>> Most ideas are impractical or have no commercial value: only about 2 percent of patented ideas ever reach the marketplace.

Profile Eric McKellar Watt

Eric McKellar Watt was a successful entrepreneur in Glasgow who built 'a sausage empire from a prison mixing bowl', as his obituary put it.

Mr Watt 'was always willing to try something new. Once he experimented with whisky-flavoured sausages. They were not a commercial success and later with a wry smile, he mused: "Let's face it. Who wants to drink their whisky out of a sausage?".'

Obituary in the Times, *July, 2001*

The two inputs to the entrepreneur process are ideas and people. If only 2 percent of ideas are commercially viable, then whether 5 percent or 50 percent of us are potential entrepreneurs, the odds on a successful business outcome are not good, at 1000:1 or 100:1 against.

All this suggests that ideas are very risky. But in the hands of the entrepreneur amazing things can happen.

The reason that entrepreneurs make ideas work for them and defeat the odds is that they draw upon their other facets. We have already mentioned Focus – Edison's perspiration – and Advantage that selects the right ideas.

Another is belief – part of the Social facet. If the entrepreneur doesn't believe in his or her idea then nobody else is likely to either. Often a weaker idea wins over a stronger one because there is an entrepreneur committed to it. Entrepreneurs beat the odds suggested by the 'idea plus people' equation.

Ideas should not just be limited to products and inventions. There can be new ideas about production, selling, marketing and distribution. When the salesman brings a deal out of nothing he is using his creative ability as much if not more so than the inventor.

Over its long history, Coca-Cola has been rich in ideas thanks to its entrepreneurs. The original inventor, Dr John Pemberton, was not an entrepreneur and never made any money out his famous drink. The first entrepreneur to come along was Frank Robinson. He invented the Coca-Cola name and its script logo and many advertising and promotional schemes. In the late 1880s 'every street car in Atlanta carried an ad for the drink'. Robinson recognised the importance of branding and mass advertising. By 1895 Coca-Cola was a national drink in the US thanks to Asa Candler, who had joined Robinson. His idea was to use other organisations to distribute and sell his syrup across the country, so saving the need for capital.

Two entrepreneurs, Benjamin Thomas and Joseph Whitehead, hit on the idea of bottling the beverage. Candler signed away the bottling rights for just $1 a gallon for the syrup – a decision that was to cost Coca-Cola millions of dollars to buy back. They introduced the new crimped cap to seal the bottles and set up bottling plants across the US.

Thomas and Whitehead 'were at the same time salesmen, cheer-leaders, advertising agents, bottlers, lawyers, negotiators, venture capitalists, chemists and accountants. They created the prototype of the American franchise system, and they brought Coca-Cola to the masses.' They were entrepreneurs.

Pendergast, For God, Country and Coca-Cola, *1996*

Opportunities

Opportunities are what makes the entrepreneur different from the inventor and those who are just 'ideas' people. Sometimes an idea translates into an opportunity but more often something has to be done to the idea first. In the last example Dr Pemberton created the idea but Robertson turned it into an opportunity.

An opportunity is one step up from an idea. Opportunities are often created when two or more ideas come together. It was the two ideas of bottling and franchising that created the enormous opportunity not only for Thomas and Whitehead but for the bottlers, of whom several became millionaires. This opportunity-sharing made Coca-Cola the first real entrepreneur generator in the US.

Opportunities can be classified and analysed. The advent of the new, such as computers, mobile phones or the Internet, creates its own set of opportunities. So do trends in culture, like concern with health and security. Government regulation and deregulation create 'million-dollar'-type opportunities.

> **Brian Souter was the son of a bus driver and he had an accountancy qualification,** so when the British government deregulated bus transport the opportunities were obvious to him.

When legislation systematically opened up the coach, bus and rail transport industries, Souter saw a series of opportunities. Through his foresight Stagecoach was an early mover in every privatisation.

Woolmar, *Stagecoach*, 1999

Souter of course did not do a SWOT analysis of the opportunity. He was mad about buses and the opportunity was obvious. It was the same for Edward Stobart. The road haulage business, like buses, was not a glamorous one, but it held the same opportunity thanks to deregulation.

> **When Edward Stobart, aged 22, split off haulage from other family business interests set up by his father, Eddie,** the timing couldn't have been better. Eddie had already created his own opportunity. He had taken orders because he was better organised than the competition. For him, deregulation of the industry was a bonus opportunity. Somehow entrepreneurs seem able to position themselves ready for the right moment.

Edward Stobart fell in love with lorries and opted to relocate the small family transport business to Carlisle. By the time he did this the law had changed – in his favour. The 1968 Transport Bill scrapped certain restrictions and allowed hauliers of any size to transport goods over any distance for the first time.

Whilst Stobart's timing was fortuitous, his move took place at the time when a horde of other small hauliers also seized the opportunity and entered the industry.

Davies, *The Eddie Stobart Story*, 2001

Edward's door of opportunity was open, but he wasn't the only one going through it. His other entrepreneurial facets helped him keep the competition at bay and create the biggest private firm in Britain with a fan club of 25,000 paid-up members. In the process he became one of the wealthiest people in the country.

Souter and Stobart were in the right place at the right time to connect their passion with the new opportunity provided by deregulation. You could say they were lucky or perhaps, in a variant of Pasteur's famous words, that 'Opportunity comes to prepared minds'.

Solutions

Ideas and opportunities may start the entrepreneur along the road but it is problem-solving ability that ensures the journey does not end prematurely. Solutions are the output of problem solving – an indispensable element of the Creativity facet.

It has links with the Ego facet that gives the entrepreneur the right attitude to problems. They always see a cup half full and not half empty. They have the courage and self-confidence to tackle giants. Richard Branson's challenge of British Airways (BA) was a classic confrontation but here is a more day-to-day example.

In the 1980s there was a strike in some UK government offices, so that income tax and VAT were not collected for several months. When the strike was over, companies received huge bills. For one small company in Birmingham, England, the bills could not have come at a worse time. They just could not pay. The tax authorities could not understand why the company had not put the money in a reserve account until the strike was over.

Confronted with this problem, the entrepreneurial managing director took action. He and his financial controller tossed a coin to see who should go to the Inland Revenue and who should go to the VAT office. But the message was to be the same. 'We can't pay you. If you demand payment now we close the business and you get nothing. If you agree to schedule the debts over six months then you might get your money.'

When the two men returned they had both done the deal. The company survived and the taxes got paid.

The Ego facet of the managing director might have given him the courage and confidence to go to the tax authorities, but he needed his Creativity to offer a solution that won the day.

Entrepreneurs are very good at turning problems into opportunities as they come up with solutions. Whilst the manager is pleased to have solved a problem and moves on to the next one, the entrepreneur often sees opportunity written all over the solution.

Armand Hammer was like this, and because of it became one of the world's richest men. It all started with his father's ill health and a failing pharmacy business. Armand had embarked on his medical studies, but he was the only family member available to take over.

Hammer was excited by the challenge, but wondered if he had the ability to turn the company around and succeed. Could he possibly even run a business and study at the same time? Never intimidated, he seized the opportunity and set out to do something useful – if for no other reason than to reward the parents who had been generous to him.

Hammer was a natural entrepreneur, and the business grew rapidly as problems, solutions and opportunities bubbled together. At the age of 21 his personal income was $1 million net – and that was in 1919. Two years earlier his father had a few dozen workers, now he employed nearly 1500.

It happened this way:

Intrigued that orders for tincture of ginger had increased by a factor of a thousand, Hammer set out to find the reason. Surprised that he even needed to ask, a customer in Richmond, Virginia, poured some ginger ale into a glass, added tincture of ginger and some ice cubes. The resultant potion fizzed away. When Hammer drank the brew he was amazed at the kick it gave him. But after all, ginger tincture contains alcohol!

These were prohibition days, and Hammer realised he was sitting on a goldmine. It is what he did next that marks Armand Hammer out as a true entrepreneur. His Creativity facet shone.

Hammer made enquiries, and soon learned that some of the leading pharmaceutical companies were already very active in making tincture of ginger.

He visited the company bankers and asked for letters of credit for over $1 million. He found out which countries were exporting ginger to America – and it was mainly India, Nigeria and Fiji – and sent out agents to buy up all future production. In effect he cornered the world market in ginger – and thus he controlled the manufacture of tincture of ginger in America. All the major pharmaceutical companies had to obtain their supplies from him.

Almost overnight the company order book shot through the roof and Armand Hammer was a very rich young man. (See Hammer, *Hammer: Witness to History*, 1988.)

The Creativity ability to see the second step – in this case cornering the market in ginger – was something that Hammer showed again and again. He was a serial entrepreneur with a strong Creativity facet.

———●———●———

In giving yourself a final score on your Creativity facet think through the three outputs of

》》》 *ideas*
》》》 *opportunities*
》》》 *solutions.*

Which of these do you consider you are best at? If you are not sure, then which of the three do you enjoy most? Try to rank them in order, putting the strongest first.

If it is ideas, then you may be more an inventor than an entrepreneur.

If it is opportunities, then you will need to be strong in the Advantage facet so that you know which opportunities to go for. You will probably enjoy starting things up.

If it is solutions, then you will enjoy the entrepreneur journey maybe more than the start-up stage. Combined with a strong Focus facet, you will make real progress.

Give yourself a final score out of 10: **my Creativity score is** _____

Chapter 11 Ego

A strong Ego facet is a must for the entrepreneur.

By this we do not mean that entrepreneurs are, or need to be, self-centred individuals who get pleasure out of cheating others and gaining at somebody else's expense. Some may be like this but most are not.

We use Ego in the broader sense to refer to the inner self, to what makes us tick and gives us purpose. Without a strong Ego facet, talent is simply wasted – and that applies whatever our talents might be.

The Focus, Advantage, Creativity and Team facets are the talents that the entrepreneur needs if he or she is 'to build something of recognised value' but it is the Ego facet that provides the temperament to do so. It is Ego that makes these talents effective.

Entrepreneurs have told us:

>>> I want to make a difference, to leave footprints
>>> I want to show my dad that I'm worth something
>>> I want to be the best
>>> I want to be rich
>>> I want something better for myself and my family.

These wants are fuelled by the entrepreneur's own ego – something within their personality that drives them forward and makes them achievers.

Some, but not all, of the wants are self-serving.

For many entrepreneurs these motivations change over time. Making a difference, being rich and wanting something better are all measures that move ahead of the entrepreneur. The entrepreneur never reaches these goals – the difference has to be bigger, the wealth greater. The better has to be even better. These ambitions all move tantalisingly forward as they are approached.

Entrepreneurs have a restless ego that drives them. Often they sell the business that they have created and plan to retire but they rarely do. They seek new challenges – ever onward and upward.

This is why we do not class the person who sits back when they have achieved a certain level of lifestyle as a true entrepreneur.

Eddie Stobart, the father of Edward the haulage business king, also had the Ego facet of the entrepreneur. In the following interview we see Eddie, aged 50, rationalising his motivations, only for his entrepreneurial ego to take over.

Eddie Stobart commented that he only planned to continue to work full-time until all his children were settled. He had never intended to devote the whole of his life to work – there were other things to do – but there always seemed a reason to keep going. He had thought he might sell up completely, but then the idea for a warehousing business came up. It required an investment of time and money, but once established, it should generate an income and look after the whole family.

It was not an opportunity he felt he could miss...

Hunter Davies, his biographer, adds that Stobart never lost his eye for a deal. There was another new business to be created before he relinquished control of the family firm.

Davies, *The Eddie Stobart Story*, 2001

Ego's shades

The Ego facet of the entrepreneur crystal has many shades. They divide into an inner group of deeper shades and an outer group of shades that others see and recognise:

» the inner group – explains what the entrepreneur is like on the inside
» the outer group – explains how the entrepreneur deals with what is outside.

It is important that these inner and outer groups are matched – each challenging the other. As the potential entrepreneur moves through to become an experienced entrepreneur the strength within grows to match the greater external challenges.

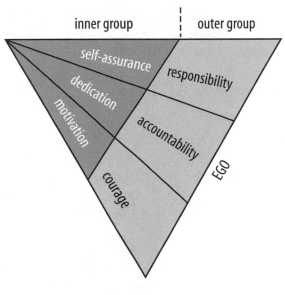

inner group | outer group

self-assurance
dedication
motivation
responsibility
accountability
courage
EGO

Ego's shades

Too many problems too early can daunt even the most driven entrepreneur.

Bill Gates, for one, almost gave up before he had started. In this reference Roberts is the inventor of the world's first PC, the Altair, for which Gates and Allen wrote the computer language BASIC.

Roberts recalled Gates coming into his office and screaming. He was yelling that everyone was trying to steal his software and he would never be able to make any serious money.

Gates had convinced himself that BASIC was not generating much revenue because too many people had obtained pirate copies and not paid anything for them. Totally frustrated and demoralised he offered the complete rights to BASIC to Roberts for just $6500. Had he taken it, Gates might have made the biggest mistake of his life for Microsoft might never have happened. The offer was declined – Roberts later commenting that he actually liked Bill Gates and his partner, Paul Allen, and did not want to take advantage of their relative youth.

Wallace and Erickson, *Hard Drive*, 1993

Gates of course recovered from this lapse in motivation and courage, though his anxiety that others might steal his software is still there. People mess with Microsoft at their peril.

The inner group of the Ego facet

Self-assurance

This is a key attribute for the entrepreneur. To have self-assurance means that you have an inner confidence in your own abilities and values. You can trust your own judgement. You know you have an instinct for getting things right. You decide on a course of action and go forward without thinking that you may be wrong. You are sure of yourself.

Self-assurance gives people an air of confidence that others see and often are prepared to follow. If an entrepreneur is not strong on the Team facet then his or her Ego facet often compensates as their self-assurance attracts a band of subordinates.

Upbringing has a strong influence on our self-assurance. Richard Branson's mother made a point of developing it in her son. As a young child she made him walk home across the fields alone whilst she drove on home. One early morning with no warning she sent him on a cycle ride that took him all day to complete. We have already noted that Jack Welch's mother 'pumped confidence into him'. Anita Roddick's father died when she was 10 years old, and she and her mother had to run the family café business together. Her mother told her 'Be special, be anything but mediocre'.

Upbringing has a strong influence on our self-assurance

Self-assurance is not a static attribute. It builds or falls as we go through life.

Jack Welch discovered this when he blew the roof off a factory. The following day Welch had to drive 100 miles and explain to his corporate chief executive, Charlie Reed, exactly what had happened. He knew what had gone wrong and he knew how to fix the problem – but this did not prevent him from being nervous. It was not only the building that had been destroyed – his confidence had also been shattered.

Reed's response took Welch by surprise and was a lesson he never forgot. This is the lesson he drew from it: the last thing people need when they have made mistakes is discipline or sanctioning. Their confidence needs restoring. They need encouraging.

Welch adopted the term 'GE vortex' to describe the intense pressure that was sometimes placed on people who had made errors. It caused them to lose their confidence, to panic and to be filled with self-doubt. He saw this happen to some very senior people, and very few of them ever recovered from it.

J. Welch, *Jack*, 2001

Entrepreneurs sometimes have this experience when their business fails. Most learn from the experience, and start again a little wiser and with an even stronger determination to prove that they can make it. The ability to bounce back is an important attribute of entrepreneurs but for some the attitudes to failure of the banks and society in general and the archaic bankruptcy laws are too much.

>>> *Were you confident as a child and have you become more self-assured as you got older?*

>>> *Do you just get on with things and decide for yourself or do you have self-doubts, checking with others before you make a decision?*

>>> *Is your self-worth something that bothers you or don't you think about it much?*

>>> *Do you bounce back when things have gone wrong or does it make you feel defeated?*

Dedication

Entrepreneurs often have within them a passion that affects all they do. Edward Stobart had two: one was customers and the other clean lorries.

Colleagues commented that they often heard Stobart say 'No problem' to a telephone request. They always knew it meant there would be a problem. Stobart had a habit of never turning down work – whatever it meant in terms of load or distance, and regardless of whether all his drivers were busy. He was not averse to unloading someone else's material to fit in a special delivery. And somehow he always contrived to deliver everything on time.

He also had a passion for clean lorries. They were cleaned every weekend, and sometimes more often. It was quite normal for them to be cleaned late on Christmas Eve. Edward declared he would not be able to sleep on Sundays or bank holidays if he left any of his lorries standing dirty.

Davies, *The Eddie Stobart Story*, 2001

This dedication served him well and became a distinguishing feature of his business.

A number of entrepreneurs have used dedication to the customer as their hallmark and it has rarely failed.

>>> *Are you passionate about some things or do you just let life go by?*

>>> *Could you stamp your passion on your business?*

>>> *How dedicated are you to your work – is it all-consuming or just one of the things you do?*

Motivation – to achieve, to win, to prove something

Entrepreneurs are strongly motivated individuals. They are self-starters. Their pushiness arises in part from their Advantage and Focus facets but over and above that is their need to achieve and to be seen to achieve.

In some cases this motivation is clear. Waves of entrepreneurial endeavour have swept across the US as new immigrant groups have come to the country. Their motivation was survival and the entrepreneurs amongst them took action.

In other cases people have responsibility thrust upon them. A parent is ill or dies, and the family business needs to be kept going, as with Armand Hammer's pharmacy and Anita Roddick's café.

Entrepreneurs are often out to prove their worth to themselves, their parents or somebody else. We know of one entrepreneur whose motivation was to buy out the company that sacked him – and he did!

Profile Howard Schultz

Howard Schultz joined Starbucks Coffee Company as marketing director in 1982. When they wouldn't listen to his idea about espresso bars he left and set up on his own. Within two years he was in a position to buy out Starbucks. When a boss won't go along with your idea there is a strong motivation to prove them wrong.

Competitiveness is found strongly in some entrepreneurs – but not all. Jack Welch says that he was always competitive. It started in childhood and was clear for all to see in his climb up the ranks at GE. The personnel chief marked him down for being 'too competitive'. When he took the helm at GE his competitiveness became a business objective. He wanted GE to become 'the most competitive enterprise on earth' – and it did.

Bill Gates's attitude to competition has got him into the law courts. One of his biographers speaks of Gates's 'relentless drive to dominate the personal computer software industry'. 'With every negotiation, Gates and Microsoft have an "I win" mentality.'

The reasons behind an entrepreneur's motivation may be complex and personal but there is little doubt that they are highly motivated and driven individuals.

The 'why' of motivation may be difficult to answer, but the 'what' is clearer. Studies have shown that the main reason why entrepreneurs set out on their journey is the need for independence – they want to be their own boss. Often they are fed up with their present boss and believe they can do better.

The second most common motivator is the challenge of the task. Like the mountain climber who has to climb a mountain because it is there – but each time making the task a little more difficult.

Perhaps surprisingly, the motivation to make money comes some way down the list. It matters only as a measure of achievement.

———————

Think through what motivates you.

>>> *Why do you do what you do?*
>>> *Are you a competitive person who always has to win?*
>>> *Do you feel comfortable as an employee or would you rather be your own boss?*
>>> *Do you crave independence or challenges?*
>>> *Do you want to be rich?*
>>> *What is your 'I want'?*

Try to summarise your motivation in life.

My main motivation is to _____

The inner group of the Ego facet is not easy to home in on. Perhaps Anita Roddick is right when she quotes Moses Znaimer: 'Being an entrepreneur is not within the realm of rational discussion. It is a burning pathological need.'

Rank yourself on the inner group of the Ego facet.
Look back over your answers to the earlier questions about self-assurance, dedication and motivation.

Do you have a 'burning pathological need' to be engaged in entrepreneurial activity or is it something you would like to try your hand at?

Give yourself two scores here, both out of 10.

First, your desire to be an entrepreneur. A low score does not matter at this stage, as once you are on the entrepreneurial track you will soon know whether this desire strengthens or fades.

My desire score is _____

Second, your inner group assessment. Do you feel that you have the psychological make-up the entrepreneur needs in terms of self-assurance, dedication and motivation? If you feel stronger in one than the other, make a note of it but put down your highest score rather than an average figure.

My inner group score is_____

The outer group of the Ego facet

The outer group all come from a key characteristic of the entrepreneur – his or her 'locus of control'.

In mathematics a circle is the locus of points equidistant from the centre. The ellipse and the parabola are similarly a locus of points in a particular relationship to fixed lines or points.

Psychologists have picked up this term and applied it to people and the way their personal control system operates. People live their lives in reference to particular fixed points.

For people with an internal locus of control, the fixed point is inside. They want to be in control of themselves and their situation. If anything goes wrong they blame themselves. They hate having to rely on other people.

Those with an external locus of control have a fixed point that is outside. They expect others to take control for them. When things go wrong they blame other people – it is never their fault.

The distinction is seen very clearly in sport. The sprinter with an internal locus of control who has a false start will blame his own lack of concentration. One with an external locus of control will blame the starting-block or the man with the starting pistol.

Entrepreneurs have an internal locus of control and from this come three important attributes:

» responsibility
» accountability
» courage.

Do you have an internal or an external locus of control?

Think through some of your own experiences as you answer this question.

Responsibility

Willingness to take responsibility for one's actions follows directly from the locus of control. If it is internal, then you will take responsibility; if external, you will expect others to do so.

At a breakfast meeting in a business incubator one of the tenants told the audience that his business was in trouble. He complained that the business plan the university business school had prepared for him was no good and that the manager of the incubator had brought him no customers.

When we asked him who was running his company he replied, aggressively, that he was.

This business owner was no entrepreneur – the support activities of the business school and the incubator had unwittingly fed his external locus of control. He had failed to realise that his business was his responsibility.

Responsibility-taking is a shade of the Ego facet that shines through for the entrepreneur. This may be difficult at first, particularly if your life has been dominated somewhat, but for the true entrepreneur this personality characteristic will eventually show itself.

Accountability

Accountability takes responsibility one step further. Accountability means that the entrepreneur holds him- or herself personally accountable for all aspects of the business.

Some entrepreneurs cover the walls of their office with performance data and check progress daily. It is as if they are the bank manager, the investor, the customer, the function heads and the employees all rolled into one – they check themselves out all the time.

Charles Forte, who built a hotel and catering empire, was like this – yet he was a man proud of his ability to delegate and work through a team.

Forte received key performance data for every division of the business every week. He ensured he had sufficient detail to appreciate the current strengths and weaknesses of every activity – hotels, restaurants, airport catering, contract catering – the lot. He was concerned with turnover, occupancy and profits. When something wasn't quite right he started asking questions…

Forte, *Forte*, 1997

Performance accountability is found in athletes as well as entrepreneurs – the common factor being that both groups have an internal locus of control and are high achievers.

Jonathan Edwards, the triple-jump champion, had failed dismally at the Barcelona Olympics and was harsh in his self-judgement. His biographer comments:

Top-flight athletes have a balance sheet and a 'bottom line' just as a business does. One column is marked 'win' and the other 'loss'. The truth cannot be hidden.

Folley, *A Time To Jump*, 2001

Athletes like Edwards feel themselves accountable for their performance and carry the agonies and pressures of that with them. Their future success, as with entrepreneurs, depends upon their ability to handle this.

This accountability is very personal.

For the athlete it is not just to their fans or the country they represent – it is to themselves.

For the entrepreneur it is not just to their customers, employees or shareholders – it is to themselves. They are their hardest taskmaster.

———●———●———

Rate yourself on responsibility and accountability.

»» *Do you find you assume responsibility easily, or does it require an effort?*
»» *Do people look to you to carry the responsibility of their decisions?*

Give yourself a score out of 10: **my responsibility score is** _____

»» *Do you feel accountable for what you do?*
»» *Do you set yourself targets and measure yourself against them?*
»» *Do you judge yourself or do you allow others to do that for you?*

Give yourself a score out of 10: **my accountability score is** _____

Courage

This is the most important in the external group of the Ego facet.

Business yields an awesome power over people's lives. It can reward them but it can also discard them. It can give people self-esteem; it can take their dignity. It can scare people, but it can also stretch imaginations. It can destroy and it can create. One outcome is stress; another is wonderful new products and services.

Law, *Open Minds*, 1998

The entrepreneur is in the thick of all this, sometimes the promoter, sometimes the victim – without courage there can be no survival, no second try.

Courage is what gets entrepreneurs started. Often they surprise themselves. Being made redundant is not a confidence-building experience, and yet it has been the trigger for many entrepreneurs to take the first step. It can happen to groups of people as well as individuals – they show corporate courage.

Profile **Chiat/Day**

When the US advertising agency Chiat/Day was merged with another large agency to create a $2 billion global operation, the London office decided to leave en bloc and go it alone. That took courage. The entrepreneur managing director, Andy Law, put it this way:

People stood together as one and mutinied. The one thing that bound people together was a desire to stay together and work with each other. The way forward as a standalone company was quite unclear, but not an immediate concern.

Law's contribution was an outline plan to start things moving.

Part of the plan was to call their existing clients and tell them what was happening. This included The Body Shop. Law comments: 'Anita Roddick, the supreme entrepreneur, asked if we needed financial help' – entrepreneurs often help each other at times of crisis.

Law, Open Minds, *1998*

But the entrepreneur needs courage for the good times as well as the bad. Building an enterprise is one challenge after another and the entrepreneur needs a 'day-in, day-out' kind of courage to persevere and to win through.

It is easy to take this routine courage for granted, especially as many entrepreneurs do not see themselves in this light. Even so it is a distinguishing mark of the true entrepreneur, not difficult to spot.

The entrepreneur's courage has three strands:

>>> the courage to confront situations
>>> the courage to face reality
>>> the courage to stand by your beliefs.

The courage to confront situations

Some managers prefer to avoid confrontation, or believe that given time most situations will change and the problems will diminish or even go away. Entrepreneurs cannot take this attitude – it is against their nature. A problem is there to be confronted.

People problems are the most difficult and require real courage. John Sculley found this when he fired Steve Jobs, the founder of Apple Computers. A year earlier he had raised a toast: 'Apple has one leader, Steve and me', but now…

Neither person was having fun; neither was enjoying what was happening. Both spoke quietly and with sadness. The split between Jobs and Sculley had become inevitable. A friendship was being destroyed and Apple itself might not even survive. Sculley's confidence was being shattered.

Jobs pleaded not to be dismissed from the company he had helped found. He would not get it. Eventually he burst out of the room, leaving Sculley alone. Wanting only to hide, Sculley retreated to one corner of the room and wondered how the situation had become so desperate.

Sculley, *Odyssey: Pepsi to Apple*, 1987

That took courage. Sculley knew he had to do it. He had told his board he would but that didn't make it any easier.

Most times courage does not have to do its job alone – it can draw on other facets. Sculley drew on Focus – action had to be taken.

Courage often calls on Creativity to find new ways of dealing with a problem. Courage faces up to problems – Creativity finds solutions.

>> **When Charles Forte was just starting out, he hit an unexpected problem.** He began to lose money. He had started one of the first fast-food operations in London, and that was in the 1930s – a man ahead of his time. He had run restaurants for his father and thought he knew how to make them profitable – it was a shock to him to find that he didn't.

Aged 23, he there and then worked out a simple money in, money out, margin formula that he used throughout his business career. His creativity had helped him analyse the problem and the solution became obvious.

He knew he had to enlarge the shop to serve more customers and increase income, and to reduce the staff to lower the wages bill. The first was relatively easy but getting rid of people required courage – he still remembered the agony of it more than 50 years later.

It was at a time when his business employed just 26 people that Charles Forte decided he had to lose three of them. It was one of the most difficult decisions he ever took. After all, he had recruited them and worked closely with them every day. They were hard workers – but in the 1930s they would not find alternative employment very easily.

It needed courage – which he found. Years later he believed that if he had not taken this decision at that time he would never have ended up employing over 60,000 people.

Forte, *Forte*, 1997

The most difficult situations to confront are those involving people, as John Sculley and Charles Forte found. Courage to deal with emotions is of a higher order than dealing with general business issues, and it never comes easily.

The courage to face reality

The self-assurance and enthusiasm of the entrepreneur are part of the Ego facet but over-optimism and arrogance can be its Achilles' heel. This can make entrepreneurs slow to pick up the signals of failure. Their desire to protect their own image of self-worth prevents them from facing reality. Like the captain of a sinking ship, they fail to believe it will actually sink.

Thinking the unthinkable and facing the reality of a situation require great personal courage. Eating one's words and admitting one is wrong is never easy, but for entrepreneurs it is particularly difficult – their own self-worth is at stake.

It is the courage part of the entrepreneur's Ego facet that saves the day. It is what enables the entrepreneur to learn from mistakes and start again.

> **One of our students set up his own business on graduation.** Despite receiving funding from 3*i*, the venture-capital company, the business had failed within two years. The bailiffs moved into his flat and took away his hi-fi equipment and everything else of value. A humiliating experience for the young man.
>
> Despite this he started again – he had learned the hard way but was not defeated. His entrepreneurial courage had seen him through.

One of the most important roles a business mentor, bank manager or any other entrepreneur enabler can play is to be the entrepreneur's reality check – but doing it in a way that does not dampen the entrepreneur's enthusiasm and self-belief.

Profile Jack Welch

When corporate entrepreneur, Jack Welch became CEO of GE he took a look at its nuclear business. He found a well-motivated team planning on three new nuclear reactor orders a year. The fact that they had had no orders for two years, that there had been a major incident at their Three Mile Island plant and were on their way to a $27 million loss had not registered.

Welch got the team to face reality. They changed their focus from hardware to service and became a very successful operation.

For years afterwards, Welch always believed his 'nuclear story' was a good reality-check. Entrepreneurs and managers should not bet on hope. Moreover self-delusion can take over an entire organisation and cause people to make stupid decisions. Whatever the circumstances and whatever the industry, it is always necessary to begin by facing up to reality.

J. Welch, Jack, 2001

The courage to stand by your beliefs

Entrepreneurs change the way business is done. They impose their personality on the company.

»» Steve Jobs fitted back into Apple Computers with ease though he had been away for 10 years. The glove was still the same shape – entrepreneurial and innovative.

»» Anita Roddick brought her campaigning environmental spirit to The Body Shop and made it distinctive.

»» Edward Stobart brought his fetish for clean lorries and smart drivers to a traditionally untidy haulage industry and in the process generated a fan club.

One of Edward Stobart's senior managers was always telling him that he had done a wonderful job with the company's image. But Edward never seemed to appreciate just what he meant. He had not set out to do anything about the company's image – he had just done what he believed in.

Davies, *The Eddie Stobart Story*, 2001

It is very easy to accept the way business is done and there is always pressure to conform. Investors and bank managers get nervous when entrepreneurs go against traditional ways of doing things.

The courage to stand by their beliefs is a characteristic of entrepreneurs. They enjoy being different.

•———•

How do you rate on courage?

This is difficult to assess – so try thinking of examples from your own experience when you have had to summon up courage to do something.

»» *What did you learn from that experience?*
»» *Did it make it easier next time?*
»» *How good are you at grasping nettles?*
»» *Do you prefer to get on with it or do you put it off – hoping it will go away?*
»» *Can you stick to your principles and your way of doing things or are you easily swayed?*

Consider the three areas of

>>> confronting situations
>>> facing reality
>>> standing by your beliefs.

Rate yourself good, average or poor against each area, then give yourself a **Courage score out of** **10** _____

●———————●

Look back over your Outer Group answers not forgetting the one about your locus of control.

Consider the rating you gave yourself for responsibility and accountability and for courage and give yourself an Outer Group score: **my Outer Group score is** _____

●———————●

Now you can put your inner and outer group scores together and come up with your Ego facet score.

This is not simply a matter of averaging the two. If there is a major difference, say three points between them, then you may need to consider the implications.

For example if your outer group score is higher than the inner group, it could be that you need to think more deeply about why you do things. A person who thinks they are high on courage but low on self-assurance could mean that their courage is actually bluff and could collapse.

If the inner group score is high and the outer group low, it could mean that there is considerable underperformance and your full potential is not being realised.

Think about this balance and give yourself an Ego facet score out of 10.

Deduct a point or two for any imbalance between your inner and outer group scores: **my Ego facet score is** _____

Chapter 12 **Team**

**We now come to two facets that are optional for the entrepreneur
– the Team facet in this chapter and the Social facet in the next.**

**Though they may be optional in that not all entrepreneurs
are strong in these facets, they do decide what type of
entrepreneur a person is.**

Without either of these two facets we have the basic entrepreneur –
only able to create economic capital but still in a way that makes a
difference and that people recognise as the work of an entrepreneur.

With a strong Team and/or Social facet the entrepreneur is also
able to create social capital.

When the Team facet is strong the social capital will be within the
team, producing a high level of mutual trust and a common purpose.
The business will move forward at a rate that the entrepreneur could
never achieve alone. When problems arise they will be shared.

> **An entrepreneur on hard times had to halve the size of his top team.**
> Such was the level of social capital in the group that when the
> entrepreneur told them the bad news each person volunteered to
> be the one to go so that the company could survive. Tears were
> shed around the board room table that day.

A strong Social facet will mean that the social capital will be created
in the community and people that the entrepreneur serves – he or
she will be a social entrepreneur meeting a social need but doing so
with a creative flair and diligent application that only the true
entrepreneur can provide.

The Team facet

The Team facet is a multiplier facet. It enables entrepreneurs to multiply
their effectiveness. It does so in two ways.

Firstly, team members can provide facet strengths that are missing in the entrepreneur. Here we have the idea of an entrepreneur team rather than the entrepreneur individual. Many people possess two or three of the entrepreneur facets. Alone they will probably struggle as entrepreneurs, but if they were to link up with people who had the facets they lacked there would an entrepreneur team with all the facets. It is perhaps not surprising that we find two-thirds of all businesses have more than one founder.

Secondly, a team is a multiplier of the entrepreneur's talent, enabling him or her to expand and grow a business in a way that is just not possible alone. Entrepreneurs who are strong in the Ego and Focus facets can find delegation difficult and approach burn-out as they try to do all the jobs. This sets a limit on what they can achieve. The Team facet heads off this problem, as Edward Stobart discovered, though it took him 10 years to find out.

Profile Edward Stobart

In 1985, Stobart started to wonder if it was all worthwhile. He never seemed to stop working. He was accepting more and more business, taking on more and more lorries, and yet at the end of it all he felt no more secure than he had in 1975. Moreover, he did not feel any better off financially. In theory his 35 employees and 26 lorries implied more revenue than 12 people and 8 lorries, but they also implied more problems and pressure. His wife complained that he was always at work, but he believed the whole business would collapse if he took more time off. The main problem: Edward was behaving just as he had 10 years ago. He was still running everything, taking all the key decisions.

Edward's situation was untenable, something had to change. He thought about splitting up the firm into owner-drivers but finally decided to go for growth. To do this he needed a management team. Edward hand-picked his team so that all the main jobs were covered and the business just took off.

The company averaged 60 percent annual growth over the next 10-year period. It was recognised as one of the top five fastest-growing medium-sized enterprises.

The business was exciting. Everyone was enthusiastic. Edward loved every minute of it.

Davies, The Eddie Stobart Story, *2001*

His Team facet had came to his aid – in fact from his biography it seems he discovered a facet he never knew he had.

The Team facet elements

The entrepreneur's Team facet has four elements. Each is distinct and can stand alone, but their combination is what really makes the difference:

- »» picking good people
- »» working through a team
- »» using experts – the extended team
- »» networking.

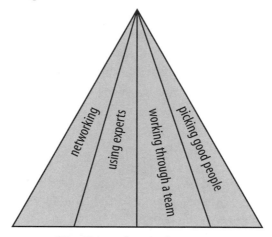

The Team facet elements

Entrepreneurs are not the only people who benefit from a strong Team facet. It is also important for the leader. Leaders have two elements of their own:

- »» gathering followers
- »» empowering others.

When these talents are found in entrepreneurs we can rightly call them leader entrepreneurs or entrepreneurial leaders.

Picking good people

Some entrepreneurs are so good at this that they believe it to be the essence of what it is to be an entrepreneur.

As Nolan Bushnell, of Atari fame, put it when speaking to engineers in Silicon Valley in the 1980s:

A guy wakes up in the morning and says 'I'm going to be an entrepreneur.' So he goes into work and he walks up to the best technologist in the company where he's working and whispers: 'Would you like to join my company? Ten o'clock, Saturday, my place. And bring the donuts.' Then he goes to the best finance guy he knows, and says, 'Bring some coffee.' Then he gets a marketing guy. And if you are the right entrepreneur, you have three or four of the best minds in the business.

Ten o'clock Saturday rolls around. They say, 'Hey, what is our company going to do?' You say, 'Build left-handed widgets.' Another hour and you've got a business plan roughed out. The finance guy says he knows where he can get some money. So what have you done? You've not provided the coffee. You've not provided the donuts. You've not provided the ideas. You've been the entrepreneur. You made it all happen.

Larson and Rogers, *Silicon Valley Fever*, 1986

Being an entrepreneur is more than having 'three or four of the best minds in the business', but it certainly helps.

Getting 'quality' people is important, but entrepreneurs have also to address their own weaknesses. They need people with strengths in those facets where they are less strong. It is more important to have a balanced team that covers all the entrepreneur facets than to have one that merely covers all functional competences. Given a choice, the entrepreneur should go for an entrepreneurial team every time and let the skill side look after itself. **[see PROFILE, JACK WELCH, p.134]**

The entrepreneur with the gift of being able to pick good people has a huge asset. 'Good people' are competent at their job but also bring other talents and attributes. Welch looked for people with the four 'Es': high Energy levels, who could Energise others, had the Edge to make tough decisions and the ability to Execute and deliver on their promises.

Working through a team

Entrepreneurs with the ability to work through a team will travel further and build bigger. We have seen that this was something that Edward Stobart discovered, but most entrepreneurs strong in the Team facet know this from the start. Linked with their ability to pick good people, it produces a powerful combination.

Profile Jack Welch

Jack Welch, as a corporate entrepreneur, was able to take the 'quality' approach to people in GE because he was strong in all the entrepreneur facets – and because he could afford to hire the best people. His catchphrase was 'We build great people, who then build great products and services'.

To make sure he got and kept the best people Jack Welch introduced the idea of differentiation.

Jack Welch categorises the top 20 percent of GE's employees as 'As', passionate people open to new ideas and who can make the business both productive and enjoyable at the same time. They make things happen; they drive change.

The next band of 70 percent, his 'Bs', are the vital heart of the business. They are critical for its everyday success. Considerable energies are devoted to helping 'Bs' become future 'As'.

The bottom 10 percent, the 'Cs', do not deliver enough and they cannot be allowed to hold the whole business back. They need to be removed.

While recognising that some think that removing this bottom layer is cruel, Welch believes the opposite. They will never achieve their potential at GE and it is kinder to help them find somewhere where they can grow and prosper.

Crainer, Business The Jack Welch Way, *2001*

Welch's 'As' sound rather like corporate entrepreneurs. This investment in the best people played a big part in the remarkable growth of GE under Welch's leadership.

When Jack Welch, at the age of 38, took over a group of GE companies with annual sales of $2 billion, 46,000 employees and 44 factories across the world, the first thing he did was to build a team.

Welch built a group of bright, smart 'turned-on' people who had complementary skills in finance, strategy, HR and law. They might have been diverse, but they were all down-to-earth and lacking in formality.

The group devoted its working time during the week to people and strategy reviews in the various plants, coming together on Friday evenings in a hotel lounge, to review the week over a few drinks. Later their wives would join them for a meal. Everyone got on with everyone else. They were all enjoying life at GE and getting well rewarded for it.

J. Welch, *Jack,* 2001

Welch's team approach was one of the key factors that got him to the top of GE and then enabled him to make GE one of the world's most successful businesses. He was strong on the Team facet.

Charles Forte, the UK hotel and catering king, had similar strengths. He may have had a strong personality but at heart he was a team player.

The arrival of Rex would complete the team that was instrumental in building the business. The group was able to avoid many potential mistakes because, although Forte believed in the importance of a clearly identifiable leader, he never believed he had all the answers himself. He believed that a team made up of the right people, who are able to think together, will be better able to make the wisest decisions.

Forte, *Forte*, 1997

But there is even more to it than greater productivity and good decision-making. Working through a team can give the enterprise an added social dimension. Entrepreneurs like Anita Roddick and Richard Branson have shown the way:

» The Body Shop has a charter which states what the business is and what it stands for. Within this, employees and franchisees are empowered to make individual contributions and help turn into reality the company's vision of a better world in which to live. The Body Shop is described as an 'extended family', in which everyone has a responsibility to make things work effectively.

» People also matter to Richard Branson. He is seen as a team player. He has a similar focus on helping people to achieve their full potential but he uses a business model that shares opportunities with others based on his strong Virgin brand. His relaxed and open style is appealing to the general public.

Using experts – the extended team

Specialists, like lawyers, accountants, bank managers, venture capitalists and business advisers all cross the path of the entrepreneur. Most of these 'specialists' have a rather different mindset to the entrepreneur so that true communication is difficult.

The following advertisement was placed in the *Financial Times* by a frustrated entrepreneur:

WANTED

A Progressive, Understanding and Positive Bank

Frustrated, knowledgeable, ambitious and totally fed up Managing Director of a progressive £6 million turnover company employing 175 people URGENTLY seeks a supporting bank.

A Bank that has vision, is supportive and positive and knows how to provide support without weakness and has a good business sense and the foresight of a Richard Branson/Margaret Thatcher type person. A Bank that can recognise and encourage potential and help to achieve success rather than generate negative attitudes and fear of failure, is URGENTLY required.

Currently the majority of high street Banks fail to provide the correct level of support to companies like ourselves and have lost their drive and direction and generally lack initiative and interest.

Financial Times, 2001

Sir John Harvey-Jones, former chairman of ICI, has said 'A consultant is someone who borrows your watch to tell you the time'.

Despite these negatives, the truth is that entrepreneurs do need the help of specialists. A DIY approach in legal and financial matters invites disaster.

The talent of 'using experts' alone is not enough. Entrepreneurs have to be able to recognise the experts amongst the specialists. Most entrepreneurs learn the hard way. They start off assuming that all specialists are experts and know what they are talking about. After losing time and money, they discover that this is not so. They find that the advice they were given was wrong, or at best inaccurate.

Entrepreneurs who are strong in picking good people and using experts have the ideal combination. They use experts as part of an extended team whose advice can be called on as and when required. There is often no need for a meeting – just a phone call or email will do – and in the process the experts often become personal friends.

Networking

For many entrepreneurs this is the strongest element in their Team facet. It links in with their Advantage facet so that they are always looking for the contact who can help them with a new business lead. They socialise for a purpose and not just for the fun of it.

Within the Team facet, networking links with finding good people and identifying experts. Entrepreneurs follow their instinct and don't wait for the CV and the letter of application to arrive.

Networking is important as a business practice. It can give the entrepreneur and his business valuable publicity free of charge. The press is always interested in good stories and the networking entrepreneur can supply them.

"Everyone you meet is another interview" – Jack Welch

In areas where entrepreneurship is now part of the general culture, such as Silicon Valley and Cambridge, the networks are extensive and of high quality. Some are formalised, but many are not. These places are like large villages where everybody knows everybody else. The meeting places are the local bars and restaurants. In their excellent book on the early days of Silicon Valley, Larson and Rogers have a chapter devoted to networks.

The oldest and most famous of these gathering places is Walker's Wagon Wheel Bar and Restaurant located in Mountain View, practically in the shadow of Fairchild Semiconductor. A number of the 'Fairchildren' spin-offs were planned here.

Larson and Rogers, *Silicon Valley Fever*, 1986

Networking has always been a characteristic of the start-up business. It is a time in the growth of a business where everybody gets involved. Later, as things develop and grow, a hierarchy often develops and there is a decrease in the level of networking within the company. This parallels the decline in the entrepreneurial spirit within the business.

We believe that there is a correlation here, and that the modern trend to reduce the levels of hierarchy and encourage networking is important for the emergence of an entrepreneurial spirit within a large organisation. When Jack Welch became CEO of GE he tackled this problem.

Profile Jack Welch

Jack Welch has likened organisational hierarchy to the numbers of sweaters some people wear. Sweaters insulate – if people wear four of them, they can't tell how cold it actually is.

He has also suggested layers in an organisation can be likened to the floors in a building, with the house walls representing functional barriers. Only by blowing them both away can you create open space where ideas flow freely, unencumbered by position and status.

J. Welch, Jack, *2001*

The entrepreneur who brings his or her networking talents into an organisation and makes them part of the business culture creates an immense asset.

The Team elements of the leader

Some entrepreneurs possess Team elements more commonly associated with the leader.

Gathering followers or even disciples is something that all leaders are good at. For the leader this talent is essential, but for the entrepreneur it is an option.

For the entrepreneur, 'followers' are those people who follow behind picking up the bits of unfinished business. They are personally committed to the entrepreneur and are resigned to the way the entrepreneur does things. They accept that that is the way he or she is, and work around it.

This ability to gather followers is not as effective as working through a team. There is not the same multiplier effect. Followers are good at running things that the entrepreneur has set up, but they will not contribute to further growth. On the plus side they do allow the entrepreneur to move on to the next venture.

Empowering others is not often found in the entrepreneur but when it is remarkable things can be achieved. It is the 'working through others' taken to the next level. When people are empowered they are able to take the opportunities identified by the entrepreneur and make them happen. They may not always grow the enterprise as quickly as the entrepreneur would, but they still go forward. But when the entrepreneur empowers a potential entrepreneur, things really move.

Profile Michael Young

Michael Young, founder of the OU, was able to establish 30 enterprises because he was able to empower others.

One of those he empowered comments that 'When Michael asked me to take over I felt inadequate but the fact that he believed in me gave me the confidence I needed. "You never know until you try" he said.'

How do you rate yourself on the Team facet?

Think through the four aspects.

Can you pick good people who are competent at their job and who have Jack Welch's four 'Es' – energy, energise, edge and execute?

Think of times when you have selected people.

» *How easy was it?*
» *Did you take on some people who disappointed you?*
» *How much was it their fault and how much yours?*

>>> When a person didn't work out, did you have a hunch that this might be the case but gave them the benefit of the doubt – perhaps because of their past achievements or qualifications?

If so, it probably taught you to trust your instincts more. Perhaps you have more of a talent for picking good people than you thought.

Give yourself a score out of 10: **my score is** _____

>>> **Can you work through a team** getting them to pull together and achieve great things? Most of us have been part of such a team at some stage in our lives. It may be rare, but when it happens it is amazing what can be done.
>>> Have you had such an experience as a team member or been able to build a team like this?
>>> Team players and team leaders are not the same thing. Which role are you most comfortable with?
>>> The entrepreneur takes the lead. Is this something you have done or feel able to do?

Give yourself a score out of 10: **my score is** _____

>>> **Can you use experts** and spot the expert among the specialists?
>>> What is your experience of working with specialists in a field that is not your own?
>>> Do you question them so that you understand what they are saying, or do you have a 'leave it to the experts' approach?
>>> Think of times when you have got it right and when you have got it wrong. As with picking good people, did you have a hunch that one expert would be better than the other?
>>> Do you see these experts as part of an extended team or are they there as outsiders to be contacted as necessary? If you have not been in the position to need experts think how you might regard them.

You should not be trying to answer like an entrepreneur here. You are trying to discover what comes naturally to you – if you just do not like *people who claim to be experts then accept it – you are unlikely to change how you feel.*

Give yourself a score out of 10: ***my score is*** _____

●——————●

>» *Are you good at networking?*
>» *Do you find it easy to mix with people?*
>» *Maybe you enjoy socialising, but do you find you pick up on things that could help you out and steer the conversation that way?*

Those strongest in this aspect of the Team facet can do this without others being aware of it. They know exactly how far to push something and when to back off.

To be a good networker you need to have a good memory for names and faces and show a genuine interest in other people. Entrepreneurs strong on networking appear very relaxed and make friends easily – but they are the right friends.

It is fairly easy to assess this element. You will know whether or not you enjoy networking.

Give yourself a score out of 10: ***my score is*** _____

●——————●

Now give yourself a score for the entrepreneur's Team facet as a whole – the leader's Team facets come later.

Look through your scores for

>» *picking good people*
>» *working through a team*
>» *using experts*
>» *networking.*

It is unlikely that you will have scored yourself very differently for 'picking good people' and 'using experts', because they require similar ability-spotting talents. If you have, then revisit the scores you gave yourself.

If these scores are significantly (three or more points) different from your 'working through a team' score, this has implications for the kind of entrepreneur you are or will become. Don't try to change your assessment but think through the implications.

There is no point in trying to work through a team if you just don't have the talent for it. It is best to recognise the fact and get on with things. Understand that you need followers.

If working through a team is one of your strengths but picking good people is not, then you simply need help from someone who is good at it. But take care in going for the first recruiting agency you find – if you are not very good at picking people you are also probably not very good at picking experts, so take care.

Take your highest score out of 10 for the four aspects of the Team facet and use it as your Team facet score.

My entrepreneur Team facet score is _____

Now we come to the two leader's Team facets.

You may have not come out strongly on some of the entrepreneur's Team facets. For example you may have been low on 'working through others' because you are a strong individualist and do not suffer fools gladly. Even so, you may still have one or even both of the team talents of the leader, making you a leader entrepreneur or entrepreneurial leader.

»» **Do you naturally gather followers?**
»» *Do you find that people enjoy helping you?*
»» *You may not be a very easy person to work with, but do people still come around and want to be part of your team?*
»» *Are you sometimes surprised how literally people take what you say and go off and do it without thinking for themselves?*
»» *Are you aware that you leave a trail of debris behind you and that you need others to tidy up, and that there is no formal delegation – people, your followers, just do it?*
»» **Do you empower others?**
»» *Are you able to recognise latent talent in others, and are you able to tap this resource to further your projects?*

>>> Can you envision others and give them the confidence to go forward?

>>> When empowered, do these people stay loyal to you or do they go their own way?

Give yourself a score out of 10 on each of these elements.

It is possible that you will score highly on 'gathering followers' and low on 'empowering others' but not the other way round. Those who 'empower others' generally 'gather followers'.

My 'gathering followers' score is _____

My 'empowering others' score is _____

Take the highest of the two scores as your leader entrepreneur Team score:

My leader entrepreneur Team score is _____

Chapter 13 **Social**

Some entrepreneurs – but not a majority – have a strong Social facet. They are able to meet challenging social needs and in so doing create significant new social capital – they make the world a better place for all of us.

Most however have the Social facet present to some degree, which is why we see many of them actively involved in charitable activities at some stage in their lives.

There are different types of social entrepreneur. Some people always focus their entrepreneurial talent and energy in a social direction. Preacher William Booth, founder of the Salvation Army, and Thomas Barnardo, the medical student from Ireland who started homes for destitute children, are excellent examples from the nineteenth century. Booth, though, showed he was also a business entrepreneur when he opened his own match factory because he felt leading manufacturer, Bryant and May, was treating its workforce inhumanely. His competing venture was a commercial success.

Others express their Social facet at a different stage in their lives. Successful business people who have a desire to 'put something back' often do much more than donate money. They take the lead and champion a new, socially entrepreneurial venture. This could be a supplementary, spare time activity or a major switch of focus. Serial business entrepreneurs who retire but retain energy and a desire to keep doing things, may devote considerable time and energy in this way.

A special and important group of social entrepreneurs seem able to operate in the business and the social world at the same time.

An early example is Richard Cadbury, founder of the famous chocolate business. In the late eighteenth century in Birmingham, England, there was not the distinction between business and social matters that there is today. This was due to the influence of the Quakers. A century of endeavour after their formation by George Fox

144

around 1650 resulted in a remarkable entrepreneur culture based on their social values. It was this holistic world that Richard Cadbury entered in 1794.

Once a sizeable Quaker community became established in an area, an effective network of businesses which all helped each other soon emerged. If one should get into financial difficulties, the others would rally round, almost acting as consultants, to help find a resolution to the problem. Once a Quaker had completed an apprenticeship the community would provide the financial support to help him establish his own business.

By the late eighteenth century these businesses, driven by the Quaker values of hard work, honesty, fair dealing, meticulous attention to detail and social equality were making a huge contribution to British industry and commerce.

Kennedy, *Business Pioneers*, 2000

The Quakers created an entrepreneurial environment in Britain in the late eighteenth century similar to that which we find today in places like Silicon Valley, but without the separation between the commercial and the social – and therefore without the excesses that that separation produces. Cadbury's business, for example, did not result in overcrowded slums because he built the town of Bourneville to provide housing and social amenities for his employees.

In Cadbury's Quaker world the business entrepreneur and the social entrepreneur were one and the same.

Victorian England was also a place where Christian values were important: the term 'philanthropist' was coined to describe what were often business and social entrepreneurs rolled into one.

Titus Salt was such a man. Like Cadbury he built a town for his workers. He called it Saltaire – it is now a World Heritage Centre.

Although Salt amassed his fortune from producing worsted and alpaca cloth, opening several mills, he became an entrepreneur by chance and necessity. He started as a wool trader, but he had a problem when he bought a large quantity of Donskoi wool for which he could not find any buyers. Local mill owners did not believe the wool could be spun and woven. Determined to prove them wrong, Salt rented a mill. He succeeded, and rented two more before opening one of his own.

Salt started with alpaca in a similarly opportunistic way. By chance he saw some open sacks of alpaca at Liverpool docks. They were awaiting return to Peru – there had been no buyers for them. He bought a small quantity, found he could use it to make an unusually lightweight cloth, and bought the rest of the consignment cheaply.

As his business grew, Salt built over 800 buildings in Saltaire, including mills, schools, public baths, a library, a chapel and homes for his employees. Everything was built to a higher standard than the norm of the day.

Today we separate the business and the social side of life. Each has its own regulatory framework. The laws for business are quite different to those for charities, and the two do not mix. It is therefore difficult for social entrepreneurs who try to run their activities on a business basis. The system makes them dependent on hand-outs even when they don't want to be.

Profile Michael Manning-Prior

Michael Manning-Prior runs a business incubator programme for young people in Wandsworth, London. Between 85 and 90 percent of the start-ups move on as successful businesses after their two-year period in the incubator.

For some years the programme was funded by grants of various kinds, often linked with the latest government initiative for getting young people into work. Michael became increasingly frustrated with having to jump through different hoops every few years for what was the same pot of government money. In the end he decided to generate his own subsidy.

He did this by converting an old factory close to his business incubator into commercial and office premises that he could rent out on a permanent basis. He used the income stream from this business activity to fund his social activity.

The inner self

A strong Social facet, working with the other facets, makes a person a very special type of entrepreneur. Many of them do not recognise that they are entrepreneurs because they just get on with the job. They are modest people motivated by a cause they express in service to others.

The Social facet is the only one that can take on the Ego facet and change its inner shades. Self-assurance, dedication and motivation are all influenced. This can bring an inner conflict for some social entrepreneurs.

> We get involved in social action by responding to the call of God to bring a taste of heaven to hurting people. Selflessly we are motivated to serve God and people in need.
>
> Yet, despite our determination otherwise, self is not so easily defeated. Though we may feel we have turned our back on self once and for all and have unreservedly committed ourselves to serving God's Kingdom, somewhere down the track all too often we start building our own empire. Whether it is seeking to create a name for ourselves or constructing a large organisation for its own sake, subtly our goal has shifted. Though the change may be small, the impact is huge.
>
> One of the root causes of this empire-building tendency lies in self-worth. As we spend ourselves on behalf of the needy, a world that does not value them, thinks equally less of us. Result: we ourselves feel undervalued and become tempted to produce something that the world does value and recognise.

In the Field, Autumn 2001

The relative strengths of the Social and the Ego facets have a critical influence. Ideally both facets should be strong with a creative tension between them. But when the Social facet dominates the entrepreneur may be meeting the social need well but will be unduly stressed when strong action is called for. When the Ego facet dominates then the entrepreneur may find the business is being developed at the expense of the social calling and feel guilty about it.

By recognising the role that these facets play it is possible to bring some understanding to the emotional tensions that are generated.

An artist has a similar tension between the Ego facet and Creativity facet. Artists grapple with the question 'Do I continue with my creative work and live in poverty, or do I commercialise my art to suit the market and make money?'

When the Social facet is dominant and stronger than the core entrepreneurial facets, the social entrepreneur will always find it difficult to accept the need for commercial viability. They may appear to acknowledge it in public and in front of the grant agency, but deep down they can resent the fact that others do not see their cause as they do and don't just give them the resources they obviously need.

Some social entrepreneurs do not succeed because this 'profit requirement versus social need' conflict is not resolved. They see 'profit' as a dirty word rather than necessary for balancing the books – and of course any money left over can always be used to improve the service or provide it to more people.

The Social facet's building blocks

The Social facet has four building blocks, each part of the whole.

They are:

>>> belief
>>> values
>>> mission
>>> service to others.

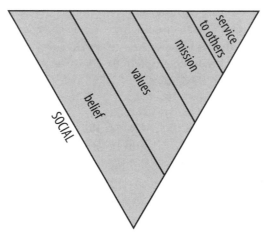

The Social facet's building blocks

Unlike the elements of the other facets they cannot be taken alone. The Social facet demands them all. It builds as one block is placed upon another.

The starting point is belief, but that belief has to be able to provide values and fuel the cause that drives the social entrepreneur. Clearly some beliefs do this better than others. Mission is built on values and defines the social entrepreneur's cause. Its expression is service to others.

Belief

Belief is that which we choose to orient our lives around. It may be belief in God or in oneself, in a religion or in a philosophy, in a political system or in humanity, in a value system or in none. Even unbelief can be a powerful belief! Whatever it is, we all have a belief of some kind that provides us with a world view and a particular way of looking at things – our mindset.

This first building block is crucial for the social entrepreneur. Only a belief that can provide values which entrepreneurs can apply will work. The step from belief to values is the first dividing line between the business entrepreneur and the social entrepreneur.

Profile Brian Souter

Brian Souter, the founder of the Stagecoach empire, is a man who takes his Christian faith seriously but considers it a private matter. His faith has given him a strong work ethic and he has not been phased by fame and fortune. So at one level belief has resulted in values. He has a modest lifestyle and gives generously to charity so that there is something of the social entrepreneur there. But his comments to a journalist show another side:

> If we were to apply the values of the Sermon on the Mount to our business, we would be rooked within six months. Don't misunderstand me, ethics are not irrelevant, but some are incompatible with what we have to do because capitalism is based on greed. We call it dichotomy, not hypocrisy.

Scotland on Sunday, *December 1991*

Some entrepreneurs who share Souter's beliefs might not like his comments, but at least he is being honest. Applying one's beliefs in the business world is difficult for those who do not have a strong Social facet, which is why the step up from belief to values is not an easy one.

Some business entrepreneurs have strong beliefs but intentionally partition their lives so that their beliefs do not affect their entrepreneurial behaviour. They feel that if they allow their beliefs to get in the way they will lose their cutting edge.

The most common expression of belief that we see in entrepreneurs is their generosity – once they have made some money. But this does not mean they have made the step from belief to values. Even people who are ruthless in business can be quite generous.

The prevailing culture also has an influence as the Victorian philanthropists demonstrate. We see a similar trend today.

The Sainsbury family 'are reckoned to give away more than £41 million a year, making them Britain's second most philanthropic family after the oil expatriate Gettys' (Kennedy, *Business Pioneers*, 2001).

Important though it is, philanthropy is not what the Social facet is about. This facet requires that belief express itself at the very least in values and an ethical approach to business.

It is just as likely that entrepreneurs who are generous with their money are responding to their Ego facet as their Social facet.

Values

The high level of corruption in business around the world suggests that not many make the step from belief to values. The book *Barbarians at the Gate* is the story of Nabisco Foods, the world's biggest management buy-out; it is so titled because of the business practices of the investors involved. The barbarians were at the gate of Wall Street.

On the other hand, values and ethics are increasingly seen as important in business. They are now accepted subjects in our business schools, and many successful entrepreneurs consider them of great importance.

Profile Charles Forte

Charles Forte, whose catering and hotel business was acquired by the Granada group in 1996 for £3.9 billion, gave this advice to his son Rocco:

> In business, cleanliness, honesty, decency, respect for other people, politeness, good manners and integrity all matter. This was true five thousand years ago; it will still be the case in five thousand years time.

Forte, Forte, 1997

Profile The Body Shop

Anita Roddick, founder of The Body Shop, has stamped her own beliefs and values on her company. Here are some points from its charter.

>» The Body Shop's goals and values are as important as the products and the profits.
>» Honesty, integrity and caring are core values and they should impact upon every activity.
>» Humanising the business community is important. The Body Shop will demonstrate that success and profits, ideals and values, are not mutually exclusive.
>» The Body Shop's concern for the world around will be manifest in several ways – by respecting fellow human beings, by not harming animals and by working to conserve the planet.

Values and ethics come naturally to the social entrepreneur through the Social facet, but even business entrepreneurs who are weak on the Social facet still see their usefulness. They apply them not because of any belief they hold but simply because they bring advantage. Honesty in the workplace means less is stolen. When people tell you the truth about a problem it is easier to resolve. A company that values its employees is likely to have a happier more productive workforce. Customers who can rely on a company's promises are likely to come back. Trust in business means less litigation and lower legal fees.

Profile Francis Fukuyama

Francis Fukuyama, who has studied the economic impact of trust in different societies around the world comments:

> One of the most important lessons we can learn from an examination of economic life is that a nation's well-being, as well as its ability to compete, is conditioned by a single, pervasive cultural characteristic: the level of trust inherent in society.

Fukuyama, Trust, 1995

Belief and values may be the important starting points of the Social facet, but the essential step is the next one. Unless a person moves from belief and values up to mission, their Social facet will never be strong. They may be socially-minded entrepreneurs but they will not be true social entrepreneurs.

Mission

Mission is about finding a cause through which belief and values can be channelled. It is an example of belief and values into action.

If there is no 'cause' then belief and values amount to virtue, which though good in itself is not enough for the Social facet. The step from values to mission is a vital one. With it comes a 'cause' and the strongest motivation a human being can experience.

J. Arthur Rank discovered his 'cause' when he was just past his fortieth birthday and this triggered his latent entrepreneurial talent.

J. Arthur Rank belonged to a happy, wealthy and successful family. His job with the family business was secure. He had several other interests and held the position of President of the National Sunday

School Union – he was anxious to find more effective ways of teaching the Christian Gospel. He used singing, band music and the occasional religious film for his work in schools. But in the 1930s his approach was seen by some as too innovative and he was once condemned for doing 'the devil's own work'.

Not dissuaded, he became passionate about the potential of film for communication, and it was this that released his entrepreneurial talent.

He foresaw that film would become a truly powerful force in society as a whole, and his commitment to the medium stayed with him for the rest of his life. Within 10 years he would own studios, cinemas and distribution rights. His business would be worth £50 million and he would be a key influence in every branch of the industry.

Wakelin, *J. Arthur Rank*, 1997

Anita Roddick was strong on values but she was driven by a cause and became a campaigner for social justice and the environment. Although her Social facet was always there, it took some time before it came to fruition but when it did it became her primary motivation.

The Body Shop opened its first branch in 1976; by 1984 it was a publicly quoted company. It was only then that Anita and Gordon Roddick realised how much power the business had for doing good. They redefined their mission; they had found a cause to champion.

Roddick, *Business As Unusual*, 2000

Service to others

Once the entrepreneur has found a cause, he or she seeks practical ways of making something happen. This is what entrepreneurs always do. They don't just talk about their 'cause', they take action. Over the years the social entrepreneur has addressed needs often well before government. Education, healthcare, child welfare, social services and prison reform were all pioneered by social entrepreneurs well before the state took them on board.

The final expression of the Social facet – 'service to others' – is part of the motivation of the social entrepreneur. Here there is an interesting interplay between the Social facet and the Ego facet. The 'I wants' are turned around and given an external focus:

- »» I want to help the terminally ill
- »» I want to help God transform the lives of drug addicts
- »» I want to provide homes for destitute children
- »» I want to create jobs for the long-term unemployed.

The social entrepreneur sees needs and translates them into opportunities. These needs are centred on others rather than on themselves.

For some, the Social facet has always been there. Even in childhood they were into helping others. But for some people there is a moment when a strong belief takes root in their lives and their Social facet comes alive – a Social entrepreneur is born.

Elliott Tepper would have been successful even if he had not had an experience that turned his life around. His parents had passed on to him 'their quintessential American values: patriotism, generosity, kindness, excellence, and the notion that hard work and drive, when accompanied by fair play, would always lead to success and happiness'.

He was 'an Eagle Scout, president of his class, New York wrestling champion, and recipient of a generous wrestling scholarship to Lehigh University'. He 'went on to study economics at Cambridge University in England and from there to Harvard' for his MBA.

All was set for an outstanding career until Elliott joined a commune in his last year at Harvard and got into drugs. After graduating he worked as assistant to the treasurer at the Boston Museum of Fine Arts but his drug habit continued. Then came his life-changing experience.

> I can remember walking one day along the banks of the Charles River...God spoke audibly to me. He said 'Give me your life.' He lifted me up in a vision and opened the heavens, showing me a glimpse of eternity and the new Jerusalem.
>
> People have asked me how much of this experience was drug induced...but I can say this. It was not an hallucination, and what was burned into my spirit has not dimmed in over twenty-two years.

Since then Elliott has built a remarkable drug rehabilitation programme. Starting in Madrid, Spain in 1983 'Betel' now has 82 residential centres in 10 Spanish cities and around the world. They are in the US, the UK, Portugal, France and India. Some 33,000 individuals have passed through the Betel centres in recent years. Between 10 and 15 percent have left fully cured and for those who have accepted the Christian faith the cure rate has been around 90 percent.

Dinnen, *Rescue Shop*, 1996; Dinnen, *Rescue Shop 2*, 2000

Elliott Tepper is a classic example of a foundation belief delivering a cause that resulted in a service to those in need. Elliott, the social entrepreneur has delivered on social capital.

———●————●———

Think through your position on belief and values.

- » *How important are they to you?*
- » *How conscious are you of your values when you decide on a course of action?*
- » *How important are the needs of others to you?*
- » *Do they challenge you or do you just ignore them?*
- » *Have you made the steps from belief, to values, to mission, to serving others or are you part way along?*

The key question is whether your belief and values have given you a mission or a cause.

If not then, unless you are trying to discover your mission, you should score yourself less than 5 out of 10 on this facet.

If you have a cause then are you expressing it in service to others or would you like to be able to?

If you are strong in this facet, you are likely to have felt the struggle with your Ego facet. Check your Ego facet score and make sure that your Social facet score reflects your relative strengths.

Give yourself a score out of 10: **my Social facet score is** _____

Chapter 14 Applying the Facets

If you are an entrepreneur, or someone with entrepreneurial potential, you will have been scoring some high marks in the self assessments in the last six chapters. The distribution of your scores between the six facets and between the sub-elements of each facet will explain the type of entrepreneur you are.

>>> So, which is your strongest facet?
>>> Where are you relatively weak?
>>> Is one of the facets particularly dominant?
>>> Are your strengths very different within the same facet?

To help understand the implications of these differences we change the analogy from the facets of a crystal to the spokes of a wheel. If each spoke is of the same length the wheel will be circular and will run well. The longer the spokes, the larger the wheel, and the more ground it covers at each revolution.

After considering this picture we look at four key points:

>>> Facets interaction: the entrepreneur character themes work together – they normally complement each other and produce a more rounded entrepreneur but sometimes they can also work against each other.
>>> The entrepreneur and the leader: all entrepreneurs who stay with high-growth businesses need leadership qualities if they are to stay effective. Equally, the strategic leaders of all large organisations need to ensure there is entrepreneurship in their organisation – they may or may not be the person to provide it.
>>> Risk: the relative strengths of certain character themes determine the entrepreneur's attitude to risk.
>>> Extreme presence: when one or more dominant character themes is present to an extreme degree there may be problems.

Measuring the spokes

The chart below presents the six facets or character themes as spokes of a wheel. For convenience we define the presence of the character theme in terms of five positions:

>» Beyond the rim – extreme
>» at or approaching the rim – highly visible
>» mid-position outwards– visibly present
>» towards the hub – present
>» at or close to the hub – weak presence or absent.

In this representation, a weak character theme is positioned close to the hub and the stronger the theme the nearer it is to the rim. The ideal is for all the character themes to have the same strong presence close to or at the rim. Beyond that the character theme can be so dominant that serious consequences follow – which is why we place it beyond the rim.

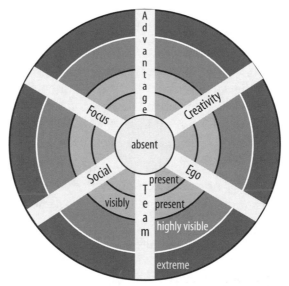

Absent	Visible	Extreme
Random	Focus	Tunnel vision
Switched off	Advantage	Ruthless
Unimaginative	Creativity	Over-imaginative
Purposeless	Ego	Self-deluded
Individualistic and independent	Team	Abdicated responsibility
Self-centred	Social	Fanatical

The entrepreneur character themes: wheel diagram

Using your facet scores from the last six chapters, you can position yourself around the wheel using the following guidelines.

You will see we have added an 'off the scale' score for the extreme incidence. This will apply to you if you scored yourself 10 out of 10 but felt instinctively this was nowhere near high enough! You will know if you are extreme.

presence	score	effect
extreme	'off the scale'	dangerous
highly visible	8–10	entrepreneurial
visibly present	5–7	enterprising
present	2–4	–
absent	0–1	–

If you are 'off the scale' in one or more facets, it should be a warning sign, which is why we describe it as 'dangerous'. Scores in the 8–10 range are what you are looking for in the entrepreneur. The enterprising person has a lower score, but is still average or above.

The table shown below the wheel describes the behaviour to be expected when the character themes are either absent or present to an extreme degree.

Matching against the facets in the figure, we can quickly appreciate that very few people would be random, switched off, unimaginative, purposeless, loners and totally selfish all at the same time – though most of us have met people with some of these characteristics!

At the other end of the scale, people with extreme entrepreneur character themes are going to suffer from tunnel vision and be ruthless, over-imaginative, self-deluded, fanatical and possibly dominating.

People weak on the entrepreneur character themes make few waves but those who possess them to an extreme degree are very noticeable and make a huge impact – often for the worst, as we shall see later in this chapter.

Facets interaction

When the entrepreneur's facets are balanced and interact in a supportive manner, the whole is greater than the sum of its parts.

One of the unique abilities of the entrepreneur is to create something out of almost nothing. He or she is able to do this because the Creativity, Advantage and Focus facets are working together.

The diagram shows how this happens. Ideas start with the Creativity facet, and are spotted as opportunities by the Advantage facet as it overlaps with Creativity. The Advantage facet ensures that the best opportunity is selected from the many. The Focus facet then discriminates and sets its target as it overlaps with Advantage. The opportunity is turned into reality by the Focus facet.

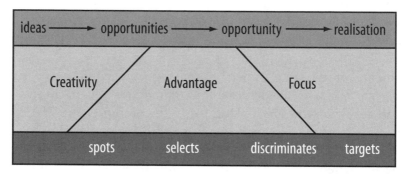

Interdependent facets: 1

Creativity is the source of ideas. Opportunities come from ideas when the ideas match the needs and desires of customers, or customers can be persuaded that they do. Spotting these matches and opportunities is a key contribution of the entrepreneur.

Spotting opportunities requires Creativity, but it is also part of the Advantage facet. The overlap shown in the diagram indicates this sharing between the two facets. Entrepreneurs see opportunities because they see the potential advantage – many other people share the information the entrepreneur has, but never spot the opportunity.

Some entrepreneurs seem to bypass the ideas stage and just spot opportunities. They are gifted and instinctive in their ability to empathise with customers. But it is still a case of Creativity and Advantage working together.

Entrepreneurs have the ability to know which of many opportunities is the one to go for. This selection is the work of the Advantage facet. Grasping the opportunity and moving forward takes place as

Advantage hands over to Focus. This enables the entrepreneur to discriminate and target effectively. Once the target is set, Focus ensures delivery and the opportunity is brought to fruition.

When difficult choices have to be made because there are too many opportunities and not enough resources, the entrepreneur strong in these three facets knows exactly what to do.

The entrepreneur never makes the mistake of 'chasing two rabbits', and we suspect the eagle doesn't either. They both know by instinct which to go for.

Our 'blob diagram' attempts to capture some of this interaction between the facets in a different way.

If an eagle goes after two fleeing rabbits at the same time, it will fail to catch either of them

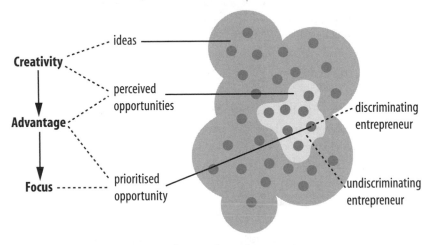

Interdependent facets: 2

Inside the larger blob are numerous ideas, shown as spots – the smaller, inner blob separates out a number of possible opportunities from these ideas. The discriminating entrepreneur realises all these opportunities, but is selective about which one(s) he or she pursues. The Creativity and Advantage facets are working well together and linking in to the Focus facet.

The indiscriminate entrepreneur on the other hand is tempted by all the opportunities. He or she cannot refuse a request or a challenge.

It is here we can see how certain character themes can work against each other, rather than for each other.

Advantage and Creativity work against Focus when too many opportunities are spotted and selection proves difficult – when too many opportunities are engaged, and adequate resources cannot be secured. Focus is lost, efforts become wasted and the enterprise loses direction. Strategic advantage may also be threatened.

Ego may also prove to be a problem and counter Focus if the entrepreneur is really wanting to make a difference, leave footprints and achieve as much as possible. In their ambition and greed, entrepreneurs may take on too much, making discrimination difficult and blurring their focus.

A similar situation is often found with social entrepreneurs. In this case it is the very strength of their Social facet that makes them want to do more and more, wherever they feel they can help. They find it very difficult to say no. Unless Advantage and Focus are both strong and working well together, discrimination will not be easy and priorities will become confused.

The interaction of the Team facet with the other facets affects the potential of the business in a variety of ways.

Unless the entrepreneur builds an effective team, he or she will become overstretched as the business grows and will lose the ability to target and discriminate – focus will be lost and opportunities will not be followed up.

Even with the 'right' team there can be a similar effect. They generate a host of new ideas and possibilities, putting the ability to prioritise under a different type of pressure. Advantage and Focus could again be stretched.

The Ego and Team facets often have a love–hate relationship. Most entrepreneurs know they can achieve more with a team than without one, but if they are temperamentally independent, or even a loner, they will find this very difficult.

We conclude this section on how the facets interact by considering how a weakness in one facet can create a dilemma for an essentially outstanding entrepreneur. We return to the Castleford Community Learning Centre that we visited in chapter 3.

The Castleford Community Learning Centre in West Yorkshire, England, provides skills training and personal development. It began as a centre dedicated to helping local women. After the miners' strike in the 1980s, and in the face of pit closures, the miners' wives sought to take control of their lives.

Once the project became successful, a raft of new possibilities presented themselves. Clients asked for more and more. Funding agencies offered more resources for additional activities. A new, larger building replaced the first (derelict) one that was used. Two additional centres were opened. The possibility of converting a listed mansion was tempting, as leisure activities could be added. More and more staff joined the founders, many of them providing voluntary support.

The outstanding and entrepreneurial leader, Margaret Handforth, who was instrumental in starting the venture after helping in a soup kitchen, scores high on the Advantage (she is close to the community and understands needs), Creativity, Ego (she has made an incredible difference), Team and Social facets. She has urgency and dedication but she finds it hard to say no. She does not discriminate as effectively as she might.

She believes Focus is her weakest character theme.

The entrepreneur and the leader

In chapter 7, when we looked at what entrepreneurs, managers and leaders do, we noted that there were some overlaps and some distinguishing differences. Now we consider the character themes responsible – though limiting our discussion to the entrepreneur and the leader. The italics in the table signify a dependency on trust, which we explain in the text below.

character themes specific to the entrepreneur	character themes shared by the entrepreneur and the leader	character themes specific to the leader
Creativity	Focus	strategic visioning
Advantage	Ego	*envisioning*
	Team	*empowering*
	Social	*influencing*

We noted earlier in this chapter that one of the unique things about entrepreneurs is their ability to create real opportunities, drawing upon their Creativity and Advantage facets. It is these character themes, essential for the entrepreneur, that we would not normally associate with the leader.

However, we also saw that it is Focus that discriminates, engages and grasps the opportunity. Focus is also a character theme of the leader.

So too are the Ego facet, including the key sub-themes of courage, dedication and responsibility, and the Team facet.

Leaders have an important role in selecting and managing their teams. Networking is also important for them, but it will not be as prominent as in the case of the entrepreneur. Moreover, the ability of the leader to find the right style of management, perhaps a coaching style, becomes increasingly significant as the business grows in size and the strategy and organisation become ever more complex. Others in the organisation have to be motivated by the leader.

The strength of the Social facet determines the field in which the entrepreneur operates. When it dominates we have the cause-driven social entrepreneur. But where a professional manager or leader is recruited to be the strategic leader of, say, a leading charity, the Social facet will inevitably be important, but it need not be the dominant one. Sometimes, of course, we see people who have a very strong Social facet promoted to a senior leadership role in an organisation such as a church or faith community. However if they do not possess other key characteristics of either the leader or the entrepreneur, they are unlikely to be effective.

The special character themes of the leader

We can identify four additional character themes that are important for the leader but which do not define the entrepreneur.

The leader must be able to embrace the long term and for this reason strategic visioning is important. Strategies are 'means to ends' – here we are saying that the leader needs a number of 'ends' or 'visions' or clear pictures for:

》》 The range of activities in which the organisation will be involved, incorporating the extent to which it will be diversified and/or international – the corporate strategy.

》》 How the organisation will compete in each area of activity, its competitive strategy – this clearly draws on the entrepreneur's Advantage facet but is more about realising the value of an advantage than about spotting it in the first place.

»» How some or all of these activities can be integrated to create synergy.

»» How the organisation will manage change and implement the strategic ideas.

Strategic visioning is clearly supported by both the creative, idea-generating talent and a person's expertise and learning. Some people are simply much better able than others to 'grasp the big picture'.

We deliberately use the term 'strategic visioning' in preference to 'vision', for it is the link between a vision, the strategic opportunities linked to that vision, and the ability to both craft and implement strategies to fulfil the vision that makes a great leader.

Strategic visioning has close links to the entrepreneur's Advantage facet, but it is on a much grander scale. A visionary can be the person who sees how a company or even an industry can be transformed, who invents some radically new product or process, or who is responsible for a major technology breakthrough – but it is the strategic element that is required for something to happen. We would describe Jack Welch as a strategic visionary for his insight into how a company as diversified as GE can be structured and managed.

So, good strategic ideas in isolation will never be enough – the real test of any strategy lies in implementation. Things have to be made to happen. Others must be convinced and their support and commitment engaged. This requires envisioning, empowering and influencing skills.

The ability to envision is the second discrete character theme of the leader. Leaders are able to communicate to others the clear pictures we describe as strategy, and to engage and maintain their support. There is a strong element of sharing to build relationships and trust.

The successful leader will not only motivate people, he or she will empower them

The leader also needs to be able to motivate those who work for and with him or her, as does the entrepreneur. This has a team element, certainly, but it operates at a deeper motivational level. As we saw in chapter 12, when we discussed the Team facet, all leaders have their disciples and followers, but not all entrepreneurs. The successful leader will not only motivate people, he or she will empower them.

We said in chapter 12 that when people are empowered they have the confidence and the will to take things on and make them happen. They are enactors and ideally they will behave intrapreneurially. For this to work the leader must believe that people want to do something meaningful in their working lives – that they have particular talents that can be enabled.

The final characteristic is influencing. This includes being able to gather together, organise and manage the necessary resources – the resourcing element of Advantage, but the means used is what sets leaders apart. They achieve things by exerting influence on people and events. Leaders get things done through other people. They have the ability to persuade others to follow their ideas and policies. Whereas the entrepreneur 'does the right things', the leader uses influence to 'get the right things done'. There are several elements to this and the term 'influence' embraces all of them.

Power is an important part of influence. Leaders must be able to acquire and use power effectively. Some leaders in certain situations are able to rely heavily on their power, status and title, commanding only limited respect – but this will never be the most satisfactory way of influencing people. Others have enormous charisma and personal power, such as Robert Maxwell (whom we discuss later in this chapter). Expertise will often help as well. In addition we cannot discount a leader's 'political ability' – which here we use to describe the ability to get things done, to make things happen within a large organisation.

Power is an important part of influence

In every case power can be used in ways people find satisfactory – the leaders for whom 'people would do anything' – and in ways they dislike. Bullying tactics, threats, hard sanctions and using an organisation for personal gain are all examples of how power and influence are sometimes used in the wrong way. Not all leaders are popular!

Strategic visioning, envisioning, empowering and influencing abilities can always help any entrepreneur in a variety of ways and circumstances, especially as organisations and initiatives grow, but they do not define the essential entrepreneur. Instead they are important determinants of the leader and therefore important for the leader-entrepreneur and the entrepreneurial leader.

Trust

In today's world, envisioning and empowering have become increasingly important for the effective leader. At the same time the relative importance of different power bases for influencing people has changed. In the past, positional power in an organisation, together with the ability to reward and coerce people, were particularly important. Today, they will rarely be adequate on their own, although their continuing significance should not be underestimated. Personal power, charisma, charm and flair have always been important, and they continue to be so. But in today's 'knowledge-based' world, and with the dynamism and uncertainty of many industries, expert power and the ability to access valuable information have become increasingly important – as has connection power, that yielded by a personal network of important contacts.

For this reason, power and effective leadership are crucially dependent upon trust – the respect and confidence people have in each other and their ability to rely on them.

A leader cannot lead effectively for any sustained period of time without the trust of his or her followers. Equally envisioning and empowering requires the leader to have trust in others. Influencing based on trust rather than coercion will have a more sustained impact. When leaders lose trust, they lose effectiveness.

The Team and Social facets of the entrepreneur – like the envisioning, empowering and influencing themes of the leader – are very clearly dependent upon trust. These two facets are not the defining characteristics of the entrepreneur, but 'Team' is the key to growth. So for an entrepreneur to grow an initiative through others, he or she needs trust.

Hence we might say that trust is the currency of growth.

These arguments also help explain why many entrepreneurs, including some who build significant businesses, are simply not trusted by others!

Trust is the currency of growth

Such entrepreneurs would be strong in the 'face' facets – Focus, Advantage, Creativity and Ego – but weak in the Team and Social facets, which require trust if they are to be effective.

Risk

We talk more about entrepreneurs and risk in chapter 18, when we look at what entrepreneurs do. For the moment we want to look behind the assertion we often hear that 'entrepreneurs take risks' and then set it in the context of the character themes.

We believe that most entrepreneurs 'handle' risks rather than 'take' risks. The word 'take' somehow implies they may not know what they are doing – that they either are unaware of or choose to ignore the inherent risks. This is not always true, but it can be true when certain character themes are particularly strong or extreme.

Some entrepreneurs do take real risks and chances. They are the gamblers who live by the motto 'nothing ventured, nothing gained'. They enjoy the thrill of the punt and often have a surprising knack of getting it right.

Other entrepreneurs, who are less adventurous, may still be seen by others to be taking risks and chances. The issue is one of perception. The observer may not be an entrepreneur, and so will have a different view of the risks involved. The entrepreneur, on the other hand, is comfortable in his or her belief that everything is under control.

We can liken this to the way people drive cars. Ignoring the obvious maniacs that are around (the true risk-takers) we normally drive within our perceived limits. We don't all want to drive at the same speed in heavy rain, snow and particularly in fog. We drive as fast as we feel comfortable driving. We know whether we have relatively fast or relatively slow reactions. In fog, some people see (or instinctively feel) what is ahead more clearly than others. But also, some people are simply better drivers than others!

Whether we are talking about real risk or the perception of risk, the character themes allow us to explain three attitudes to risk that are captured in the following statements often made by entrepreneurs.

>>> What risk?
>>> I can handle it.
>>> It won't happen to me.

What risk?

Some entrepreneurs are not risk-aware. This is linked with their strong Ego facet that makes them self-confident people in charge of their own destiny. They expect to have setbacks and difficulties but they see these as par for the course and not as things that they could have avoided if they were more aware of the risks.

A strong Ego also means they are high on courage and there is a thin line between someone who is courageous and someone who is foolhardy.

Having said that we do believe that some entrepreneurs have a kind of risk blind spot, due to the make-up of their Ego facet. This gives them remarkable boldness when others can see the risks and pull back.

> **A friend describing his successful entrepreneur brother, told us that he was completely oblivious to risk.** He likened it to running across a frozen lake when the ice had broken up. No single piece of ice would carry a man's weight but his brother leapt from one piece of ice to another and somehow got to the other side. It never crossed his mind that he might fall in and drown.

I can handle it

Many entrepreneurs, because they are strong on Creativity and Ego, take the view that 'you can't plan for the chaos of an uncertain world'. They believe that the best route is to be equipped with good resources, stay vigilant, watch out for danger and deal with eventualities as and when they arise. Too much advance planning delays action, perhaps to the extent that one never sets out!

Creativity, innovation and courage can be used to find a way around obstacles and setbacks. There are always 'many ways to skin a cat' and problem solving is one of the elements of the Creativity facet. Rather than plan for every eventuality these people prefer to trust in their ability to deal with the unexpected. Successful entrepreneurs manage in the face of adversity.

Some entrepreneurs, as well as interested observers, speak of calculated risk. Although there is unlikely to be a formal risk analysis, entrepreneurs strong on Advantage have the knack of weighing up risks and reaching the right conclusion. They seem to know when it is 'a bridge too far'. It is this instinct that makes them good negotiators – they know how far to push a deal.

It won't happen to me

For many who are not entrepreneurs this is seen as a naive approach, but it is the attitude of many entrepreneurs and perhaps surprisingly, events often prove them right. Luck seems to be on their side.

This attitude arises because of a combination of the Ego facet and the Advantage facet. Entrepreneurs strong on Ego will have incredible self-belief – extreme courage – and will think they are invincible. Their Advantage facet adds to this a belief that the opportunity is so good that it can't fail.

When entrepreneurs with this attitude have to face failure they find it very difficult and some never recover. Those who do are all the wiser and learn from their mistakes. They still take risks but believe they now have the experience to handle it.

Extreme presence

After brief comments about what happens to each of the six facets when they are present in an extreme form, we will consider three cases of how extremes in several facets at the same time produce the 'shadow' side of entrepreneurship.

Extreme Focus is about tunnel vision, about being able to see only one thing and ignoring information that might be of vital importance. It is about everything being urgent – there is an obsession with time. It is about being hyperactive and always stretched.

Extreme Advantage means wanting to grasp every opportunity going by. Entrepreneurs like this need Focus to keep them on course.

Extreme Advantage can also distort decisions. Judgements are made based on the question 'What's in it for me?' Customers, employees, suppliers, even friends and family are regarded as pawns which can be easily discarded and sacrificed to satisfy the entrepreneur's personal wants and desires. Such people are ruthless.

The extreme form of Creativity is over-imagination. Entrepreneurs like this have an endless source of ideas, but are unlikely to be able to discriminate between those that have value – as potential and realistic opportunities – and those that will go nowhere.

They may be too far ahead of their time, envisioning things that are not feasible with today's technology, but that may happen at some stage in the future. A number of science fiction writers are extreme on Creativity.

Inventors who cannot ground their ideas into firm, marketable products are also likely to be singularly high on Creativity.

An extreme Ego is the most difficult facet to cope with, especially when it is combined with greed. It is likely to swamp the other facets and subvert them to its own ends. An otherwise moderate Team facet can be swamped, resulting in a group of weak dominated subordinates. Entrepreneurs with an extreme Ego facet always believe they know better. Their arrogance means that they don't listen to anybody and charge along the track unaware of the true situation. Such people can live in a fantasy world and can be seriously self-deluded.

Entrepreneurs with an extreme Ego facet always believe they know better

In the short term they may be very successful and create an extremely high-growth business but inevitably things will 'boil over'. Arrogance and an unrealistic belief in one's ability to handle a crisis will mean that the situation can only deteriorate very rapidly. Delusions always have to face their moment of truth.

Extreme presence of the Team facet is seen when one of the four elements that make up this facet dominate the others. Thus, someone extreme in networking will spend all their time meeting people and speaking at conferences and will neglect the business. Those extreme in using experts will have consultants running their business for them and regard the home team as incompetent.

Being extreme in picking good people will mean a team of outstanding individual players all competing with each other. Those extreme in working through a team will delegate everything. In each instance, there is an element of abdicating responsibility.

The extreme Social facet results in an obsession with a cause which can amount to fanaticism. There is an impatience with those who do not share the same passion. Clients are forced to accept the service whether they need it or not, like the person running a hostel for the homeless who opposes all efforts to help the homeless to find jobs, in case they become no longer homeless!

When all these characteristics are present in the extreme we have a potent brew – and it can be seriously dangerous.

Those who have these characteristics will be very driven, very ambitious and very profit-oriented – they will be ruthless, having to win at all costs. They are likely to take big risks, which if they pay off, will reinforce their extreme behaviour.

Sometimes we find entrepreneurs who have an overwhelming sense of their own rightness – and who then surround themselves with managers and assistants who are really only second-rate sycophants. Such entrepreneurs are extreme on the Ego facet. They can truly confide in very few, if any, of their managers and assistants. There is inadequate debate and only the entrepreneur's views and opinions are seen as credible.

When this goes hand-in-hand with the tunnel vision and the manipulation of others and of situations for personal gain – greed – then we have a powerful mix.

It is often the case that an extreme presence of Ego is the damaging factor. When we categorised the character themes in terms of talent and temperament, we said that the Focus, Advantage, Creativity and Team facets are talents, and the Ego facet is temperament. What we have is a situation where a person's temperament is destructive. Instead of temperament helping a person to exploit his or her talents positively and effectively, it is either preventing the talents coming through properly or forcing them to be used destructively.

We now give the story of Robert Maxwell as an excellent example of a once-successful entrepreneur who was extreme on Focus, Advantage and Ego, and probably also Creativity.

Then we consider the criminal entrepreneur and history's tyrants. They also show what extremes in the character themes can lead to.

The late publisher and media-magnate Robert Maxwell was born in poverty in Eastern Europe. He found his way to England in World War II and enlisted. After the war, a decorated hero, he was determined to 'become rich and famous – and to belong'. He was, for a time, a Labour MP, but lost his seat.

After problems with his first major business, he was declared unfit to be a director of a public company. But he bounced back.

Physically a big man, he was a larger-than-life figure who dominated those around him. He enjoyed publicity and notoriety. He courted other public figures.

But his business affairs became more and more complex and he was eventually found to have used shares owned by the Mirror Group Pension Fund as collateral for a loan to another of his companies. The shares never belonged to him – he simply had access to them. His actions left many pensioners without a pension. Apparently senior managers who worked for him, and who suspected at least some of the truth, were clearly afraid to expose him.

Determined to build a global media empire, his last major acquisition was a contested bid for the US publisher Macmillan. He paid an over-the-odds premium price. 'The battle had not been about commercial sense, but about a man's place in history.'

He eventually died when he fell overboard from his luxury yacht. The nature of his death has remained a mystery.

The criminal entrepreneur

Most criminal activity implies an absence of the Social character theme. Criminals are taking something from others and from society. They are destroying lives and destroying social capital.

Some successful business entrepreneurs are successful in part because they have broken the law. Other people with a number of the entrepreneur character themes present choose to focus their talents and energy on criminal activity instead of business. In many ways, successful gangsters are entrepreneurs.

After all, if there is such a thing as the 'perfect crime', what would be required?

>>> carrying out the crime with a degree of ruthless precision, making sure nothing or nobody gets in the way – Focus
>>> spotting a lucrative opportunity and an appreciation of how to achieve the desired outcome without detection – Advantage and Creativity
>>> extensive press coverage of the achievement and admiration for the daring involved – Ego
>>> pulling together and controlling all the resources required to execute the crime – Team.

The more we consider aspects of criminal behaviour, the more we see evidence of the entrepreneur character themes in some form.

Many minor criminals – rather than the true professionals who are very focused – are impulsive. This implies a lack of self-discipline and someone who is very low on Focus.

Serious criminals are often fearless, which would represent an extreme form of courage, part of the Ego facet.

Some are aggressive, which we can easily link to a need for domination, the extreme form of Ego.

History's tyrants

History has been peppered with warlords who have sought to dominate parts of the world, if not the whole world. When we study them we begin to see that they do many of the things that entrepreneurs do, and they manifest many of the character themes at the extreme.

They do things that all entrepreneurs do. They

>» want to make a difference
>» exercise creativity and innovation
>» spot and exploit opportunities
>» find the resources they need
>» develop and utilise networks
>» show determination in the face of adversity
>» handle risk, and
>» control events.

But they show some of the consequence of the extremes in their character themes. Tyrants do not put the customer first – they put their personal objectives at the forefront. Their desired outcomes are not financial, social or aesthetic capital, but power and domination. Their style is to acquire and maintain power with ruthlessness, making sure few of their followers present any threat to them. They want to rule, rather than simply make a difference. Their challenge – and skill – is one of harnessing the talents of other military leaders whilst keeping them loyal and subservient. They will often rely on personal charisma to achieve this.

Modern-day cult leaders often behave in exactly the same way.

Chapter 15 Some Real Entrepreneurs

This chapter presents seven entrepreneurs – a number of them will be familiar figures.

In each case a brief profile is provided, followed by a series of comments – often quotes from the entrepreneurs themselves – in the context of the Focus, Advantage, Creativity, Ego, Team and Social facets.

We have deliberately avoided drawing conclusions about the nature of each person profiled. This is a task for you!

- » What can you learn about the person from their facets?
- » Where are they particularly strong?
- » Do they seem to have any weak facets?
- » Do their facets seem to complement each other, or is there any evidence of one character theme hindering another?

We begin with an international figure, and typically the person most British people would nominate as the archetypal entrepreneur.

Born in 1950, the son of middle-class parents, Sir Richard Branson attended a public school. He dropped out at 16 to develop his youth magazine, *Student*. He was able to sell advertising because he persuaded a number of well-known personalities to write articles for him. *Student* provided the foundation for his Virgin empire.

He realised he could sell records by mail order if he promoted them in his magazine. Music retailing, Virgin Music (a recording label), Virgin Atlantic (Branson's airline), Virgin Radio, Virgin Rail, Virgin Cola, cinemas, financial services and a mobile telephone network have all followed. His major failure has so far been his inability to secure the National Lottery franchise.

Branson has always been able to attract publicity as a larger-than-life figure, aided in no small way by his powerboating and ballooning adventures. He has started over 200 companies which he keeps separate but networked as the Virgin empire. He has always preferred start-ups to acquisitions. Over the years he has also sold several businesses, most notably Virgin Music, and minority stakes in others, often to raise money for new ventures. Virgin was floated as a listed company in 1986, but Branson soon bought it back again.

Branson the entrepreneur

Focus

Branson is the opportunity spotter and deal-maker, rather than the project champion who sees it through personally. Focus may not be his strongest facet, but he does have an ability to focus when it matters. He got it right when he published *Student* and again when he found an empty upstairs room in Oxford Street and started his music business.

Both could have gone wrong but he carried them through. He targeted well and delivered.

Advantage

Branson is about opportunity. Sometimes the ideas are his; quite often they are offered to him.

In 1984, American Randolph Fields approached Branson and suggested they start a business-class, transatlantic airline. Branson was not convinced by Fields's business model, but he liked the idea of an airline, and in a matter of weeks he began to set up Virgin Atlantic Airways.

Whilst he sometimes appears to be instinctive, Branson does look for opportunities in markets where he feels the dominant competitors have become complacent and 'taken their eye off the ball'.

'The most critical thing with any new venture is delivering a tremendous value to the customer, so that it enhances all the ventures we've done before it.'

The growth of the Virgin empire was built on music. Even though Branson at one time thought about buying Thorn EMI, when the same company later offered him a substantial price for Virgin Music, he did not hesitate to sell. He knew he could usefully redeploy the money to his other businesses, in particular the airline. Branson is a man who sees and takes opportunities.

Creativity

Virgin has a unique, Branson-driven culture which 'embodies learning and fun'.

'You only live once and you might as well have a fun time while you're living.'

Earlier, in chapter 10, we recounted how Branson persuaded a reluctant Mike Oldfield to perform in a sell-out concert. When Oldfield appeared to lose his nerve and threatened to pull out at the last minute, Branson offered Oldfield his Bentley car, something he knew Oldfield coveted. When most others would have gone to the lawyers to deal with a breach of contract, Branson came up with a novel solution.

Ego

'If you start a company from scratch, and you don't have any financial backing, the only thing that matters is survival. And you have close shaves.'

'The challenge of learning and trying to do something better than in the past is irresistible.'

'All those concerned with Mr. Branson have to accept that he is an adventurer – he takes risks few of us would contemplate' (the *Financial Times*).

"I love to learn things I know little about"

Team

With the exception of his airline, Branson is not renowned as a hands-on entrepreneur. He attracts and employs experienced managers and steps back. But somehow they all know they work for Richard Branson. They are part of his team.

He has created a devolved, informal culture across Virgin which people enjoy.

Social

Branson is a trustee of several charities, including the Healthcare Foundation, which has focused on AIDS. He has contributed to several high-profile fundraising events, such as the televised Comic Relief.

Sir Ken Morrison is a billionaire and an elite member of the richest 20 people in the UK. Taking over his family business, he has expanded it to 100 Morrisons supermarkets and 75 petrol stations. The company head office remains in Bradford, where the company began. Prices are the same – and competitively low – in every store. One analyst described the management style as 'faceless Yorkshire nutters' – and maybe there is an element of uniqueness, as nobody from Morrisons has moved to take over another major retailer.

Now 70 years old, Ken Morrison still works six days a week and he is renowned for his thriftiness. He started work at the age of seven, and recalls that when he was a young boy his father would give him a pair of new shoes and then demand that he work in a store to pay for them.

Morrison the entrepreneur

Focus and Advantage

'He is by far the best retailer in Britain. Morrisons presents a simple proposition and does it better than anyone else…he is tough, shrewd and ruthless' (Allan Leighton, former chief executive, Asda).

There is no sophisticated analysis when searching for new store sites – 'We just get on a bus and look for chimney pots'.

'When it gets to numbers, Ken says he doesn't know about that side of things and passes you on to the finance director' (comment from an analyst). One wonders…

'He understands his customers very well…the thing you notice about the stores is that they are in tune with their customers' (Terry Leahy, chief executive, Tesco).

'Instead of asking customers "Is everything all right?" he asks "How can we make it better?"' (Victor Watson, former chairman, John Waddington).

Creativity

The in-store layout features a market hall concept, which replicates the style of open street markets and is popular with customers.

Team

Asking questions and listening is seen as one of Morrison's greatest assets. 'He lets people get on with their jobs – he is a good delegator. He has been doing empowerment for years' (Victor Watson).

Sir Alan Sugar was born in Hackney, London in 1947. His father was a tailor, but his uncle ran a successful retail business. His uncle acted as his mentor and he began buying and selling electrical goods in his late teens. Amstrad (Alan M Sugar Trading) was started in 1968. The business model was based on designing low-cost consumer products which Sugar had manufactured in the Far East and which were then marketed aggressively. Hi-fis were followed by computers, satellite dishes and mobile phone emailers.

A true serial entrepreneur, Sugar has seen his fortunes rise and fall, and his net worth exceeds £500 million. He has an 'uncanny insight into consumer wants' which he satisfies with products at affordable prices. Throughout his life he has 'put something back' with charitable donations and, more recently, by encouraging young people to think about doing something for themselves. On entrepreneurs and entrepreneurship he says 'you have to recognise who's good at it and who isn't. It's in-built in you, like a musician's or artist's talent. You can't go into WH Smith's and buy a book and just become an entrepreneur. You've got to have some killer instinct in you.'

Sugar the entrepreneur

Focus

'You have to have discipline when you work for yourself – there's no one else to report to on a Monday.'

'He growls and jumps and likes to provoke – but he is 100% focused on what he wants to achieve.' – Sir Stanley Kalms, retired Chairman, Dixons.

"You have to be good at figures – and be a good salesman"

Advantage

'There's no luck involved in my business success – it's a case of smelling the market. You have got to have a nose for certain things.'

Creativity

Amstrad has always been noted for its innovative products, which typically follow the leaders in a particular industry, but provide low-price competition.

Ego

'He hates bullshit, always wants to avenge a slight and trusts only those who have come up the same way as him, with the same values' (comments from one journalist).

Sugar bought control of Tottenham Hotspur Football Club (which he has now sold) to 'save the club my dad loved'. His period as chairman was controversial, and he lost the support of many fans.

Team

Amstrad boasts a preponderance of managers from north and east London, mostly from non-affluent backgrounds, and many from immigrant families: 'We can all trade, do a deal and make it stick'. Despite its size and diversity, Amstrad has always retained the image of the trader entrepreneur.

Sugar is very hands-on and is reported to be tough on employees who fail him: 'He can't delegate'.

Brent Hoberman is a team entrepreneur, a visionary with a complementary partner. He has a wide circle of friends and he socialises extensively – he is a classic networker. Now in his early thirties, he was born in Cape Town but was educated at Eton and Oxford. His maternal grandfather was a successful entrepreneur in South Africa.

He worked as a consultant before becoming involved in the start-up of QXL, the online auction house. In 1998, together with Martha Lane Fox, a fellow consultant with whom he had worked on projects, he secured the funding to begin lastminute.com, one of the UK's best publicised e-commerce businesses. In three years the company has acquired a French competitor and floated – but the share prices have not maintained their opening value. The company name came from Hoberman's reputation for doing everything at the last minute.

Hoberman the entrepreneur

Focus and Team

He is 'a bit disorganised, always leaping from one thing to another' (comment of a friend).

Hoberman's weakness in Focus was compensated for by Fox, who is well organised. She is recognised as a motivator of people and she concentrates on the day-to-day operations of the business. She comments that Brent 'sells ideas, but can immerse himself in the details'.

Advantage

Lastminute is about 'owning the market'. He 'moves fast to seize opportunities'.

The business provides a site where customers can pick up late bargains in travel, accommodation and entertainment. At the same time his suppliers can find a market for slow-moving goods. Everyone can benefit. A classic win–win situation.

'In every business story there's an element of luck...if you think about all the risks you never do anything. That's why lots of people have great ideas they never do.'

Creativity

Hoberman has been described as a 'great visionary'.

Ego

Hoberman was always 'ambitious, driven to prove himself, working on business plans even at University, using his parents' contacts and resources to realise his goals' (view of a friend).

'He is full of determination and ambition, unfazed by rejection ...he is a confident networker with a drive to believe a gamble [like lastminute.com] cannot fail' (comments from his friend Rogan Angelini-Hurll).

'You'll never meet a complacent entrepreneur, it's an oxymoron. Every milestone you achieve, you want to achieve more.'

Mike Tamaki is a New Zealand entrepreneur in the tourism industry. He is part Maori. One of his early jobs was a coach driver – he drove tour buses around Rotorua, his home town on the North Island – but he longed for a business of his own. He saw an opportunity to buy a small bus and start his own tour company, but he lacked the cash. Unable to borrow it from traditional sources, he persuaded his brother, Doug, to join him and to sell his prize possession, a Harley-Davidson motorcycle, to raise the funds for the bus. The Tamaki brothers set out to offer more intimate, friendly tours than their larger rivals, although they were covering the same destinations. The business was slow to take off, but eventually it did. The brothers expanded, diversifying into adventure trips – rafting and so on. These largely did not work and were abandoned.

Traditional tourist attractions in Rotorua include a visit to a Maori *marae* (a meeting house) and a *hangi*, a feast cooked in the traditional Maori way using white hot stones in a pit. These meals were normally cooked in hotel grounds. Tamaki has now built his own Maori village outside Rotorua and buses tourists there for entertainment, including a *haka* (the Maori challenge dance) a traditional culture and craft exhibition and a *hangi*. Successful, he has become something of a legend amongst the Maori population. Most visitors are foreign tourists, but local Maoris who go are visibly moved from the poignant reminder of their heritage. He has plans to set up a Maori cultural theme park in Christchurch, on the South Island, thereby tripling his turnover. An energetic, charismatic man who is full of ideas, he is held in check by his quieter brother and his wife.

Tamaki the entrepreneur

Focus

'Entrepreneurs [like me] just want to get out there and do it – fighting those who try to stop them.'

He lost his way by following the wrong opportunities but quickly realised his mistake and refocused: 'We had overstretched our resources'.

Advantage

'We began with a dream – more intimate tours based on our own personality. We knew we could improve on the things people weren't happy with.'

'You have to go through the windows of opportunity when they are there for you. You have to take the risks.'

'We set our basic standard deliberately high – as a bench-mark – so any would-be rivals would find it hard to copy us.'

"The secret is to get everything right"

Creativity

Persuading his brother to finance his new venture demanded creativity.

'I am constantly thinking about new business ideas. My mind is always going 100%. I see things and think "we could do that".'

Ego and Team

'Entrepreneurs are there to inspire. It's important to surround yourself with people with business acumen – people who counter-balance your enthusiasm.'

Tamaki respects the contribution of his brother and wife. His son, who is more like him, has also joined the business.

"Our business is all about relation-ships"

Social

There is a very strong cultural and educational underpinning to the business. Tamaki is keenly committed to explaining the Maori heritage to his visitors and doing it in a serious way which does not offend the Maori people.

Jack Welch retired in 2001 from his post as chairman of GE. During his 20 years as head of the largest company (by value) in the US, he had developed a reputation as a corporate entrepreneur who had transformed the culture of an industrial giant and created a business full of entrepreneurs. At the same time he had fostered extensive integration and collaboration in a diversified conglomerate – GE manufactures turbines, aero engines, white goods and lighting, for example, as well as owning NBC Television and a huge financial subsidiary. Businesses had been bought and sold by Welch, and some operations had been drastically down-sized but GE's market value rose from $13 billion to $550 billion in the process.

Interestingly, GE began in 1889 when two existing companies were merged – one was Edison Electric, which had been formed in 1878 to commercialise Thomas Edison's breakthroughs with electric lighting.

Welch graduated as a chemical engineer and joined GE in 1957, aged 22. He had chosen a smaller university rather than a major, as he had 'a better opportunity of standing out'. At a major he would have been 'bottom of the pit'. In 1968 he became GE's youngest ever general manager, and his division quickly developed a reputation for innovative new products and effective team working. He once promoted a middle manager two levels for losing a lot of money in a new venture – to emphasise that mistakes have to be made when a company ventures into 'new and uncharted waters'. Punishing failure ensures people are afraid to take risks.

Always keen on sport, he was extremely competitive but not exceptionally skilled. He had major bypass surgery when he was 60 years old but returned to work, active as ever.

Michael Bonsignore, retired chairman of Honeywell, described him in a *Financial Times* interview as: 'tireless, brilliant, fearless, ruthless, heartless and sharply focused on making money for GE's shareholders'.

Welch the entrepreneur

Focus

Academically, Welch did not stand out as an exceptionally clever college student – but he did have a real ability to focus and complete his work, whilst his fellow students struggled to finish their theses. He mused that it was his impatience that drove him to hit his targets.

He was aged 35 years when he began to think that one day he could end up as CEO of GE. From that point he had a single focus – to run GE. A decade later he landed the top job.

Advantage

'The idea of quantum change is not just reserved for the fast, new start-up in Silicon Valley. It's for everyone, everywhere.'

Welch became convinced that anything that GE did that made their customers more successful would, in turn, help their own revenues and profits. He declared that it would be a central tenet that GE would serve its customers everywhere.

Creativity

'GE is a bubbling cauldron of ideas and learning…my job is to find great ideas, exaggerate them and spread them like hell around the business with the speed of light.'

Ego

He acknowledged that his mother taught him to be independent and to seek to control his own destiny. He valued the self-confidence she instilled in him – it gave him courage and 'extended his reach'.

The competition for the CEO post at GE (which he won) was inevitably brutal because it was complicated by serious organisational politics and a number of big egos, 'mine included'.

Team

He wanted people in GE to have sufficient self-confidence to express different, perhaps opposing, views.

He believed that people who coach others improve themselves in the process.

Employees who could not operate as team players, regardless of their individual talents and value, simply did not belong in GE under Welch.

'Our job at GE is to deal with resources – human and financial. The idea of getting great talent, giving them all the support in the world and letting them run is the management philosophy of GE.'

Welch certainly saw himself as a liberator, inspiring others to realise their responsibility and talents. His key slogan was 'Control your destiny or someone else will'. But everyone knew who was really in control. He had chosen his own men to push through his reforms and weed out 'resistors'. He had replaced a republic with a monarchy.

Samson, 1996

Eric McKellar Watt died in 2001 at the age of 81. He had built 'a sausage empire from a discarded prison mixing bowl'. He may not be as well known as the others in this chapter, but he is important because he represents the large band of entrepreneurs who are 'out there' but whom we often fail to recognise as entrepreneurs. They are the people who are more than businessmen with the skills and talent to keep a business ticking over. They are the people who build something of recognised value because they can't help it. It is part of their nature.

His business had humble beginnings in a tiny Glasgow shop; Watt used the discarded bowl to mix the first ingredients. Eventually he was to build a substantial meat products business with the strap-line: 'McKellar Watt for meatiness'. He was an innovative businessman from the very beginning, willing to experiment with new ideas and abandoning them if they failed.

We mentioned in chapter 9 that he tried whisky-flavoured sausages and that customers were less than enthusiastic. 'Let's face it,' he rationalised, 'who wants to drink their whisky out of a sausage?'

"Who wants to drink their whisky out of a sausage?"

McKellar Watt the entrepreneur

Focus and Advantage

In true entrepreneurial fashion, McKellar Watt built a meat products empire from a micro-business start-up. He began with recycled utensils, resources that were adequate but hardly the best.

Could he have achieved this without Focus and Advantage?

Creativity

Significantly, he could laugh about his failures. Habitually he simply moved on to something else.

Ego

He wanted to 'beat whatever system was conspiring to make his life difficult'. In 1939 he defied his father, volunteered for the army and took a commission as a captain in the Royal Service Corps. He saw active service in Montgomery's 8th Army, and in 1942 he and his patrol were caught up in sniper fire. He spent the next 18 months in an army hospital, 'having his body rebuilt and learning to walk again'. A female doctor told him he would never drive a car again. A week later he persuaded a friend to bring a car to the hospital – and he proceeded to drive it around the compound. As he drove past, the doctor gave him the thumbs-up sign.

He was pleased and amused when a journalist once wrote: 'Beneath the tough, unyielding exterior of Eric McKellar Watt beats an even tougher, unyielding interior. Other men, known for their strength, poise and confidence have emerged from sessions with him white, trembling and sapped of all vitality.'

Team

Watt appears to have been an autocratic businessman, and certainly not someone who suffered fools gladly. And yet he was seen as a generous and loyal employer.

'On one occasion his managing director was summoned to receive a Christmas gift. He expected a bottle of whisky or perhaps a piece of glassware. Instead he was handed the keys of a new car.'

———

Now it's your turn again.

Review any biography, autobiography or story of an entrepreneur that you can get your hands on. It might even be an obituary.

- ⟫ *Where can you see evidence of the facets?*
- ⟫ *Where is this person particularly strong?*
- ⟫ *Are there any obvious weak character themes?*
- ⟫ *How do you think this has affected what the entrepreneur has done and achieved?*

Chapter 16 Releasing the Entrepreneur

We have referred several times to the idea that entrepreneurs are hidden in the woodwork and that given the right conditions they will emerge. Another analogy is that there is a well of entrepreneurial talent waiting to be tapped, rather like the oil deposit that you know is there somewhere – but you have to drill down and find it before it can gush to the surface.

If this could be done with entrepreneurial talent and we were able to release the entrepreneurs in our midst then there would be nothing special about Silicon Valley or the Cambridge Phenomenon – it would be happening everywhere, an entrepreneur culture would be the norm.

In this chapter we consider how all this might be achieved but we do so with two provisos:

>> we are dealing with a natural process
>> ends come before means.

Whatever steps are taken to release the entrepreneurs in our midst, whatever mechanisms and facilities we put in place, we must always remember that we are dealing with a natural process.

The emergence and growth of the entrepreneur is like the flower in the garden whose growth is part of a natural process – from seed to seedling to full flower. Adverse conditions can prevent or delay this natural process, but get the conditions right, employ a good gardener and flowers will be blooming everywhere. Nature will have done its job. Releasing natural talent works in a similar way. Some entrepreneurs will emerge whatever happens, but do a little digging and watering and there will be an abundance.

The gardener might build a greenhouse to care for his seedlings and save them from frost. At the right time he beds them out in the open and they continue their growth. The greenhouse and the prepared garden are all means to an end. The outcome is the healthy flower. In our experience, projects designed to promote entrepreneurs and enterprise often fail to achieve their potential because what should be means have become ends in themselves. A business generator facility with all the resources imaginable is no use unless it is generating businesses. An expensive and well-appointed business incubator or innovation centre is of little value if it is not full of entrepreneurs growing successful businesses.

With these provisos we look at how the entrepreneurs can be encouraged out of the woodwork. We look at four aspects:

>> smart luck and hard luck
>> entrepreneur cultures
>> building an entrepreneur culture
>> giving half a chance.

Some entrepreneurs emerge from the woodwork because of 'smart luck', and others because of 'hard luck', but these are not large groups. It is entrepreneur cultures that really cause entrepreneurs to emerge in numbers. In fact, many emerge who are not true entrepreneurs but the culture treats them kindly and they usually find their niche.

It is the entrepreneur cultures that really cause entrepreneurs to emerge in numbers

Between these two extremes is the entrepreneur's support infrastructure that aims to provide the 'half a chance' that he or she deserves in an environment that is generally hostile.

Smart luck and hard luck

Some people find themselves in the right place at the right time. If they have a strong Advantage facet they will see the opportunity in front of them and grab it with both hands.

Profile Charles Dunstone

Charles Dunstone is in his mid-thirties; he founded the Carphone Warehouse retail chain at just the right time. Depending on share value, he is worth around £200 million.

'When people ask Charlie Dunstone why he has been so successful, he likes to crack a joke. "I'm the luckiest man since Ringo Starr," he says.'

'What makes an entrepreneur successful? The smart ones say luck. But of course, it's more than just that…'

Davidson, Smart Luck, *2002*

'Smart luck' is a good way of describing what made entrepreneurs like Charles Dunstone. Their success is far more than just blind chance, they have to be smart to see what in hindsight might be obvious and then turn that perceived opportunity into a reality.

Sometimes the opportunity is so good that building a business may not be very demanding. The founder's Advantage facet will have identified the opportunity and the Focus facet helped to target the opportunity but he or she may not be all that strong in the other entrepreneurial facets. Such people are more opportunists than they are entrepreneurs and are not likely to repeat their success.

'Hard luck' has probably produced as many entrepreneurs as 'smart luck'. It is a strong trigger to entrepreneurial instincts. When things can't get worse and the only way is up, the entrepreneur stirs. Redundancy or, worse still, expulsion from one's homeland, have all helped people to discover their entrepreneurial talents – they have had to in order to survive.

Ram Gidoomal arrived in the UK in 1967 as a 16-year-old refugee. His father had left Kenya the previous year with only £3000 in his pocket. They had lived in a palace in Kenya – now all 15 of them were crammed into four rooms over a corner shop in Shepherd's Bush, West London. The family's entrepreneurial skills soon showed as the corner shop became a money-spinner. It wasn't long before they had a chain of corner shops across London.

Ram become a successful entrepreneur in his own right and in recent years has turned his hand to social entrepreneurship. In 1989 he founded the Christmas Cracker Charitable Trust, and in 2001 was appointed chair of the London Sustainability Exchange.

He came to public notice as leader of the Christian Peoples Alliance and as its candidate for Mayor of London. The *Times* commented that 'If this were an election on policy alone, Gidoomal would win by a landslide'. As it was, he achieved the highest percentage of votes outside the main three political parties.

His book *UK Maharajahs* shows his interest in the entrepreneurial talents of his fellow Asians.

No doubt a study of the 'corner shop' opportunity in the 1960s and 1970s would not have shown this to be the best business opportunity around but families like the Gidoomals knew about trading and for them it was an ideal low-cost start-up opportunity. Their strong Advantage facet told them that. They gained their competitive advantage by staying open until late in the evening and working unsocial hours. Their strong Focus facet meant that hard work and perseverance was part of their nature and they achieved great things.

The courage from the Ego and Creativity facets means that entrepreneurs thrive on adversity. They can keep going when the things get tough and they know how to survive. These are characteristics that refugee groups like the Kenyan and Ugandan Asians so clearly demonstrated.

Entrepreneur cultures

From smart luck and hard luck, which produce only a few entrepreneurs, we now move to cultures where entrepreneurs are everywhere.

'Two hi-tech start-ups a week for five years' is what happened in a town in East Anglia, England when an entrepreneur culture took hold. The banking community, more accustomed to handling the business accounts of the local farmers, had to learn about hi-tech companies rather quickly. The joke in the mid-1980s was that bank managers were afflicted with 'technology glaze' – mention words like 'micro-chips' and 'computers' and their eyes glazed over and you knew you'd lost them. Barclays Bank took this problem so seriously that they set up a training programme for their managers on 'how to handle hi-tech accounts'.

The Cambridge Phenomenon originated from six spin-off points: three in the University of Cambridge (the physics, engineering and computer science departments), two private research consultancies and one government Centre of Excellence.

It was here that local entrepreneur cultures first developed. Over time they coalesced and spread to include other places and the area as a whole. Frequent articles in the *Financial Times* with racy headlines like 'The place where anything grows' made the business world and the general public aware that something was happening in this university city. It also gave the entrepreneurs that began to emerge from the woodwork a real sense of belonging – they were part of an entrepreneurial movement.

A similar story could be told of the origins of Silicon Valley, the place where a modern entrepreneur culture first took hold. *Silicon Valley Fever* by Larson and Rogers, published in the mid-1980s, tells the story. The subtitle 'Growth of High-Technology Culture' is well chosen.

We will consider later in this chapter whether it is possible to create an entrepreneur culture and so achieve the release of hidden entrepreneurial talent on a large scale. In principle we believe it is, but it requires a 10–20-year timescale, and that is too long for most economic developers and governments.

One of the main drivers of an entrepreneur culture is the influence of peer groups

One of the main drivers of an entrepreneur culture is the influence of peer groups. The simple adage that 'if he can do it, I can do it' applies. This can be particularly strong within an academic community, such as David's, the university lecturer in chapter 2. When the professor bought a new red Porsche through his company, David and his colleagues took note. They thought that maybe they should have a try at being entrepreneurs.

There is a similar effect among the business community when career employees suddenly realise that they too can start a company and make money for themselves.

Bob Noyce, one of the founders of Intel, the world's most successful computer chip company, is in this category. On his first step into the world of the entrepreneur with Fairchild Semiconductor, he commented:

Suddenly it became apparent to people like myself, who had always assumed they would work for a salary for the rest of their lives, that they could get some equity in a start-up company. That was a great revelation, and a great motivation too.

Hanson, *The New Alchemists*, 1982

Bob Noyce was changing his big company mindset for that of the entrepreneur. It happened because an entrepreneur culture was developing in the area. He saw that others around him in Silicon Valley were setting up their own businesses and becoming very rich. He was experiencing the 'peer group effect'.

The entrepreneur culture in Silicon Valley developed from four spin-off points. Stanford University pioneered the way as early as 1912, but the real starting point was in the late 1930s when Professor Fred Terman, a true entrepreneur enabler, suggested that his students Bill Hewlett and Dave Packard consider exploiting a business opportunity around Hewlett's end-of-year project. Thus the Hewlett-Packard company was born. Others followed from Stanford University over the years.

The second spin-off point was a number of key companies that just seemed to spawn start-ups. The most notable of these was Fairchild Semiconductor. In the 1960s it became a technology beacon and created more spin-off businesses than any other company. At a conference of semiconductor engineers held in Silicon Valley in 1969 'less than two dozen of the 400 present had never worked at Fairchild'. Its influence was all-pervasive at that time.

The technology of the microchip was an important opportunity trigger to what was happening in Silicon Valley and this needs to be factored in to the entrepreneur culture equation. With the momentum gathering pace the last two spin-off points came into being.

The first of these was the Homebrew Computer Club, an informal network formed in the mid-1970s. It immediately attracted a remarkable blend of technological and entrepreneurial talent. Apple Computers is the most well known of the Homebrew spin-offs.

The second was a collection of restaurants and bars where people gathered informally to talk about the latest technology and its business opportunities – Walker's Wagon Wheel Bar and Restaurant close to Fairchild Semiconductors, the Cow Girl Bar in the Sunnyvale Hilton Inn, The Peppermill near Intel's headquarters and the Lion and Compass owned by Nolan Bushnell the entrepreneur founder of Atari.

A sales manager at Intel said:

> I can go to The Peppermill at eight in the morning and always meet somebody I know. After all this is Silicon Valley. All of my customers and all of my competitors – and that's about 500 people – eat breakfast there regularly. In fact I have to be careful about who is sitting in the next booth; you can gain a lot of information by overhearing conversations. The Peppermill is just a giant meeting place.

Larson and Rogers, *Silicon Valley Fever*, 1986

This social type of spin-off point plays to the networking strength of the Team facet as we have already noted. Entrepreneurs just love these places – it seems to bring them alive.

Building an entrepreneur culture

The most effective way to release the entrepreneur is to build an entrepreneur culture and let nature do the rest. Here we consider the key elements involved in this process which, we believe, given time, commitment and perseverance can be made to happen.

The key elements are:

>> spin-off points
>> entrepreneur enablers
>> product/service excellence
>> community networks
>> visibility.

A region does not need many spin-off points to begin the development of an entrepreneur culture. Rather like lighting a barbecue, you look for the coals that have started to glow and work on those to get the fire going.

As we have said spin-off points are important because of the peer-group effects that develop in them.

Within all spin-off points there is certain to be at least one entrepreneur enabler. These are people who think in entrepreneurial terms and are keen to help entrepreneurs along the road. They are often found in institutions like banks, universities or local authorities. Entrepreneur enabler bankers played important roles in the entrepreneur cultures that developed along Route 128, Boston, US, and in Cambridge, England. We have already noted the enabling role of Professor Terman at Stanford University in Silicon Valley.

Entrepreneur enablers have many of the facets of the entrepreneur but are probably lacking in one of the 'face' facets – the most common omissions being the Advantage and Ego facets, which makes them risk-averse, preferring the security of the institution.

For a region to have a serious possibility of developing an entrepreneur culture it needs to have some speciality or expertise that allows its entrepreneurs to achieve excellence. Even quite small communities have been able to bring entrepreneurs out of the woodwork because of a local expertise. The town of Laguiole in the Aveyron region of France has a special expertise in the manufacture of jack-knives, and now this is an industry that seems to employ the whole town. Many entrepreneurs have emerged and they are proud of their corporate branding – the 'Bee' logo at the base of the handle shows it is a Laguiole knife. Montebelluna in northeastern Italy had specialised for many years in making leather hiking boots of high quality. As prosperity returned after the Second World War they began making ski-boots, for which there was an increasing demand. The timing of the 1956 Winter Olympics in Cortina, Italy could not have been better. Soon a whole industry developed in the region as entrepreneurs emerged to exploit the opportunity.

The fourth factor important in the creation of an entrepreneur culture is the development of community networks amongst potential entrepreneurs and entrepreneurs who have actually taken the plunge and started their own business. Sometimes, as we have noted in the case of Silicon Valley, these networks become so strong that they constitute spin-off points in their own right.

Any network is in effect a mini-community. At first it may be a network of just a few people, but when it is a network of entrepreneurs things don't stay that way for long. Entrepreneur networks show an amazing ability to multiply because entrepreneurship is contagious.

> **Any network is in effect a mini-community**

The final factor, visibility, is about spreading the message around that something special is happening in a region. This may be in the form of publicity provided by a friendly newspaper. In Silicon Valley it was the *San Jose Mercury News*, in Cambridge, England, the *Financial Times*. Visibility can also come from a building or facility of some kind, like the Stanford Research Park or Cambridge Science Park. Anything that will attract international visitors will do the trick.

These factors together enable a critical mass to develop in a region. When this point is reached there is take-off, and entrepreneurs appear from everywhere. The size of this critical mass depends upon the business environment in the region. If this is positive and supportive then the critical mass will be much smaller and take-off will be earlier than it would be if the business environment was harsh.

Universities are an interesting case in point. Universities often build an anti-entrepreneur wall around themselves and wonder why so few people bother to climb over it. They put restrictions on what their staff can and cannot do and have intellectual property (IP) rules that give the academics and researchers few rights. Yet they seem surprised when only a few of their staff bother to spin off businesses to exploit their research work.

Red tape is another issue that creates an unhelpful climate for the entrepreneur. Just as entrepreneurs are often uncomfortable in classrooms, they are unhappy filling in forms. The business plan demanded – and rightly so – by potential funders is about their limit. In certain regions business grants are available for particular initiatives – but many entrepreneurs never access this funding because of the red tape involved. They find it difficult to penetrate the rules and regulations – and anyway, they have other things to do.

Employment law and Health and Safety regulations seem to get ever more complex. Filling in forms for grants might be an option, but there is no escape from government legislation. Compliance can be extremely complex, time-consuming and expensive. The entrepreneur gets frustrated with the whole process, having a business to run.

Some 'rogue entrepreneurs' see this as an opportunity and cut corners to steal an advantage. Enforcement of rules and regulation is therefore required to try and stop this, but this can be heavy-handed and can defeat the object.

We accept that regulation is needed to curb the worst excesses and to improve conditions in the workplace, but the trend for more rules and regulations rather than less does not bode well for encouraging the release of entrepreneurial talent.

Giving half a chance

Now we come to the practical things that can be put in place to give the entrepreneur half a chance.

Here we consider three support elements:

>>> premises
>>> money
>>> business advice.

Entrepreneurs need premises to operate from, money to grow the business and business advice to ensure that they don't 'shoot themselves in the foot'. In the past all of this has been very expensive and has seriously limited the number of entrepreneurs who have emerged and survived. In recent years things have begun to change as the needs of the entrepreneur have been recognised.

Premises

Entrepreneurs never know how much space they will need for their start-up business or how long they will need it for. Large buildings with long leases are of no use to them. Also, they cannot necessarily afford the office equipment, telephone systems and so on that they would like. Their businesses are just not big enough to carry that level of overhead.

This problem was solved by the invention of what has become known as the business incubator – also called the innovation centre, particularly in its early days.

They first appeared in significant numbers in the US in the 1980s. By 1985 there were 117 in 28 states. Since that time they have spread across the world. There is an active business incubator programme in China and Israel has a successful business incubator programme to encourage Jews emigrating from Russia to start their own businesses.

Business incubators are buildings which provide the entrepreneur with a range of small rooms or units, some as small as 10 m². Units can be rented at short notice on an 'easy in, easy out' basis. Central services are to a high standard, with reception, telephone and photocopying facilities that the start-up company could not otherwise afford.

Business help and advice is also available, but the greatest benefit is being with other entrepreneurs, all eager to make a success of their enterprise.

The two most important critical success factors for a business incubator are to have an entrepreneur enabler running the place and a coffee shop in the building around which an informal entrepreneur community can develop.

The success of this formula has been remarkable. Results gathered by the UN from business incubators across the world have shown that on average businesses in incubators have a survival rate of 80 percent over a five-year period, turning the normal 20/80 success to failure ratio on its head.

Business incubators certainly give their tenant entrepreneurs more than half a chance.

Money

Giving the entrepreneur half a chance on the financial side has proved to be a much more difficult task. It is true that a thriving venture-capital industry has developed on both sides of the Atlantic and there is now more money than ever available for start-ups – but that is only half of the story. Venture capitalists are not known as 'vulture capitalists' for nothing! Their expectation of an annual return on their investment of 40 percent and an exit from the investment in three years does no favours for the entrepreneur.

There is now more money then ever available for start-ups

Venture capitalists like to claim that they have 'sparked the greatest burst of entrepreneurial activity the world has ever seen'. Maybe they helped, but it is the entrepreneurs who have done the work.

The venture capitalists who first appeared in Silicon Valley did seem to have the right approach. They certainly took risks and were in for the long haul. They spoke in terms not just of investing but of building companies. They saw their primary aim as growing a successful business. Capital gains were their reward not their goal.

Somewhere along the road this sentiment seems to have been lost. In our view this is the biggest unresolved area. Many entrepreneurs never make it because they are spending all their time fundraising when they should be running their business. The term 'burn rate' has been coined to define the rate at which a start-up business burns the money that has been invested in it. This gives the entrepreneur an operational horizon that is rarely more than a year, so that any medium-term financial planning becomes guesswork. Only entrepreneurs strong on the resourcing element of the Advantage facet and the courage element of the Ego facet are likely to make it.

Many of the people running venture funds have never started their own business, nor are they entrepreneur enablers, so that difficulties and misunderstandings are bound to arise. Perhaps the best sign of improvement is in the role that business angels are beginning to play in the funding process. All are wealthy individuals and most have created the wealth themselves. They are often entrepreneurs with a great deal of experience helping other entrepreneurs to follow in their steps.

Business advice

It is part of the nature of the entrepreneur not to sit in the classroom or take advice from other people. Providing business advice to entrepreneurs is therefore inherently difficult. They learn best from their peers or from people they respect. Those strong on the Team facet, who can pick out competence, have a strong advantage here. Without this strength the entrepreneur is likely to have one or two bad experiences and then write off all advisers as being of no use.

It is here that the idea of entrepreneur enablers is so important. Such people immediately empathise with the entrepreneur and their help is well accepted.

The banks and various government agencies offer a wide range of advice and support services to the entrepreneur. They have business advisers and mentors that work with the entrepreneur to help on a day-to-day basis. There are training courses covering every business topic. Despite all these efforts the entrepreneur often feels alone. This is because their strong Ego facet means that they don't easily seek advice and prefer to learn the hard way. Part of the problem is that these support services, many of them free, are used by people who are not really entrepreneurs and the focus is on imparting technique and skills. We do believe that entrepreneurs need support, but it has to be available as and when they need it and in a form that they can understand and accept. We believe that this is best done by entrepreneur enablers who themselves have been trained in understanding and working with the entrepreneur.

Chapter 17 Releasing the Corporate Entrepreneur

There are four different levels of organisational achievement – we might describe this as the hierarchy of achievement and relate it to an elevator. The most entrepreneurial organisations start at the top and stay on the top floor. Others start lower down. Some start quite high but then fall away as the early spirit of entrepreneurship is lost. Those on the lower floors really need to move upwards rather than risk sliding further down – for the bottom floor is not sustainable in the long term. In order to move up, these organisations need corporate entrepreneurs.

The four levels are:

» The entrepreneurial organisation – the ambitious and proactive organisation that grows and prospers because it creates and seizes opportunities. Change, sometimes quite radical, will be evident. Naturally the most lucrative opportunities will occur in high-growth and emerging industries, which by their nature are relatively high-risk. The entrepreneurial organisation thrives in this environment.

» The survivor organisation – the less ambitious organisation that survives without major upheaval in a state of acceptable 'normality'. It does this by dealing effectively with environmental pressures and opportunities – vigilant, but with an emphasis on reaction. It may not aspire to be the leader of change in an industry, rather preferring to follow what it sees as relatively lower-risk strategies. For companies in low-growth or even declining industries, there are opportunities for limited growth and these will be seized by the most entrepreneurial competitors.

» The underperforming organisation – the organisation that is allowed by its stakeholders to underperform. Its achievements are below those that might be expected. Its performance fluctuates but it manages to deal with problems as they occur in order to return to 'normality', but it is not really in control of its own destiny.

» The inadequate organisation – the organisation that performs inadequately, because it fails to resolve crises, and ends up needing 'radical surgery'. It may or may not survive.

Entrepreneurship is fully at the heart of the entrepreneurial organisation that grows and prospers because it is, by nature and definition, proactive and driven by opportunities. The 'survivor' organisation may demonstrate some entrepreneurship, but on a much more limited scale as it opts to 'play safe'. Organisations that underperform may periodically demonstrate entrepreneurship in dealing with the setbacks they face, but they are not truly entrepreneurial as they are fundamentally reactive.

Of course, proactive and entrepreneurial organisations may fail if they make errors of judgement and create crises for themselves. They take risks which overstretch their resources and capabilities. The lower-growth, survival approach has its merits as long as the organisation does not lose out to more ambitious rivals.

Arguably, too many organisations are allowed to underachieve or perform inadequately. Managers may believe it wise to avoid strategies that are seen as high-risk, but such organisations can be vulnerable to entrepreneurial rivals. If we can release more corporate entrepreneurs and make organisations more innovative and entrepreneurial, we can move more organisations up this hierarchy of achievement.

To accomplish this we need both entrepreneurial leaders and entrepreneurial employees scattered throughout the organisation – intrapreneurs. But it would be unrealistic to suggest all leaders should be entrepreneurs and all employees intrapreneurs. We have already established that entrepreneurs and leaders share certain character themes but others separate them. Whilst we can all be more creative and innovative, some of us will be reluctant to go further, to take on more responsibility and champion new initiatives.

We use the term 'strategic leader' for the person at the head of the whole organisation and those who head identifiable businesses and divisions within large corporations.

The entrepreneurial strategic leader may be an entrepreneur or someone who encourages and rewards entrepreneurship in others – a growth entrepreneur or an entrepreneur enabler.

In this context we can also separate the ideas of 'stewardship' and 'entrepreneurship'.

entrepreneurial strategic leaders	stewards
transformers	consolidators
venturer enablers	manager enablers
intrapreneur enablers	

Strategic leaders who are stewards rather than entrepreneurs preside over organisations and businesses where the strategic thrust is one of continuing to exploit opportunities spotted in the past. Sound cost management and limited, incremental change will dominate. Analysis will be preferred to aspiration. The entrepreneurial organisation will be more aspirational and focused on the future. From time to time it is likely to make dramatic changes to its strategies, structure and/or style.

So what types of corporate entrepreneur are we looking to release? Transformers – entrepreneurial leaders who

» transform the fortunes of an organisation with new strategies and styles of management
» change the rules of competition in an industry
» turn around a company in difficulty
» encourage venturing and intrapreneurship by cultivating an organisation in which this can and does happen.

Venturers – who establish and grow

» a new business within or alongside an existing organisation
» a spin-off business from an established organisation – as either a management buy-out, a buy-in or an initial public offering.

Intrapreneurs – who

» create, nurture and develop new ideas, products, services and processes that make a real difference to the organisation and its relative success.

We saw in chapter 3 that transformers are at the top of the corporate entrepreneur's triangle, and intrapreneurs are at the bottom. Because we need an entrepreneurial leader – who may not actually be a full entrepreneur – to foster venturing and intrapreneurship in an organisation, this time we will look at the transformer first and then work down to the intrapreneur.

Releasing corporate entrepreneurs will involve elements of both 'push' and 'pull':

» 'Push' happens when entrepreneurial leaders foster venturing and intrapreneurship and thus release corporate entrepreneurship. But who pushes for the appointment of entrepreneurial leaders to the top posts in the first place? We look at alternative strategic leader styles in the next section.

» 'Pull' is more reactive. It happens when market forces and competition make innovation and change inevitable if the organisation is to survive. This is happening more and more as markets and industries become increasingly global and business environments change faster and less predictably. Market forces, then, can help release the corporate entrepreneur.

But where is innovation and corporate entrepreneurship most and least likely to happen? There is a belief that it is least likely where an industry is very competitive and also where it is controlled by a small number of leading organisations. In very competitive industries margins are tight and rivals are fearful of initiatives that might increase their costs without them having a real opportunity to raise prices correspondingly. In non-competitive industries it is easier for complacency – however misjudged that might be – to develop. Governments have views and policies to deal with competition and so they have a contribution to make here in releasing corporate entrepreneurship. Their challenge is to encourage competition – but perhaps only up to a certain point!

Releasing transformers

Industry transformers, who rewrite the rules of competition in an industry, and organisational transformers, who change strategies and style in a radical way, will appear from time to time. Sometimes they are general business growth entrepreneurs who break in and surprise everyone in the industry. Richard Branson did this when he began Virgin Atlantic Airways.

However, entrepreneurial leaders who are minded to drive through radical change are sometimes promoted to the top job, as happened with Jack Welch. This will often be seen to be happening when a company is in real difficulty and needs turning around – and few observers will express surprise when it happens in these circumstances.

But what about when a company is doing well – as was the case at GE when Welch became CEO – and stewardship might be seen to be the preferred choice in the interests of shareholders?

The choice of a strategic leader falls to other directors, invariably influenced by the company's major shareholders, who, in the case of large organisations, are likely to be City institutions. Are they inclined to select an entrepreneur? Quite possibly not. When boards of directors and company shareholders deliberately appoint entrepreneurial leaders they are taking a risk and speculating that a transformer will generate faster and stronger growth. There is an element of bravery, but the pay-off from success can be huge.

When organisations get into difficulty and results are disappointing, it is not unusual to see a change of strategic leader. The first choice might well be a company doctor, often someone with a finance background, who is required to 'stop the rot' and restore financial stability and viability. This is of course essential – but what comes next? Future growth will require a transformer who can identify and pursue new competitive opportunities. The company doctor will not always be an entrepreneur, and so the risk is that the organisation is stabilised but fails to have a prosperous future.

The downturn in fortune could be the result of strategic mis-judgements as distinct from poor operational controls. Whatever the reason, it is quite usual for organisations in difficulty to divest businesses. Astute strategic leaders will also, from time to time, divest businesses that no longer fit the desired corporate portfolio. The business could simply be sold to a new parent, or it could be released in a different way and headed up by a venturer. When this happens, corporate entrepreneurship is again being released.

Intrapreneurs champion entrepreneurial initiatives and promote innovation

Intrapreneurs champion entrepreneurial initiatives and promote innovation throughout organisations. They have to be recruited, encouraged and rewarded – a challenge for every strategic leader. Whatever the natural style of the strategic leader, and his or her approach, the need for inno-vation, intrapreneurship and occasional venturing is not in question. For some leaders, fostering this type of corporate entre-preneurship themselves will be natural – for others it will require the appointment of senior people whose talents and style complement those of the leader but are nevertheless different.

Put simply, strategic leaders vary markedly in their style. Different styles can all succeed in particular circumstances. However, where a strategic leader is not an entrepreneur, it is essential that he or she finds ways of making the organisation entrepreneurial if it is to prosper in the long term.

To put the entrepreneurial leader as transformer in context we next look at different styles of strategic leadership and then consider the special case of the turnaround champion.

Strategic leader styles

All strategic leaders have a dominant style which influences the culture of the organisation. They are not all transformational entrepreneurs; it would be inappropriate to argue that they all should be.

We can identify six broad leadership styles – all leaders will have some element of each one, but the relative strengths and the pattern will vary from leader to leader. There is no single, preferred style that works better than the others. Circumstances matter and therefore, sometimes, a change of style is needed.

The six styles are:

- » the aspirational visionary style – which provides direction
- » the analytical style – the source of 'thoughts' and plans
- » the public relations style – which underpins a highly visible profile
- » the tactical, operational style – which implies hands-on involvement
- » the financial engineering style – with tight control systems
- » the HR style – which brings about a supportive environment and a 'coaching' style of management.

Let's first consider two leader entrepreneurs – growth entrepren-eurs who have started significant, but very different, businesses and stayed at the helm.

Richard Branson's dominant style is public relations – his driving ambition appears to be to build a brand with the visibility of Coca-Cola and McDonald's – strongly backed by aspiration and people management. He has made Virgin a globally recognised brand and unashamedly courted publicity. He is not a 'coaching manager' himself, but he has created an organisation that behaves in this way. His high Team score is based on his ability to spot and recruit talented managers to work with him.

Anita Roddick is driven by a desire to support the environment and the third world – she is primarily an aspirational visionary. She also demonstrates the public relations, operational and HR styles. The Body Shop name is widely recognised; Anita Roddick travels the world in search of new product ideas for the business; there is considerable support for the franchisees who run the shops.

In both of these cases the financial engineering style is relatively low in the order. Branson was uncomfortable with City expectations when Virgin was a public company in the 1980s, and he bought back control. Roddick has also criticised City analysts, and she reputedly relied on her husband and business partner, Gordon, to mastermind operations.

Are Branson and Roddick popular and visible in part because they are different from many other corporate leaders?

Profile Jack Welch

Jack Welch mixes vision, financial engineering and HR as his dominant styles. He has transformed GE into an entrepreneurial company by radically changing its corporate strategy, its structure and its predominant style of management.

GE is a company made up of small companies where people are very much encouraged to take on intrapreneurial challenges.

Up to his retirement in 2001, Welch retained his title as the 'World's Most Respected Business Leader' in an annual poll conducted by the *Financial Times*. The 'top ten' for that year included four outstanding entrepreneurs (Bill Gates, investor entrepreneur Warren Buffett, Michael Dell and Richard Branson) as well as two clearly entrepreneurial leaders: Nobuyuki Idei of Sony and Andy Grove, the man largely responsible for the growth of Intel.

In the UK, *Management Today* publishes annually a similar list of the most admired companies and strategic leaders, selected by their peers. Lord (John) Browne, CEO of British Petroleum, was the winner in 1999, 2000 and 2001. He was then ninth in the *Financial Times* world rankings. Browne is clearly very successful: he has presided over the mergers of BP with Amoco and Atlantic Richfield, and the subsequent rationalisation. He has also helped restore the fortunes of BP after a period of turbulence and uncertainty.

But Browne does not appear to be an entrepreneur himself. He has a science background and he has been described as a 'private man', studious, neat and intellectual. He does not court publicity. Persistent, he 'leads the business with a rational assiduousness that borders on obsession'.

Browne was 'selected to control BP with a rigorous control of process and technology…and control is what he is good at'.

Management Today, *December 1999*

Lord (Arnold) Weinstock, when head of the UK's General Electric Corporation (GEC), was sometimes criticised for his relatively low-risk strategies and his accumulation of a 'cash mountain'. His dominant style was financial engineering, and we can also see clear evidence of analysis. After he retired, his successor, the more obviously entrepreneurial Lord Simpson, set about transforming GEC. He divested the defence businesses, refocused GEC on telecommunications, spent GEC's cash on acquisitions and changed the name to Marconi. When the growth in telecommunications slowed, GEC's profitability and share price collapsed. The outcome has been closures and redundancies – and another new strategic leader who is having to act as a company doctor.

We may not think of financial engineering and analysis as entrepreneurial styles – for fundamentally they are not – but that does not mean they cannot result in successful businesses if the leader concerned ensures there is a flow of new ideas from somewhere and mechanisms for doing something with them. After all, we have to accept that every industry is under threat from 'rule changers'. IBM was set back – but recovered – when PCs threatened the dominance of mainframe computers. Intel is currently fighting hard against emerging Asian entrepreneurs who have discovered new ways of manufacturing semi-conductors. In pharmaceuticals the biotechnology companies, most of them entrepreneurial start-ups, continue to gain ground. Companies need enterprise and entrepreneurship if they are to survive!

Where the tactical, operational style is dominant, this implies that someone is reluctant to let go of the detail. Some entrepreneurs find it difficult to take a back seat – and release other corporate entrepreneurs – when the organisation they have built from scratch grows and prospers. If they fail to do this, further growth potential will be constrained.

We cannot demonstrate that entrepreneurs have to be appointed as strategic leaders for corporations to succeed, but there is evidence they can make a real difference.

Releasing turnaround champions

Turnaround champions are a different type of transformer entrepreneur. They are required when companies are in difficulty. Maybe a company was entrepreneurial in the past, but it has lost its way.

There are normally three needs:

» a new strategic leader to provide fresh direction and impetus
» new sources of added value and competitiveness
» tighter financial controls and systems.

As we have said, it is firstly essential to slow or stop the decline with tighter systems and often some rationalisation, maybe divestment of some activities. Costs have to be reduced. A new base from which new growth can emerge is the requirement. In this respect it is like careful pruning in a garden.

The organisation then needs entrepreneurs to identify and champion new opportunities, new products and new services. Recognising this, and bringing it about, does not always happen.

Archie Norman replaced a strategic leader at Asda who had made strategic misjudgements. His story appears in chapter 20. Norman successfully released the entrepreneurship in the Asda staff.

Releasing corporate venturers

We have already said that corporate venturing takes two main forms:

» A company comes up with a new idea and feels the best way to exploit the opportunity is to create a separate, spin-off business. The story of British Airways and Go in chapter 19 is an ideal example.

>>> A company decides to refocus its portfolio of activities, divesting some of them. If they are sold to another corporation, entrepreneurship may not be released. If new, independent businesses are formed, the release of entrepreneurship is a real possibility.

Releasing the corporate venturer can thus be achieved by a corporate parent setting up a new business, spinning off a business or selling a business to either its existing managers (a management buy-out) or to a new management team backed by financiers (a management buy-in).

Profile **Tetley**

Between 1970 and 1995, tea consumption in the UK dropped from 4.5 to 3 cups per person per day. Tetley, owned by Allied Domecq, succeeded Brooke Bond as market leader. The business was sold to its managers in 1995. The new company was re-floated successfully in 1998. Before and after buying the business, this management team:

- >>> reduced the number of plants
- >>> introduced new premium products
- >>> targeted key international markets in China, Russia and Poland – all big tea drinkers
- >>> introduced round tea bags and later bags with drawstrings
- >>> established an alliance with Tata of India, the world's leading tea maker. Tata had the tea, Tetley the superior bagging technology.

Profile **Kingfisher**

In the 1980s, Geoffrey Mulcahy led a management buy-in at Woolworth. Under his leadership the underperforming business was renamed Kingfisher and it acquired Comet (electrical goods) Charlie Browns (car parts) and Superdrug (pharmaceuticals) and opened the leading DIY chain B&Q.

In 2002, coincident with the retirement of Mulcahy, the splitting up of Kingfisher was completed. In 2001, Superdrug had been sold and Woolworth demerged as an independent company. Finally, the remaining electrical goods and DIY businesses became two separate companies.

Sometimes corporate venturing is described as being analogous to the spider plant. A healthy plant spawns new offshoots from time to time. Although the embryo plants develop roots of their own they are linked to the mother plant by a strong umbilical cord. Until this cord is severed their growth is limited. However once given independence at an appropriate time, planted in fresh compost, and nurtured, growth can be rapid. Strong, healthy plants are the outcome. This metaphor highlights the importance of seeing venturing as a positive, proactive strategy rather than one reserved for when the company is in difficulty and needs cash.

Releasing intrapreneurs

Innovation

Innovation is about making ideas work. It builds on creativity. It happens when something new, tangible and value-creating is developed from ideas. The innovator may not be the person who has the idea in the first place – rather he or she is the person who sees the opportunity and does something about it.

In some organisations employees are encouraged to innovate. They are encouraged to be intrapreneurs. They have access to resources and success is rewarded. When this happens, entrepreneurship is again being released.

Historically, science has been our main source of innovations. Advances in scientific knowledge have led to technological breakthroughs. Increasingly, though, 'marketing' has taken over the reins, and a systematic search for new market opportunities linked with new technologies in the design and development of new products. However, we have moved on again. Now the most successful organisations are able to capture the knowledge and imagination of their employees and leverage this into new opportunities.

Everyone knows how to do their job better – it's just that they are very rarely asked

It has long been said that everyone knows how they could do their job better – it's just that they are very rarely asked. However, we must never forget that new ideas do not become winning opportunities overnight, and that some employees are not enthusiastic about being innovators. They are not looking for greater empowerment and the attendant responsibility.

We may also be tempted to imply that innovation and intra-preneurship is an excellent way for an individual to make a mark inside an organisation – but people can also impress by finding ways to reduce costs, and this may well have a shorter timescale. Reputations can be built in different ways – the way of the entrepreneur is not the only one. However, whilst prosperous futures might be built on top of a base of cost reduction, they are not built out of cost reductions.

Intrapreneurs

Intrapreneurship happens when we recruit, spot and use people with entrepreneurial talent – and who are, or can be, motivated to use their abilities and initiative to champion a new venture or project leading to a new product, process or service. All organisations have these people – potential entrepreneurs who prefer not to start a business or venture of their own – but they don't always recognise or encourage them.

These are the words we see used to describe the innovator and the intrapreneur:

>>> strategically aware
>>> ideas-driven
>>> creative
>>> flexible
>>> innovative
>>> good at networking
>>> individualistic but able to work well in teams
>>> persistent and courageous.

– they are familiar words!

The innovator and the intrapreneur exhibit many of the behaviours of the entrepreneur, because, quite simply, they possess at least some of the entrepreneur's character themes.

Sometimes the relative strength of the themes will be less than in the case of the true entrepreneur. This is true for many of us – and we have the potential to be far more enterprising than we are. Partly this is reluctance on our part; more often it is the failure of large corporations to properly utilise the talent they possess.

On other occasions the intrapreneur simply prefers the large organisation environment to going it alone. If he or she is then frustrated by a lack of freedom, he or she will underachieve or leave and join someone who does recognise talent.

Organisations can release intrapreneurship if they search out the right people, encourage them and find ways of providing the resources – particularly time and money – they will need.

Building the intrapreneurial organisation

The intrapreneurial organisation is where:

"It should be easier to ask for forgiveness than to request permission in the first place" – Pinchot, 1985

» people are encouraged to find time to be creative
» there is an active search for new ideas, ahead of competitors
» there are simple core rules that provide a framework but which do not stifle individuality and invention
» successful individuals are recognised and rewarded
» setbacks are handled so people are not discouraged
» there is extensive networking and sharing in a supportive and non-threatening environment
» people feel encouraged and energised
» risks are handled effectively
» people are 'pushed outside their boxes' and comfort zones
» there are effective mechanisms for deciding which ideas are worth pursuing.

If an organisation is to succeed with intrapreneurship it must deal with four key issues:

» The strategic and structural environment has to be 'right'. The purpose and direction implies a realistic vision that is widely understood and shared. Formal systems and controls do not stifle innovation and people are free to make limited changes. Inhibitive internal 'chimneys' are pulled down so people can collaborate and share ideas readily.
» An appropriate workforce has to be built. Enterprising people – with entrepreneurial talent and temperament – have to be recruited. They will be trained in key skills and there will be an appropriate reward system. The organisation's main heroes are the entrepreneurial ones.
» The workforce is backed by the necessary support systems. Teamworking is commonplace, people collaborate and network naturally, information is shared and learning is fostered. After

all, several people in the organisation may be thinking along the same lines at the same time concerning future possibilities.

»» Successes are visibly rewarded and mistakes are not sanctioned so harshly that people are dissuaded from further initiatives.

An intrapreneurial organisation will often feature a relatively flat structure with few layers in the hierarchy – too many layers tend to slow decision-making down. The culture and atmosphere will be one of collaboration and trust. The style of management will be more coaching than instructional, and mentoring will be in evidence. Ideally it will be an exciting place to work. The leader's enthusiasm will have spread to others.

We must remember, though, that effective intrapreneurship is not that easily achieved, and that many organisations set off down the road but fail to reap the anticipated rewards.

Balancing control (to ensure current activities and strategies are implemented efficiently) with flexibility (to foster and embrace changes to the same strategies) can imply different cultures, which are difficult to achieve without tension and conflict.

Another difficulty frequently lies with finding the appropriate reward and remuneration systems to ensure fairness. It is a brave organisation that only awards bonuses to the visibly entrepreneurial people.

Managers in established companies often find it difficult to handle setbacks and disappointments when initiatives fail. But there always has to be the risk of failure – albeit temporary – when experimenting with new and unproven ideas. Whilst intrapreneurs often have the security of large company employment, such that the penalty for failure is to some extent protected, the rewards for real success are unlikely to equal those of the true entrepreneur. Nevertheless, 'Increased competition in global markets and the pressure for innovation is forcing Britain's large companies to look for methods to stimulate ideas for new products' (Terazano, 1999).

Innovation and intrapreneurship will not happen if

»» we underestimate the importance of encouraging creativity
»» we fail to put in place mechanisms for harnessing new ideas, prioritising potential winners, resourcing them and tracking their development
»» we as organisations fail to realise what we already know.

But we must not underestimate the importance of innovation and intrapreneurship… 'It used to be the big that ate the small. Now the fast eat the slow'(Geoff Yang, Institutional Venture Partners).

Effective organisations – where people have fun and contribute

As individuals, we cannot often choose what we have to do at work, but we can influence or choose how we do it.

The 'how' is a reflection of the attitude we bring to the situation. Are we switched on or switched off?

Effective work requires an element of fun and irreverence. Work can (and should) be made to feel something like play for those involved – without ever losing sight of the underpinning serious purpose! This is the basis of the all-important **creativity**. Staying in touch with the key purpose of the activity implies a realisation of, and commitment to, the **advantage**.

Of course, play bonds people together as a supportive **team**.

People thus become involved and engaged – both with each other, and, just as importantly, with customers, who they will treat appropriately, recognising their importance. Customer engagement is then another manifestation of the **advantage**.

For all this to happen people's endeavours must be **focused** and directed. The focus should not be inward-looking, with personal problems and with internal competition to the fore. Instead it should be external, helping customers and 'defeating' or out-performing competitors.

Chapter 18 What Entrepreneurs Do: See it, Seize it, Move it, Do it!

To build our model of the entrepreneur process we use 10 key action factors associated with entrepreneurs and entrepreneurship.

1. Entrepreneurs are individuals who make a significant difference

'Do you want to spend the rest of your life selling sugared water, or do you want a chance to change the world?'(Steve Jobs recruiting John Sculley to Apple).

Entrepreneurs translate what is possible into reality.

Put another way, they transform an idea, which might be simple and ill-defined, into something that works. They have their own ways of dealing with opportunities, setbacks and uncertainties to 'creatively create' new products, new services, new organisations and new ways of satisfying customers or doing business.

As Joseph Schumpeter argued, entrepreneurs disturb the status quo. They make a difference because they are different from most of us. They initiate change and enjoy it. For the entrepreneur it is always 'onwards and upwards'. Barriers and problems that would stop or hinder most of us are for them a spur and a challenge. They get involved directly in the whole operation, they are 'hands-on' people, they 'push the cart'.

The remaining nine action factors all contribute to an entrepreneur's ability to make a difference. Obviously not all entrepreneurs display these factors equally strongly, but they are all present to some degree, and a few of them to an outstanding degree. It is the combination of these action factors that enable the entrepreneur to make a significant difference.

"If we did all the things we are capable of doing, we'd literally astound ourselves"
– Thomas Edison

2. Entrepreneurs are creative and innovative

The best way to forecast the future is to invent it!

Creativity and innovation are the distinguishing marks of the entrepreneur. Entrepreneurs are imaginative and set off in pursuit of their dreams. This is why they disturb markets and can challenge the large established businesses.

It is the entrepreneur who 'thrives on chaos,' as guru Tom Peters once described today's business world.

Creativity is a continuous activity for the entrepreneur. He or she is always seeking and seeing new ways of doing things, often with little concern for how difficult they might be or whether the resources are currently available.

But Creativity in the entrepreneur is combined with the ability to innovate – to take an idea and make it work in practice. Seeing something through to the end – and not being satisfied until all is accomplished – is a central motivation for the entrepreneur. Indeed, once a project is accomplished entrepreneurs seek another 'mountain to climb', because for them creativity and innovation are habitual – something that they just have to keep on doing.

"My golden rule is that there are no golden rules"
– George Bernard Shaw

3. Entrepreneurs spot and exploit opportunities

For entrepreneurs the cup is always half full. For others it is frequently half empty.

A story is told of a shoe manufacturer who, many years ago, sent two of his marketing graduates to the interior of Australia to see if they could come up with new product ideas for the undeveloped aborigine market. The first responded: 'There's no business here; the natives don't wear shoes of any type!' The second was more enthusiastic about the prospects: 'This is a great opportunity; the natives haven't even discovered shoes yet!'

People's perceptions about opportunities vary. How often do we only see an opportunity in retrospect? The 'good idea' was always there to be spotted, but for many of us it is a case of 'Why didn't I think of it first? It's so obvious!'

Entrepreneurs are able to see or craft opportunities that other people miss, even though the data or information that generates the idea is often there for all to see. They are able to synthesise the available information and clarify patterns that escape others. They are comfortable with ambiguity and they can bring clarity by piecing together previously unrelated messages and signals. Not only do they see the opportunities, but they also seem to know, as if by instinct, which of the many is actually worth pursuing.

In some cases opportunity and need is widely recognised and talked about. We have been told that great wealth awaits the person who designs a reliable and low product cost vending machine for french fries. The inventor might be the person who solves the problem, but it is the entrepreneur who exploits that opportunity and turns it into a reality. Those gifted few who, like James Dyson, are both inventors and entrepreneurs, have a special edge.

4. Entrepreneurs find the resources required to exploit opportunities

Entrepreneurs are never put off by a lack of resources. They know that they can get hold of whatever they need. They have a special talent for this.

John Paul Getty was once asked why he was so successful. His reply: 'Some people find oil; others don't'.

In business, too many executives spend money they have yet to earn in order to buy things they don't need to impress people they often dislike.

John Paul Getty was once asked why he was so successful. His reply: 'Some people find oil; others don't'.

Entrepreneurs are able to find resources because they have the right contacts and can innovate and adapt. They are not afraid to phone people up out of the blue and 'beg, steal or borrow' as appropriate.

Entrepreneurs are pragmatists who find and put together the minimum resources required for a job.

You will never hear entrepreneurs complain that they have a resource problem. They just get on and solve it.

5. Entrepreneurs are good networkers

Learn from the mistakes of others – you won't live long enough to make them all yourself

Learn from the mistakes of others – you won't live long enough to make them all yourself.

We have seen that entrepreneurs know where to find the resources they need and that they use their contacts to the full. They are able to do this because their networking skills give them a wide range of people that they can draw on. They will know who has access to what and who the experts are. Rather than exploiting such people, they have a network of friends that stay with them over the years. They help each other.

A young man who had recently come from Italy to a new town in the UK wanted to start a small ice cream business. He went to a local solicitors' practice and was helped by a junior. Over 25 years, the new business grew and diversified. The entrepreneur always retained the same solicitor – who in turn became the senior partner in his firm.

Profile **Silicon Valley**

One of the key factors in the growth and prosperity of Silicon Valley was the networks that formed. Bars and restaurants became favourite places for 'talking shop'. The famous Homebrew Club mentioned in chapter 16 began in the garage of a computerphile, and soon reached a membership of 500 enthusiasts. It was informal and open to all. Members shared their ideas freely. Hardware and software exchanged hands without charge. It was a catalyst for entrepreneurial activity as people helped each other.

Many small businesses rely on networking for their marketing. They cannot afford the advertising that large organisations employ, so they use contacts to glean information and open up market opportunities.

Inside large organisations successful intrapreneurs form their own network of contacts to manage the 'innovation and change' projects they initiate.

6. Entrepreneurs are determined in the face of adversity

If you think you can, you can. If you think you can't, you're right.

Entrepreneurs are motivated to succeed; they possess determination and self-belief. Above all, they are courageous. On the one hand, this is a major reason for their success. They refuse to be beaten and persevere when 'the going gets tough'.

On the other hand, this also explains why some would-be entrepreneurs fail. They have too much faith in their own ability and refuse to accept they might be wrong. Their Ego facet gets out of control, and they fail to see the warning signs until it is too late.

If you think you can, you can. If you think you can't, you're right

Successful entrepreneurs are also able to deal with unexpected obstacles, the kind that cannot be predicted in a business plan. Most companies experience three or four life-threatening crises in their early years. To survive this period the true entrepreneur must deal with these crises and win through. He or she has to be an 'overcomer' – able to resolve problems under pressure.

Entrepreneurs use their creative and innovation skills in these difficult times. Somehow they really do turn problems into opportunities.

7. Entrepreneurs handle risk

We invariably associate entrepreneurs with risk, but here we need to use our terms carefully. As explained in chapter 13, entrepreneurs have a number of different attitudes to risk. Some have a blind spot regarding risk, others think they can handle it and the rest think it can't happen to them.

Whilst entrepreneurs may well take risks that other less enter-prising people would avoid, as their risk threshold is higher than normal, relatively few fall into the category of mere adventurers who take chances intuitively or simply at the toss of a coin. Such ventures will sometimes pay off handsomely, but more often they fail, because they are always based more on hope than judgement.

Some entrepreneurs choose not to worry unduly about trying to avoid the risks in a venture. They know that forecasting and planning involves guesswork as much as judgement, and that procrastination is not an option. So they seize the initiative and accept the risk. They have great faith in their ability to deal with setbacks and difficulties when they arise. They remain flexible and vigilant throughout, learning and changing as they implement their ideas.

To become innovative and find better ways of doing things or new things to do, large organisations need to encourage their employees to take risks. But this is not easy. The idea that employees will be honoured for their successes and punished for their failures is so inbred into most organisations that people opt for the safe route and don't take any risks. The intrapreneur is the only person who can unlock such a situation and develop a culture in which risk-taking is acceptable.

In summary, perhaps we should argue that entrepreneurs are not risk averse. They prefer to find ways of saying 'yes' rather than 'no', and are willing to accept responsibility for their decisions. They handle risk effectively.

8. Entrepreneurs have control of business

People fall into three categories:

- » those who make things happen
- » those who watch things happen
- » those who are left to ask what did happen.

It is easy for a business to get out of control, and for directors and managers to feel that the business is running them. Entrepreneurs do not allow this to happen. They are not control freaks, but they pay attention to detail and develop their own key indicators of performance that they monitor carefully.

Some entrepreneurs keep a loose rein on the business whilst others manage it very tightly, but both know exactly the state of their business. They seem to have a knack for knowing what is important and what to keep an eye on. They are able to see 'the wood for the trees', but they also know which trees to watch. In this way they are able to exercise strategic control over their business.

"There are two times in a man's life when he should not speculate – when he cannot afford it – and when he can" – Mark Twain

9. Entrepreneurs put the customer first

It is perhaps fairly obvious that entrepreneurs put the customer first, and yet most studies of entrepreneurs do not mention it directly. Instead they speak of the need for market knowledge or observe that the best entrepreneurs are salesmen.

The market for any new enterprise or initiative is always a difficult place, with surprises just around the corner. But entrepreneurs thrive on this uncertainty and generally end up making a success of a product or in a market sector that was quite different from the one they started with. This is because they listen to the customer.

Entrepreneurs are anxious to retain their customers, recognising that finding new customers to replace lost ones is far more expensive than maintaining good customer care. They are as quick to find out why they have won a sale as to understand why they have lost one. They are able and willing to respond to what the customer is telling them.

However, they also recognise that customers can – and sometimes must – be led and persuaded. Market and customer research can find out why customers are dissatisfied, but customers are not always going to be able to point the way to real improvements. This is where entrepreneurs' creativity comes in.

"It's not the employer who pays the wages. Employers only handle the money. It's the customer who pays the wages"
– Henry Ford

10. Entrepreneurs create capital

Creativity and innovation, resource acquisition, control of the business, networking and the other action factors, are all part of the entrepreneur's intellectual and emotional capital. They are the currency that the entrepreneur brings to the table and uses to generate new kinds of capital external to him- or herself. These are:

>>> financial capital
>>> social capital
>>> aesthetic capital.

The entrepreneur is generally associated with financial capital, but we want to include as entrepreneurs those who create social and aesthetic capital. This is because we see people operating in these areas who are clearly entrepreneurs by our definition. They 'create and innovate to build something of recognised value', where that value is in the social or aesthetic area. It is less easy to measure social and aesthetic capital than financial capital, but it can be done.

"The value of a man should be seen in what he gives [to the world] and not what he is able to receive" – *Albert Einstein*

These action factors help us to understand the entrepreneur process, which we discuss next. They also form the basis of the business health check set out in chapter 21. But alone they do not help us to identify the potential entrepreneur. To do this we need to implement the facets approach described earlier.

It is entrepreneur character themes that unlock the action factors of the entrepreneurial process and reveal the entrepreneur. The correlation is given below:

Character themes		Action points
Focus	8.	Have control of the business
Advantage	3.	Spot and exploit opportunities
	4.	Find resources
	9.	Put the customer first
	10.	Create capital
Creativity	2.	Create and innovate
	3.	Spot and exploit opportunities
Ego	1.	Make a difference
	6.	Be determined in the face of adversity
	7.	Handle risk
Team	5.	Network effectively
Social	3.	Spot and exploit causes (opportunities)
	10.	Create (social) capital

The action factors and the entrepreneur process

We have been considering what entrepreneurs do – their action factors. We now want to place them within the entrepreneur process. We do this using two process models. [see FIGURE, opposite]

The starting point in this first model is the motivation to make a difference (action factor 1). There are other motivators for the entrepreneur, but this we believe to be the most important.

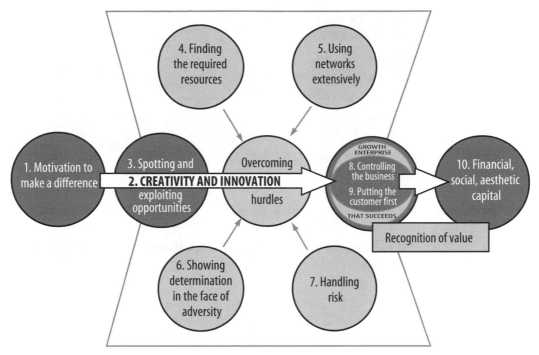

The entrepreneur process: model 1

The ability to create and innovate (2) is the life-blood of the process – without this vital blood flow the process would not happen. The first step in the process is to spot and exploit an opportunity (3); as things move forward, obstacles appear.

We group the next four action factors around the way in which the entrepreneur deals with these obstacles. The entrepreneur finds the required resources (4), uses networks extensively (5), is determined in the face of adversity (6) and handles risk (7). Using the talents of creativity and innovation, the entrepreneur turns the obstacles into opportunities.

All these contribute to a growing enterprise that succeeds because the entrepreneur knows how to control the business (8) and is consistent in putting the customer first (9).

The outcome of the entrepreneur process is the creation of capital (10), which can be financial, social or aesthetic.

Whilst entrepreneurs are motivated to make a difference, they also want to be recognised for their achievements and contribution. Visibility, recognition and reputation matter to the entrepreneur.

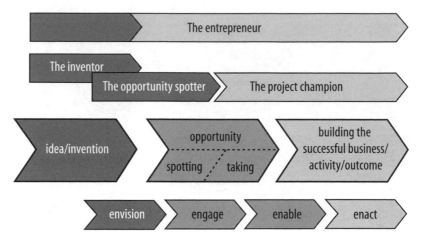

The entrepreneur process: model 2 – see it, seize it, move it, do it!

See it – envision

The first stage in model 2 is spotting the opportunity. The person who sees the potential for an idea may not have come up with the idea in the first place – but then the creator of the idea may not know how to exploit it, or even see it as something that could be exploited.

The opportunity spotter sees the gap in the market and provides the strategy for exploiting the opportunity. It could be an opportunity for making money, for creating something of perceived value for the community (social entrepreneurship) or for adding to our artistic or aesthetic environment.

Whilst business and some social entrepreneurs respond to external opportunities, other social and most artistic entrepreneurs are driven from within to search for ways in which they can exploit their personal gifts and talents.

As we have noted, social entrepreneurs are invariably engaged by a cause in which they believe. Artists are engaged by the desire to create and express themselves.

Seize it – engage

The second stage is grasping the opportunity. This is the role of the project champion. It is their first task.

The opportunity spotter may well be minded to engage the idea and take it forward, and if capable of doing this effectively, then he or she is an entrepreneur. The entrepreneur can run with both stages, and is both the opportunity spotter who can see it and a project champion who can seize it.

If an opportunity spotter does not have these implementation capabilities, he or she will need a partner who is able to do this well. The baton has to be passed from the opportunity spotter to the project champion if it is to come to fruition.

Move it – enable

Project champions are people who make things happen and do whatever it takes. They gather together the necessary resources and know where to find help and support.

As a business or initiative grows, more and more people must come on board. Moulding them into an effective team is part of the enabling process.

Do it – enact

It is this team that ultimately enacts the venture and delivers the outcomes. The true entrepreneur provides effective leadership to this team.

Project champions are single-minded in their endeavours, and everything they do is focused on moving forward and getting the job done. When the project is the creation of an enterprise, they put all the pieces together to make the whole.

The bottom bar of model 2 summarises these points as four stages or activities:

>> envisioning – seeing an opportunity
>> engaging – taking the opportunity
>> enabling – gathering the resources necessary to move it on
>> enacting – building the business or the activity.

In other words: See it, seize it, move it, do it!

Many of us do see at least some opportunities – we might even be described as 'ideas people' – but we do not possess either the abilities or the inclination to exploit an opportunity and build something distinctive and valuable. At the same time, others are extremely capable implementers. When provided with a challenge, task or project they can organise and lead a team, manage the necessary stages and bring everything to a successful conclusion. They simply need a good idea or a defined goal.

It can be difficult, frustrating or even traumatic when opportunity spotters are not natural project champions but remain in charge of a project and fail to engage the necessary help and support.

In this context, it has been commented that 'a visionary without the skills required to implement the vision is one of life's cruellest concoctions!'

Small business people typically spot a limited opportunity for something they can do, and choose to exploit it – but essentially that is where it stops: the opportunity does not have real growth potential. These people are not true project champions. Such people are unlikely to keep finding further new opportunities to graft on to the business.

Intrapreneurial managers who champion change in larger organisations are often project champions acting on behalf of their organisations. They are encouraged to come up with new ideas and see them through to fruition.

●———●

To what extent would you describe yourself as an:

- »» *envisioner*
- »» *engager*
- »» *enabler*
- »» *enactor?*

Are you an opportunity spotter or a project champion?

To be an entrepreneur you need to be both!

The next two chapters feature examples of entrepreneurs in the airline and retail industries. You will see evidence of the entrepreneur process in action, alongside the facets of the individual entrepreneurs.

Chapter 19 **Airline Entrepreneurs**

The airline industry has always attracted entrepreneurs, with differing results. In recent years Richard Branson has built a successful international airline, beginning with a couple of leased Boeing 747s, as well as several other businesses. He has helped change the industry view of service and value for money. Virgin International now flies many long-haul routes, and Virgin Blue competes in the low-price sector of the Australian market; Virgin Express, however, has been less successful in Europe.

At the same time, many remember Freddie Laker's failed attempt to take on the giants of Britain and America with his cheap fare transatlantic Skytrain. A true pioneer, Laker grew his business too quickly and was driven out of business when his rivals reduced their prices and he could not cover his debts. More fail than succeed in this intensely competitive and international industry.

Others have seen different opportunities. At the opposite end of the scale are any number of small air-charter businesses which fly passengers, such as businessmen and jockeys, point-to-point in small, light aircraft.

When entrepreneur and ex-Vietnam war pilot Fred Smith devised the business model for Federal Express, he saw an opportunity to use aircraft to provide a reliable overnight courier service, something for which customers would pay a premium price.

However, today's sustainable competitive model is the so-called budget airline – the low-cost, no-frills, cheap-fare sector. The ability of these airlines to retain their customers and their business after the terrorist attacks in the US in September 2001 is testament to this.

From this sector we have selected four quite different examples of entrepreneurs in action.

- Herb Kelleher changed the rules of competition in this industry, and set new standards that others have copied.
- Michael O'Leary succeeded in turning around a company in difficulty. He is a corporate entrepreneur.
- Stelios Haji-Ioannou comes from a wealthy and entrepreneurial family. He too was attracted by the industry, but he is a serial entrepreneur. His airline is one opportunity amongst many.
- Barbara Cassani is a corporate venturer who set up a new airline with funding from her employer, BA, championed a management buy-out only to see the funders sell the business one year later.

We explain what they have done and achieved, bringing out important elements of the strategy and the entrepreneur process. As we tell their stories we can also see examples of the entrepreneur character themes and behaviours, reinforcing that it is the person, rather than the idea or the particular business situation, that defines the entrepreneur.

Herb Kelleher began Southwest Air in 1971 when he was 40 years old, with a simple intention – to 'fly people safely, cheaply and conveniently between Dallas, Houston and San Antonio', three key cities in Texas. He would succeed where many others had failed. Kelleher set out to compete against coach and car travel rather than the other airlines.

'From day one Southwest challenged the assumption that permanently reduced fares would cut revenue.'

Herb Kelleher was the son of a Campbell's Soup manager in New Jersey; he had been a champion college athlete and a successful lawyer in Texas before he started the airline. The idea for Southwest Air, however, had come from Rollin King, an investment adviser friend (and co-founder of the business) who spotted the gap in the market after a conversation with a banker. Significantly, King had already started an unprofitable air charter service. For the first seven years Southwest Air employed a salaried CEO with industry experience, Lamar Muse, but then Kelleher resigned from his law

'From day one Southwest challenged the assumption that permanently reduced fares would cut revenue'

practice and took over full control in 1978, as Muse and King had disagreed over strategy.

In its thirty years as a low-price, no-frills airline, Southwest Air has prospered and grown to become the fifth-largest carrier in the US. It serves over 50 cities in 27 states and has some 2500 flights every day.

No staff have ever been made redundant, which is very unusual in this industry. The outcome is staff loyalty, customer satisfaction and a willingness to be innovative, because people do not fear for their jobs.

The winning strategy, competitive advantage and success is based on a number of factors:

»» Frequent and reliable departures.
»» Relatively short journeys by US standards, now averaging 450 miles; this has increased as the airline has grown in size and destinations.
»» Where relevant, the choice of smaller airports nearer to city centres in preference to international airports which are further away from the centre.
»» Very low prices.
»» Automated ticketing and direct bookings (without travel agents), and now using the Internet extensively.
»» Limited frills, with no seat assignments, no videos and just one class of seating. Kelleher realised that if people board the plane in the order they check in, passengers would turn up early to try and secure their seat of choice. Take-off delays would be reduced.
»» Fast gate turnarounds, to maximise the time the planes are in the air. Less food and hot drinks on board means less mess, less cleaning and faster turnaround between flights – as well as fewer cabin staff.
»» A standardised fleet of Boeing 737s, to simplify maintenance.

Southwest Air is now the only significant short-distance, point-to-point carrier in the US. Others have certainly tried to compete, but have been unable to make the equivalent impact. On several occasions it has won the US Department of Transport's coveted Triple Crown award of best on-time record, best baggage handling and fewest customer complaints. Every new route and destination is immediately popular, and as a result Southwest Air has been consistently profitable for over 25 years, a unique record for an airline anywhere in the world.

Kelleher himself is a very focused and energetic man who follows a 'punishing work schedule'. Dedicated, he has been known to stay late at night with mechanics working on a problem. Profit-oriented, and aware of the bottom line, he has commented that 'market share has nothing to do with profitability ... market share says we just want to be big, that we don't care if we make money'. Confirming his desire to make a difference in this industry – his ego – he has frequently expressed great pride in Southwest Air's achievements.

Kelleher is a renowned 'people person'. A heavy smoker, he often has an alcoholic drink in his hand, and he is 'worshipped' by Southwest Air staff as a larger-then-life figure. Through profit-sharing schemes employees own over 10 percent of the company's stock, and he has made 'working in the airline industry an adventure'. Southwest Air is dynamic and responsive; employees accept empowerment and are motivated to work hard and deliver high levels of service consistently. Rules and regulations are minimised to allow staff the freedom to deal with issues as they arise. Southwest Air is full of entrepreneurs.

'We've never tried to behave like other airlines. From the very beginning we told our people "Question it. Challenge it".'

Southwest Air recognises where its competitive advantage originates: 'We are not an airline business with great customer service – we are a great customer service organisation that happens to be in the airline business.'

'Ask employees what's important to them. Ask customers what's important to them. Then do it. It's that simple.'

The frequent flyer programme, unusually, rewards passengers for the number of individual flights, not the miles flown.

But it is never that simple! Southwest Air is also renowned as 'one of the zaniest companies in history'. Creativity is rife. From the very beginning, Kelleher encouraged flight attendants to crack jokes during in-flight emergency briefings, but, at the same time, operate with very high safety standards. He was determined that passengers would enjoy their flights. Some of the planes are decorated externally to reinforce the fun image. Three planes, promoting major sponsor Sea World, are flying killer whales; another is painted with the Texas flag; one more is christened Arizona One, a spoof of Air Force One. Flight attendants have been known to hide in the overhead lockers as passengers come on board, startling them as they open up the lockers. Kelleher himself often appears in fancy dress for certain flights and special occasions and in company advertisements. He has made a rap video for employee training. A special on-board prize for the passenger with the biggest hole in his sock would be quite typical.

"At Southwest we don't want clones – everyone is expected to colour outside the lines"

Consequently, a sense of humour has become a key element in the recruitment process. People are 'hired for aptitude and trained for skills'. During their training, employees are given a book with sections on jokes, games and songs – but they are all encouraged to develop an individual style.

Kelleher is dedicated and focused and, wanting to make a difference, he is in possession of a strong ego. He has always had the courage to be different. He is creative and innovative and he understands the contribution people can make. When he was introduced to an idea he saw the opportunity and activated it. He appreciated the advantage and understood competitive strategy. He then stayed focused on that. Truly profit-oriented, he has been extremely successful in a dynamic and cruel industry in which many competing airlines have failed.

Ryanair is now the fastest growing European low-cost, no-frills airline and the first to really copy the Southwest Air model. The business was originally started in Dublin in 1985 by the Ryan family as a rival to Aer Lingus. Ryanair was providing meals and two classes of seating – as did Aer Lingus – but at a lower price. In its first four years it lost I£20 million.

Michael O'Leary joined the company in 1991 and helped to change the strategy and the company's fortunes. He had been to the US and met Herb Kelleher. Ryanair adopted the Southwest Air model and it worked. In 1993 O'Leary bought an 18 percent shareholding and took over as chief executive. At this time Ryanair was carrying 650,000 passengers a year.

The low fares expanded the market. Ryanair concentrated on destination airports in the UK and continental Europe which offered low landing charges. They selected Beauvais – to the north of Paris – for this reason. Hubs at Stansted, Frankfurt and Charleroi (south of Brussels) have been added to Dublin.

A good proportion of sales are via the Internet, and the company was floated on the stock exchanges in Dublin and New York in 1997 – its valuation at the time was $500 million. One year later its stock was also listed on the London Stock Exchange.

The number of passengers grew to 5 million in 1999, and the 7-million mark was passed in 2001. Operating 36 Boeing 737s, O'Leary's target is 14 million passengers by 2004. This would make Ryanair comfortably the fifth largest carrier in Europe.

Who is Michael O'Leary?

Now in his early forties, he is an ex-accountant who never completed his final examinations. Having worked for KPMG, he left to set up his own business in the early 1980s. He began in property development, buying and selling newsagents, but he also provided tax consultancy. One of his clients was Tony Ryan, a co-founder of Ryanair.

O'Leary is happy driving older cars and dressing in the rugby shirt uniform sported by Ryanair cabin staff. He has a 'brazen can-do style' and is very focused on the company's strategy and on what matters to customers. He understands his market. Whilst safety cannot be compromised, it is something of a given: the 'business is about fares, fares, fares'. As a hobby, O'Leary breeds bloodstock and Black Angus cattle.

The best-known British low-price, no-frills airline is EasyJet, begun in 1995 by a 28-year-old Greek entrepreneur, Stelios Haji-Ioannou, the son of a wealthy shipping magnate, with financial backing from his father. His father was a self-made multi-millionaire who had begun as a trader in Saudi Arabia before he started a shipping business in Athens. He was to create, and later sell, the world's largest fleet of supertankers.

Haji-Ioannou intended to 'make flying in Europe affordable for more and more people'. Parodying BA's claim to be 'The world's favourite airline', EasyJet now calls itself 'The web's favourite airline'. Over a third of its bookings come via the Internet; the rest are direct over the telephone. There are no commissioned travel-agency bookings, no tickets and no on-board meals.

When passengers with a reservation check in at the airport, they are allocated a number based on their time of check-in, not when they pre-booked, and this determines the order in which they board the aircraft. There are no seat reservations.

Hub airports in the UK are the relatively uncongested and quick-turnaround Luton and Liverpool; destinations are concentrated in Scotland and continental Europe, including Athens, Barcelona, Geneva and Nice. All the aeroplanes are relatively new Boeing 737s, painted white and orange and featuring EasyJet's telephone number on the side. The airline became profitable for the first time in 1998 and was floated successfully in 2000. Its valuation was £860 million.

Stelios had studied in the UK, at the London School of Economics and City University, and then worked for his father for a short while. He began his first business, Stelmar Tankers, in 1992. EasyJet's strategy was modelled on Southwest Air, but Stelios claimed he had also been inspired by Richard Branson and Virgin Atlantic. Like Branson, Stelios flies on his own planes and talks to the passengers – in his case several times a week, as he commutes to Luton from Nice, which is close to his home in Monte Carlo. A television 'docusoap' on EasyJet, which began in 1998, has continued to show that Stelios is regularly present at Luton (his headquarters) and is willing to help resolve passenger problems. It also shows how he enjoys wide visibility and acceptance as someone who has made a difference.

Claiming to be a shy, private person, Stelios says he has polished a number of small-talk subjects to give him the confidence to deal with strangers.

I lead by example. I believe that people will do things if they see their boss doing exactly the same things...the best way to motivate a team is to convince them they're always under attack...having an external enemy is the best way of focusing their mind on results, rather than fighting each other and becoming complacent...I'm keen that important information is available to everybody in the company...there are no secrets.

The EasyJet 'product' is, in reality, a package of services, many subcontracted in. EasyJet provides the planes and their crews, and markets and sells the flights. As a company, it is focused. Check-in and information services, snacks (for passengers to buy before they board the aeroplane), baggage handling and fleet mainte-nance are all bought-in from specialists.

More recently, the serial entrepreneur Stelios has personally diversified into other activities, all based in some way on the Internet. EasyEverything, when it opened in London, was the world's largest Internet café; it had 400 screens and lower prices than its rivals. The chain has since expanded. In 1999, Stelios announced plans for financial services via the Internet, which he christened EasyMoney; and in early 2000 he unveiled Easy Rent-a-Car, where cars can be rented only via a website. The cars are all small Mercedes and, although there are various extra charges for insurances and so on, the basic hire charge is lower than its main rivals. Since then he has introduced EasyValue, a price-comparison website, and is said to be thinking next of EasyCinemas.

In 2002, Stelios announced that he would step down from day-to-day executive control within the next 12 months to focus on his other businesses, which are much less profitable – especially the Internet café chain. His successor will be Ray Webster, a seasoned executive Stelios recruited from Air New Zealand.

Go was an entrepreneurial initiative conceived by Robert Ayling when he was chief executive of BA. It was a start-up company wholly owned by BA, which invested £25 million in the venture – not all of which was to be spent at once!

Go was to provide a low-cost, limited-frills service on selected European routes from a base in Stansted. Whilst BA and Go served the same destinations, the product on offer was different. BA wanted to compete with Ryanair and EasyJet without compromising its existing image and strategy. The prices would be competitive with its main rivals, and much lower than BA's, but Go would sell food and drink on board and provide seat allocations. In these respects Go 'broke ranks' with the Southwest Air model replicated by Ryanair and EasyJet.

Yet again, Boeing 737s were the chosen planes. Some pilots were recruited from BA, but the staff were largely new recruits. Telephone sales staff would provide a round-the-clock service.

Barbara Cassani was to run the new airline. Born in Boston in 1960, Cassani had been a management consultant in Washington before moving to London. She was the youngest child of three; her father was a bacteriologist who had become a laboratory equipment salesman. As he had moved around in his job, she had attended several schools. 'Hard work was the family motto' – her father continued to work well into his seventies.

She joined BA in 1987 and had a number of posts before being made general manager for BA in New York in 1993. Four years later she was restless and looking for a new challenge. Feeling hemmed in by BA's organisation structure and style, she had told Ayling she might leave to start her own business, and he believed she might be the right person to champion Go. She was invited to return to London and investigate its potential.

Ayling believed she had 'energy, intelligence, motivational skills and ambition' and knew she was 'very up-front with people', straight rather than 'touchy-feely'. She was a thorough organiser who 'led from the front and kept things simple'. She also had a real sense of urgency and could be impatient. A focused person, she believed in using time effectively – as a working mother married to an investment banker, she had to.

Cassani came to believe that budget airlines are about 'personalities and profile', and that image is vitally important, as the competing products are not differentiated. Interestingly, Stelios Haji-Ioannou was provoked into a reaction, and he claimed that BA was subsidising Go unfairly. This began a 'war of words' in the two companies' advertisements, which has persisted.

Go was begun in 1998 at Stansted in open plan offices with an informal style of management. Systematically spending BA's £25 million, over 30 routes were opened, and a second hub was established in Bristol. By early 2001, although there were accumulated losses, Go was trading profitably. By this time

Ayling had left BA and the company's strategic priorities had changed. BA was now focusing more on first- and business-class passengers, and Go no longer seemed as important. Having behaved entrepreneurially when it made sense to do so, BA was now willing to sell Go.

In June 2001, Go was the subject of a management buy-out financed by 3*i*. Turnover had reached £160 million a year with nearly 3 million passengers. The company was valued at £110 million, with BA receiving £80 million immediately and the remainder being dependent upon future performance. Cassani acquired a 4 percent stake and remained as chief executive. Another 18.5 percent of the shares were made available for 19 senior managers to purchase, and for future share-option schemes for all current and future employees. The company was looking for an initial public offering in two years time.

In the event, 3*i* would recoup its investment in just one year. In Spring 2002 EasyJet negotiated to buy Go for almost £400 million and thus became a larger airline than Ryanair. Some critics argue it will lead to a rise in prices – but Ryanair is still in the competitive frame. A multi-millionaire from the deal, Cassani opted to leave rather than work for EasyJet. Some Go managers joined EasyJet; others followed Cassani. Many of them had become instant millionaires through their shares and options.

It becomes an interesting debate as to whether 3*i* was truly funding entrepreneurs when it supported the management buy-out, or strategically investing for the best return. Regardless, the release of corporate entrepreneurship was reinforced at the time.

The other debate concerns the price EasyJet has paid to acquire its rival. There is always the risk of overpayment – an almost fourfold increase in Go's value in just one year is remarkable. But the value of market leadership may be significant in years to come. If EasyJet's new management team becomes overstretched trying to fuse together two airlines with slightly different strategies and clearly different cultures, it is always possible that entrepreneurship and value might be destroyed, albeit temporarily.

In these four stories, we have seen evidence of a number of important character themes of the entrepreneur.

We have seen:

» How successful entrepreneurs are able to stay **focused** on key business issues, initiating strategic actions and maintaining the momentum of change and growth.

» The importance of a clear and winning strategy, one which promises and delivers something valuable for all stakeholders, but especially the customers. This is competitive **advantage**.

» **Creativity** and innovation in action.

» The desire of certain people with a strong **ego** to make a difference with the things they do and achieve. They are agents of change.

» How people are at the heart of business success and how they must be motivated and led effectively. Successful businesses are dependent on effective **teams**.

Chapter 20 Retail Entrepreneurs

In this chapter on retailers we look at four entrepreneurs and one entrepreneurial organisation.

» The late Sam Walton, founder of retail giant Wal-Mart, was arguably the world's greatest retailer. In him we see further evidence of the character themes of the entrepreneur.

» New Zealand's largest non-food retailer, Stephen Tindall, similarly exhibits the character themes, but in him we also see evidence of a strong social element.

» Archie Norman is a corporate entrepreneur who successfully rejuvenated the supermarket chain Asda.

» Our fourth story charts the rise and decline of Marks & Spencer (M&S), a truly innovative retailer for many years. We see how a loss of outstanding entrepreneurial leadership can cause attention to be drawn away from the key contributions an entrepreneur brings to an organisation. The question is: with renewed entrepreneurship can M&S regain its prominent place in the high street?

» Finally, the example of Gerald Ratner highlights that there is a potential danger when a particular character theme is present to an unusually high degree. Ratner possessed a very strong ego and this contributed towards his personal downfall – his family company has survived without him leading it.

Sam Walton: the world's greatest retailer

» **Sam Walton was a truly great retailer. His Wal-Mart stores provide huge ranges and choices of household goods.** Prices are kept low through scale economies and a first-class supply-chain network. Despite their size the stores seem friendly, and Walton employed people simply to answer customer queries and show them where particular goods were shelved. A visionary, he was focused and dedicated. He worked long hours and 'talked retailing outside work'. Strong on the people and team elements, and willing to take measured risks, Walton sought to learn from other organisations. In this respect he was opportunistic but reflective. He never claimed to be an original thinker, and he networked widely to find his new ideas.

Born in 1918 in Missouri, and raised in relative poverty, Walton started earning money by selling newspapers when he was very young. As a footballer he showed he was highly competitive, a trait which again proved valuable when he started his career in retailing. After he graduated in 1940 he began selling shirts in a J.C. Penney store. Because of a minor heart murmur he was not drafted for the war effort, and instead worked in a gun-powder factory. Afterwards, in partnership with his brother, he took on the franchise for a Ben Franklin five-and-dime store in Arkansas.

The two brothers bought additional outlets, abandoned counters in favour of self service, established central buying and promotion, and quickly became the most successful Ben Franklin franchisees in America.

In 1962, the same year that K-Mart began opening discount stores in larger cities, Walton began with discount stores in small towns. Both had seen the concept pioneered elsewhere. Walton's principle was simple – mark everything up by 30 percent, regardless of the purchase cost. This proved to be a winning formula and his advantage. He toured, observed, absorbed and learned to develop his 'buy it low, stack it high, sell it cheap strategy'. Walton's first Wal-Mart store opened in Arkansas in 1962; turnover now exceeds the figures for McDonald's, Coca-Cola and Disney combined! With 3600 stores in the US alone, and with annual sales of $85 billion, Wal-Mart is the world's largest retailer. It is exceeded by only the Indian National Railways, the Russian Army and the British National Health Service in terms of numbers employed. Yet the wealthy Sam Walton is alleged to have driven himself around in a pick-up truck and to have been a mean tipper!

With annual sales of $85 billion, Wal-Mart is the world's largest retailer

Growth was gradual in the early years, but there were 30 Wal-Mart stores by 1970. Once Walton opened his own distribution warehouse (another idea he copied), growth exploded. In addition, Wal-Mart was the first major retailer to share sales data

"We got
big by
replacing
inven-
tory with
information"

electronically with its leading suppliers. 'We got big by replacing inventory with information.' Wal-Mart has always been careful to contain the risk by 'not investing more capital than is justified by results'. But Walton was always willing to try out new ideas, quickly abandoning those which did not work. He successfully combined emergent strategy with his vision to create a potent organisation and formula. He was creative and innovative.

Walton's very strong ego was manifested in three guiding principles: respect for individual employees, service to customers ('exceed their expectations') and a commitment to excellence. An intuitive and inspirational retailer, Walton was also a cheer-leading orator and inspirer. He preached that 'extraordinary results can come from empowering ordinary people'. His showman style was also reflected in 'glitzy store openings'. He created a 'culture that in many ways represents a religion – in the devotion it inspires amongst its associates and in the Jesuit-like demands it makes on its executives'. Following the lead of the John Lewis Partnership in the UK, Walton called his employees 'associates' and personally spent much of his time in stores exchanging ideas with them. Profits were shared with employees. 'Ownership means people watch costs and push sales.' Walton provided support for many good causes, but largely anonymously. He possessed the Social character theme, but kept it low-key.

Recognising his own weaknesses, Walton recruited an analytical businessman, David Glass, to be his second-in-command. Glass commented once that Walton 'wasn't organised – I saw one store he was running with water melons piled outside in temperatures of 115 degrees'. Glass has continued as CEO after Walton's death.

Founded by an individual entrepreneur, Wal-Mart has become an entrepreneurial business; its growth and prosperity has continued after the death of the founder. Wal-Mart is now expanding selectively into other countries, and acquired Asda in the UK in 1999. Asda is discussed later in this chapter.

Stephen Tindall: the benevolent retailer

New Zealander Stephen Tindall first dreamed of becoming a doctor – but placed in an advanced class at primary school he fell behind with reading and lost his self-confidence. Later discovering he had a natural ability as a swimmer, he trained hard and became a long-distance champion. He regained his self-confidence and became head boy at his grammar school. His grades were too low for medical school, so he opted to study for a degree in physiotherapy.

So far in his life he had demonstrated focus, dedication, determination and tenacity.

Friends at university persuaded him to think instead about a career in business. Stephen's great-grandfather had opened one of Auckland's leading department stores, which was still run by his cousins. He joined, starting at the bottom. He stayed for 12 years, rising through merchandising to become promotions manager. During this time he studied part-time for a business diploma.

Tindall had always enjoyed talking to people and he quickly showed he had a natural affinity with customers. He also travelled the world in search of new product opportunities. He was looking for a new advantage. Demonstrating profit orientation, he openly expressed disappointment that profits at Courts were decreasing as turnover went up. The company, he believed, needed to reduce its overheads.

In 1982 he opted to start his own business, scraping together NZ$40,000 to do so. The Warehouse was born. It was to become New Zealand's largest non-food retailer. By the late 1990s there were 95 stores – 71 for general merchandise, 24 for stationery – and NZ$1 billion in sales.

Tindall leased premises and obtained slow-moving stock from an import wholesaler on sale-or-return arrangements. He believed that with tight stock control – and for this he invested most of his start-up capital in information technology – low prices, strong presentation and promotion, he could move the stock. He proved he was right – and when he needed to discount his prices even further he renegotiated his sale-or-return deal. He had his advantage.

Soon there were more stores. Then he moved from North Island to South Island. Full-time staff joined his casual part-timers. The Warehouse was a popular employer with extensive employee benefits.

He looked after his staff as well as his customers. His mission statement included the words 'where people come first and quality is affordable'.

His stores were essentially large sheds which were

painted bright red. They had concrete floors and aisles stacked high with merchandise. Eventually the product range spread to include clothing, electrical goods, music, hardware, furniture, shoes, toys and gardening equipment – all at bargain prices, because he always bought in bulk. The logo was 'where everyone gets a bargain'.

He advertised extensively, with a promotion budget of 3.7 percent of turnover, nearly four times the retail average for New Zealand. Full-colour brochures were regularly posted through letterboxes.

The first Warehouse Stationery store – for office supplies – was opened in 1992, painted bright blue.

The company was floated in 1994. Existing shareholders retained 80 percent of the stock, with Tindall and his family holding control with 53 percent. The 14.5 percent sold to outside investors and the 5.4 percent to employees at favourable prices raised NZ$54 million.

In 1996 sales grew rapidly but profits fell. Tindall openly confessed that the business had grown too quickly and controls had been lost. The whole management team accepted a salary reduction. Within a year the situation had been turned around again.

In 1995 Stephen Tindall demonstrated his Social character theme. He put 23 percent of Warehouse shares into a charitable trust, the Tindall Foundation. The dividends they earned would be used to support groups – many of them volunteer groups – who work to support families, employment generation and the environment. Initially this meant NZ$3 million a year, but now it is over four times this amount.

The idea was always 'a hand-up not a hand-out', with a philosophy of helping those who wanted to help themselves. Tindall had wanted to 'start putting something back' when he saw the relative poverty of many people in the Philippines, from where he was buying extensively. He had started an educational foundation there.

A leader who dislikes hierarchy, Tindall now spends half his time at the Warehouse and half with the foundation.

The story of Stephen Tindall illustrates all six character themes:

» Tindall had a clear and focused strategy, with distinctive competitive advantage. He himself was focused and behaved with urgency, making things happen quickly – too quickly at one time. But he knew how to rectify the situation.
» The merchandising strategy reflects creativity and innovation.
» He 'dreamed of building a better New Zealand for every-one'. He possessed a strong ego.
» His 'people come first' philosophy confirms the team element of the business.
» Finally, the desire to 'put something back' adds a social dimension to the Warehouse.

Archie Norman: the corporate entrepreneur

Archie Norman is, in fact, the entrepreneurial strategic leader who 'made a difference' at Asda by pioneering change and instilling a new culture. Asda is the UK's third-largest supermarket group, behind Tesco and Sainsbury. Its initial growth and success came in the 1960s when it began to open out-of-town supermarkets – large stores at that time, but relatively small in today's terms – largely in the north of England, where the company has always been strongest. Asda's head office is still in Leeds, but the company has now developed nationally. In the 1980s Asda began to diversify, first into furniture retailing and then into carpets. This was followed by the acquisition of kitchen supplier MFI in 1985; two years later MFI became a management buy-out when the promised synergies proved illusory. Shortly after this, Asda bought 60 stores from Gateway and struck a deal with George Davies (the entrepreneur behind the growth and temporary fall of Next) which gave Asda the exclusive rights on a range of George-branded clothing. By the early 1990s Asda was, however, trading at a loss. Analysts concluded that the company lacked a strong corporate identity and it had become a reactive follower in its main industry.

A new chairman was appointed in 1991 and he recruited Archie Norman to be the new CEO. At this time, Norman was 37 years old. Originally a McKinsey consultant, he was then group finance director with retail group Kingfisher. When Norman became non-executive chairman in 1997 – after being elected a Conservative MP for Tunbridge Wells – Asda had regained its popularity and profitability. Together with his deputy – and successor for a time – Allan Leighton, Norman had transformed the company.

Although Norman 'took best practice from elsewhere and Asda-ised it', it was always believed that he used Wal-Mart as his model, and so perhaps it was no surprise when Wal-Mart acquired Asda in 1999. David Glass, CEO of Wal-Mart commented of Asda: 'I have not seen such passion for a company amongst its employees – except at Wal-Mart'.

What exactly had Norman done? Furniture and carpets had been divested at the earliest opportunity. The business had been split into two distinct parts: the (large) supermarkets – Asda owns some of the largest food stores in the UK – where the non-food ranges were strengthened, and smaller, local, stores with a limited range of grocery products. The whole business was refocused on 'ordinary working people who demand value'; advertising used the slogan 'That's Asda Price!' to reinforce an average saving of some 5 percent against Tesco and Sainsbury prices.

High productivity and high levels of service have been derived from a committed and involved staff, who have seen many changes in their working lives. People are known as 'colleagues'. A successful suggestion scheme, Tell Archie!, generated 45,000 suggestions in five years, and Norman read them all. Incentives are linked in to the scheme, and employees can also benefit from share options and training at the Asda Academy. Since 1995, colleague circles have also provided an effective forum for staff involvement in customer service innovation. 'A failing organisation is almost invariably an organisation that ceases to innovate and to experiment because innovation and experimentation are risky' (Archie Norman). At head office there are no reserved parking spaces, and everyone works in large open plan offices. Staff are encouraged to wear Asda baseball caps when they do not want to be disturbed by their colleagues. In relative terms, store management has grown at the expense of head-office staffing.

Marks & Spencer: the rise and stutter of a retail empire – a story of lost creativity and innovation

Marks & Spencer (M&S) is a well-known and revered high-street retailer in the UK. All its products are exclusive – there are no outside brands on offer. Every shopping centre developer wants M&S to open a store, as they always attract customers. Throughout its history, M&S has had several 'strategic leaders', but some – entrepreneurs – stand out from the rest.

In 1985, management author and guru Peter Drucker summarised M&S as

probably more entrepreneurial and innovative than any other company in Western Europe these last fifty years…may have had a greater impact on the British economy, and even on British society, than any other change agent in Britain, and arguably more than government or laws.

But recently this great retailer has stuttered.

The original foundations of the business lay with a young, Jewish immigrant and his Leeds market stall. Michael Marks had a poor grasp of English, a clear disadvantage for a trader in a noisy street market! Opportunistically, he turned his disadvantage into a strength. He had a sign on his stall: 'Don't ask the price – it's a penny', and for a penny he provided the widest range and best-quality items he could find.

The early growth of M&S was built around clothing, and its reputation owes much to the popularity of its underwear! But it built a second reputation for foods, pioneering chilled, fresh varieties. Other ranges such as cosmetics, homeware, gifts and furniture were added gradually and systematically.

This philosophy of 'value for money' has pervaded through the generations and been sustained with innovation and change. The market stall led to a store, and then to stores on most high streets in Britain. The Spencer name came from Marks's first partner, Tom Spencer, who acted as the company's accountant.

However, the Marks family became related to the Sieff family through marriage and it is these two families who dominated the business for most of its history. Indeed, Simon Marks, Michael's son, who controlled the business from 1916–64, and Marcus Sieff, who succeeded him, are regarded as 'retail geniuses' and the people who established and cemented in place M&S's high-street dominance. They were both entrepreneurs.

M&S has always sought to be innovative in upgrading and adding value to its existing ranges.

M&S has always sought to be innovative in upgrading and adding value to its existing ranges

In the 1930s M&S pioneered a new form of inventory control when it designed perforated tags in two identical halves. Half was torn off at the point-of-sale, dropped in a box and then sent to the Baker Street (London) head office – where it was used to direct store replenishment. Over time this enabled M&S to introduce sophisticated replenishment from out-of-town warehouses and reduce the in-store stockrooms in favour of more direct selling space.

There has been some international growth in countries such as France, Belgium, Canada, the US and Hong Kong. The development has been gradual, with one of the objectives being to introduce new types of competition. Some mistakes have been made as part of the learning process, and sales in some countries have been disappointing, but the risks were generally contained in order not to threaten the UK interests. International growth proved to be a strategy which M&S reversed.

The foundation for the unique products and competitive prices was the M&S system of supply-chain relationships, a considerable proportion of these being with UK manufacturers for much of its history. Generally, where they have been successful, the arrangements with suppliers have been long-term and non-contractual. They have been based on mutual trust and common understanding. M&S was always actively involved in product specification, material sourcing, quality control and production scheduling at its suppliers. M&S has typically been a supplier's most important customer. It has worked so effectively because the M&S reputation for fair dealing – with its suppliers, customers and employees – was seen as too valuable to put at risk.

In recent years M&S has – somewhat controversially – included more and more goods sourced overseas, sometimes for particular innovation and quality reasons, but mostly to lower costs.

In addition, M&S provided a comprehensive benefits package for its employees, and became 'the place to work' on the high street. With redundancies in recent years, this reputation has also been tarnished.

Simply, the networking and team strengths had diminished.

At the end of the 1990s, this long-established business was suffering sales and profits declines. Critics argued that:

» Too many product ranges were no longer the winners people associated with the company – it had lost touch with its core customers. M&S had lost focus.

» The 'value' element had been partially lost as margins had been deliberately increased beyond the 10 percent maximum that Marks had always insisted upon. Some of the advantage had been lost.

» Its management needed strengthening at all levels – since the mid-1980s the company's strategic leaders have not been descendants of one of the founding families, and in the 1990s there was a perceived arrogance at the top. The entrepreneurs had disappeared; arrogance and complacency had replaced ego.

Senior management changes became normal as results did not improve. To help restore creativity to its crucial female fashion ranges, M&S recruited the help of George Davies. A wealthy man, Davies has invested £21 million of his own money into his Per Una range for M&S. An entrepreneur, Davies has insisted he retains total control over design, manufacture and display of his products. Sales of Per Una clothes were ahead of target from the first day they were launched in 2001.

Gerald Ratner: a risky ego trip

The story of Ratner's recounts a business which has managed to survive the fall from grace of a high-profile entrepreneur, who has himself made a comeback – a serial entrepreneur through necessity as much as choice.

Gerald Ratner was born in 1949 and became joint managing director of the family business of jewellery retailing in 1978. By 1984 he was sole managing director, and by 1986, chairman. He saw a real opportunity in critical mass and in product standardisation across a range of stores for low-cost, lower-quality fashion jewellery. He realised that some people will treat jewellery as discardable rather than a lifelong investment. He used Focus and Advantage to the full.

A major competitor, H. Samuel, was acquired in order to yield the critical mass. To ensure standardisation, everything was sourced centrally. Staff at head office experimented with window designs and layouts, and when they were satisfied they took photographs which were sent to every branch. Exactly the same layout, down to the position of an individual ring on a tray, had to be replicated in every branch. The business invested in advertising and promotion. Later on, Ratner's bought other retail outlets – such as Zales (jewellers) and Salisbury's (principally leather goods) which were acquired from Next.

Ratner was very aggressive. 'I was a complete megalomaniac, very ambitious, very competitive. If another jeweller opened, I'd do anything to put him out of business.' The strategy worked, but it was always replicable. His rivals could follow – some did, even if they were smaller and less profitable. He was never a major threat to the expensive and exclusive specialist, of course.

Speaking at an Institute of Directors' Conference in 1991, Gerald Ratner claimed that his company was able to sell sherry decanters at really low prices because they were 'total crap'. Ratner's continued success relied on its reputation for slickness and efficiency; denigrating his company's products in this way would prove a 'bridge too far'. The tabloid newspapers seized on the comment and were very critical, and the company's previously strong image was damaged; profits became losses. The group name has subsequently been changed to Signet, and although the company has been turned around by a new management team and trades profitably again, the name Ratner's has disappeared from the high street. Ratner himself was forced to resign, devastated by the reaction to what he saw as a light-hearted, throwaway comment.

There is always a potential danger if a character theme is exceptionally strong. Ratner had made a difference to jewellery retailing. He was strong on the Ego facet. Unfortunately his ego was so strong that he deluded himself into believing he could say almost anything and get away with it. He was wrong!

Ratner spent four years recovering from this setback, saying that 'my esteem was low for a long time'. He did find work, though, at one time letting office space for a property developer in Canary Wharf.

In 1996, Ratner spotted a new entrepreneurial opportunity. He saw that one of the richest towns in the country, Henley-on-Thames, did not have a health club. The sixth bank that he approached was willing to back his proposed new venture; he also had financial support from friends. Reflecting his project-championing skills, he advertised for members and signed up 500 prospects before he committed himself to a lease on a warehouse he planned to convert. He planned a luxury, upmarket health club – and he knew he needed to open without delay. Once other property developers realised there was a gap in the market, they might try and beat him by being first to open.

He began work with a colleague/partner who was destined to be the general manager after it opened. In the end there were tensions, and Ratner took over control of day-to-day responsibilities. Perhaps Team is not a particularly strong character theme with Ratner.

Changes to the specification were made as the conversion progressed; Ratner decided to add both a crèche and a pool. The target break-even increased from 700 to 900 members. On the day of the official opening the complex was not completely ready, but Ratner went ahead anyway. It was reopened two months later, when it was fully complete; and very quickly the membership topped the thousand mark.

Ratner said he was determined that this time his style and approach would be more restrained. 'My ambition has gone,' he claimed. Well, maybe not altogether, because he was soon talking about the prospect of opening more clubs.

In 2002, Gerald Ratner set out to raise money to build a new business selling jewellery over the Internet.

Chapter 21 **Now it's Your Turn!**

So far this book has been about recognising the entrepreneur within. Now it is time to release it – to achieve your potential and go with your talents. It may be you will have to pull yourself out of a rut or take some particular initiative. This may test and challenge your temperament but it is all part of the process.

It may be that you do not feel you have the necessary entrepreneurial facets to really succeed as an entrepreneur or that your enterprise or the company you work for does not offer you sufficient opportunity.

As a final test of these issues we invite you to consider:

» The relative strength and distribution of your entrepreneur facets. Are you or could you be an entrepreneur? Or are you perhaps more of an entrepreneur enabler?

» The quality of your business or other initiative – or any project you are working on – when measured against the entrepreneur action points.

» Whether your organisation is one that welcomes corporate entrepreneurs and intrapreneurs and helps them to feel at home.

When you have worked your way through these evaluations please do not simply treat them as an interesting piece of personal research. Think about what they imply and what they say about you and your organisation.

We conclude by suggesting that you set yourself three practical first steps to help you to achieve your potential.

Are you an entrepreneur?

Your facets self-assessment

To remind you of the areas in which you made up your assessment, we show a summary of the elements that make up the facets.

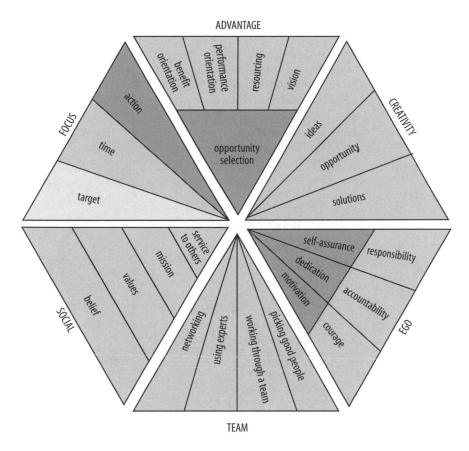

Facets of the entrepreneur: complete hexagon

In chapters 7–13 you were encouraged to give yourself a score for each of the elements and come up with a final score for each of the six facets character themes. We now suggest that you transpose all your scores – an overall score for the theme and the sub-element scores from which your overall score is derived – onto the summary table overleaf.

First evaluation chapter 7	Score	Detailed evaluation chapters 8–13	Score	Final evaluation	Score
Focus (p. 71)		Target (p. 85) Time (p. 86) Action (p. 88)		Focus (p. 88)	

Advantage (p. 71)		Opportunity
		  selection (p. 93)
		Benefit
		  orientation (p. 95)
		Performance
		  orientation (p. 98)
		Resourcing (p. 98)
		Vision (p. 98)
				Advantage (p. 98)	

Creativity (p. 71)		Ideas (p. 112) Opportunities (p. 112) Solutions (p. 112)		Creativity (p. 112)	
Ego (p. 72)		Entrepreneur desire (p. 120) *Inner Group* (p. 120) Responsibility (p. 123) Accountability (p. 123) Courage (p. 129) *Outer Group* (p. 129)		Ego (p. 129)	

Team (p. 72)		Picking good
		  people (p. 140)
		Working through
		  a team (p. 140)
		Using experts (p. 140)
		Networking (p. 141)
				Team (p. 142)	

Social (p. 73)		Belief (p. 154) Values (p. 154) Mission (p. 154) Service to others (p. 154)		Social (p. 154)	

We now suggest you carry out three separate but linked analyses of your scores to assess the implications.

First-pass evaluation

Look at your six facets scores down the right hand side in the summary table. If you have a set of scores between 8 and 10 – and with no 'off-the-scale' extremes – you clearly have all the makings of a successful entrepreneur. You may already be one!

If all your scores are 6 and above, with some in the 8+ band, you could also think of yourself as an entrepreneur – but with one proviso:

you need one, and preferably two, of your higher scores to be in the 'face' facets – Focus, Advantage, Creativity and Ego. It is these character themes that define the entrepreneur.

If all, or most, of your scores exceed 4, but you can't really boast any high ones, you are clearly enterprising but probably not a true entrepreneur. You have the potential to be innovative and enterprising, and you should look for suitable opportunities.

Second-pass evaluation

The next step is to look at your score for each individual character theme in turn.

Focus is critical for the entrepreneur. It deals with the all-important project championing role. It is about action and making things happen. Without an above-average score on Focus, you are probably not an entrepreneur. However, there are three aspects of Focus – target, time and action – relating to your ability to prioritise, your sense of urgency and your desire to activate. Your Focus score can come from a strength in any one of these, but target Focus is arguably the most influential. Check how your overall score is made up and what it says about your ability to Focus.

The main element of Advantage is opportunity selection, knowing which opportunity is potentially the most valuable and why. You will know if you have the knack for doing this. Check your opportunity selection score. Ideally it should not be less than 7 out of 10. People who find themselves in the right place at the right time may only discover they are not very good at opportunity selection when they try their second venture. This is one of the most important evaluations in this assessment of your facets strengths, so think about it carefully. Those who aspire to be entrepreneurs must not be weak in the Advantage facet.

The four sub-elements of Advantage build on this ability to select opportunities. You will have assessed yourself on benefit orientation, performance orientation, resourcing and vision. To take full advantage of the ability to select opportunities you will need to possess these four talents to a similar degree. Beware of a lower score on resourcing as this is something that lets down many would-be entrepreneurs. They fail because they are not able to solve the inevitable problem of lack of resources.

Creativity encompasses ideas, opportunities and solutions. If you score yourself high on ideas but much lower on opportunities and solutions, you may be more of an inventor than an entrepreneur. A relatively low score in Advantage (relative in the context of your scores overall) would reinforce the inventor classification. Solutions, along with your earlier Focus score, cover project championing.

For Ego, we asked you to provide separate scores for the inner and outer groups, and suggested that they should be in balance. A gap between them of just 1 or 2 points is acceptable, but it should certainly not be more than 3 points.

A strong (but not extreme) score on Ego defines your temperament as an entrepreneur; therefore a low score should cause you to ask questions. It is not inconceivable that you have entrepreneurial talents (in Focus, Advantage and Creativity) but lack the temperament to exploit these effectively.

Entrepreneurs always face setbacks and hurdles – it is part of an entrepreneur's life! Your ability to face these challenges is defined by your courage. So a high score in courage is ideal, and a low score should have you wondering.

Your Team score is based upon your scores for picking good people, working through a team and using experts. If you can combine your strengths across these three you will have a powerful vehicle for magnifying your entrepreneurial talents. Never forget that this is one area where technique can help enormously. Training courses can be particularly helpful for addressing certain team issues.

However, the fourth element, networking, is slightly different. True entrepreneurs build networks of useful contacts by instinct. They know who could be useful to them, why and how – benefit orientation is an element of their Advantage facet. They are good at relating to other people and building relationships. Part of this is a gregarious nature and it builds on the self-confidence and self-assurance elements of the ego. It is less easily trained.

A high Team score implies a potential to grow. Without effective support the entrepreneur must inevitably be held back.

Finally, your Social score depends upon how you have climbed the ladder of beliefs, values, mission and service to others. For the social entrepreneur, belief and values provide a mission and a desire to give service to others. A lower Social score might mean that there is a social element to your business and your style. Put simply, Social has a marked influence on the direction of a business.

Third-pass evaluation

Now, finally, it is important to look at the distribution of your six scores. Which are your higher ones, and which your lower?

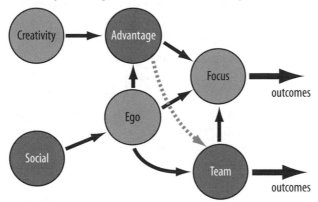

The facets relationship diagram

You will see from this commentary and the relationship diagram that the balance of your scores is significant.

Start with the Creativity–Advantage–Focus channel, which runs across the top and is a major driver of outcomes. As we have seen, Creativity provides the opportunities but Advantage and Focus are the exploitation skills. The true entrepreneur is both an opportunity spotter and a project champion. Therefore any marked imbalance in your three scores could be significant.

Ideally your three scores should be roughly equal. If they are an 'increasing funnel' – in other words, Focus is higher than Advantage, which in turn is higher than Creativity – this is OK. You may not come up with a huge range of ideas and opportunities, but you will be minded to exploit the opportunities you do spot.

If the opposite is the case – your 'score funnel' reduces – and Creativity is your highest score, then you have a problem. You will probably spot a lot of ideas, but not discriminate particularly well and be limited in your ability to exploit them. You could end up with an ideas or an opportunities bottleneck.

Next consider your Ego score. Ego feeds Advantage, Focus and Team. For this reason, Your Ego score really needs to be quite strong.

We have already said that if your Ego score is low, you may have entrepreneurial talent without the supporting temperament.

If, on the other hand, it is higher than your scores for Creativity, Advantage and Focus, then you may have another, different problem. It could have a distorting effect as temperamentally you overestimate your true talent. This can lead to misjudged risks and decisions.

Your Team theme feeds Focus and helps drive positive outcomes. Along with high scores for Advantage and Focus, a high Team score implies a high-growth business with fresh opportunities coming along all the time – habitual entrepreneurship.

However, a high Team score can sometimes compensate for a relatively low Focus score, as long as Creativity and Advantage are relatively high. In this case, the wise entrepreneur builds a strong and effective team with people who can make things happen.

We have said that without a relatively high Focus score you can't really be a true entrepreneur. And individually you can't. However, you can show real enterprise and build a strong entrepreneurial team and appear to the world to be the entrepreneur at its heart.

Here Team, instead of Focus, is exploiting Advantage in order to drive the positive outcomes. The dotted arrow on the diagram illustrates the point.

Your Social score can feed and dominate your Ego – in fact, it is the only character theme that can. If you are particularly high on Social it will have a major impact upon who you are and what you are looking to achieve from your business or your social initiative.

●────●

Now you will understand something about the entrepreneur within.

Maybe you already are an entrepreneur – running your own business or social project – or a corporate entrepreneur within a large organisation, be it private or public sector – and this has confirmed what you already knew. At least you will understand more about why you are successful.

Maybe you wondered if you had entrepreneurial potential and needed confirmation before you took a leap forward. Perhaps you have received that confirmation. But maybe you have learned enough about yourself to know that you are wise to think of yourself as a member of an entrepreneurial team, exploiting your talents and strengths but recognising your weaker spots.

It may be that you could excel as an entrepreneur enabler – someone who helps entrepreneurs along, giving them support when they need it, pointing them in the right direction or just simply encouraging them. Entrepreneur enablers play a crucial role in helping entrepreneurs to emerge. They are the people behind the spin-off points – those places which produce a steady stream of new businesses and which are so vital to the building of an entrepreneur culture in a region.

Typically, an entrepreneur enabler has high scores in two or three of the entrepreneur facets but lacks in others. Most commonly they are weak on Advantage or some aspects of Ego, such as courage or motivation. They may also be weak on Focus. This is not a criticism – it is just the way some people are.

But the entrepreneur enabler does, however, have something extra – the ability to talent scout and coach at the same time. People with this developer character theme enjoy enabling others, helping them to achieve their full potential. The entrepreneur enabler, because of the presence of some of the entrepreneur facets, directs this developer theme specifically towards the entrepreneur.

Entrepreneur enablers are often found in institutions or in the public sector where they can play to the entrepreneurial strengths they do have, where there are structures in place that support them and where they have access to people they can develop.

If you are neither entrepreneur nor entrepreneur enabler, you may still be an enterprising person. Creativity is the main facet here, which, combined with Focus, Advantage or Ego, produces different kinds of enterprising person. Perhaps you are one of these. If so, you have an important role to play in stimulating others and helping new ideas and initiatives along.

Your business/project health check

If you are going to be a successful entrepreneur you need the relevant facets – but you also need a good business or project proposition.

The following questions are derived from the 10 action points outlined in chapter 18.

Begin by allocating up to a maximum of 10 marks for each one, using the following criteria, and using the table which follows:

》 my answer is strong and convincing – 9 or (exceptionally) 10
》 my answer is reasonably convincing – 7 or 8
》 my answer is generally positive, but there are some doubts in my mind – 5 or 6
》 my answer is relatively unconvincing – I really need to do something about this – 3 or 4
》 I am at sea with this one – you've really got me thinking – 1 or 2
》 no idea at all – 0.

You are looking for an overall score of at least 65.

Question	Score
1	
2	
3	
4	
5	
6	
7	
8	
9	
10	
Total score	

1. Are you clear what it is you want to **achieve** with your business/project/initiative – for example growth, wealth, visibility and high profile, or survival?

   It doesn't matter what it is, as long as you are clear and positive about your answer.

2. How **different** is your (business) idea?
   Is it, for example, 'unique' on a local basis?
   Is it, essentially, a 'tweak' or an improvement on something similar?
   Could it be copied relatively easily by rivals?

   Your score here should be dependent on the extent of the perceived difference.

3. Would others see your initiative as genuinely **innovative**?
   In what way? Can you justify your claim?
   How might you sustain innovation?

4. Are you clear about the **opportunity** you are addressing?
    Do you know who your target customers are, and are you able to reach them?
    Do your (target) customers **recognise**, appreciate and value what you can do for them?
    Are they willing to pay you a suitable premium?
    You should halve your score for this question if these details are not articulated in a proper business plan.

5. What is your relationship with your **customers**?
    Are you sure you know what they expect of you?
    When did you last lose a customer?
    When did you last let a customer down?
    When did you last give real satisfaction that you know was appreciated, because the customer told you so?

6. Have you got access to the **resources** you need, such as money, people, premises and coaching?
    How do you get them – do you beg, steal, borrow or buy?
    Base your score half on the existence of the resources and half on the Creativity you used to acquire them.

7. Do you have a strong **network** of contacts?
    Do you claim to have 'know how', 'know who' and 'know where'?
    Do you keep records (formal or informal) of your contacts?
    What do you do with your collection of business cards?
    Who should you know that you don't know (well enough)?
    Add 3 bonus points if you have a proper system for maintaining regular contact with your network.

8. What was your most recent business **setback** and how did you deal with it?
    How well did you cope?
    How did you feel about it – positive, relieved or dispirited?
    What is your greatest fear about the business – and is this something you believe you can deal with?
    Add another 3 bonus points if you genuinely see this fear as a challenge rather than a problem.

9. If someone asked you, could you quickly identify the three most significant **risks** you face?
    Do they involve money? Employees? Customers? Your own limitations?

What is the extent of the possible downside?

What (if anything) are you doing to minimise the potential impact of these risks in the future?

What help might you need to deal with these risks in the future?

Add 5 bonus points if you can demonstrate plans to deal with these risks – but deduct 5 if you have done nothing to deal with the risks you face.

10. Are you in **control** of your business?

Do you know your cash and inventory situation today?

Do you know how much profit you made in the last month?

To what percent of capacity is your order book full in the next three months?

What is your maximum capacity, and what is involved in working at that level?

Corporate health check

You have evaluated yourself as an entrepreneur and carried out a health check on your business/project idea.

If you are a corporate entrepreneur you also need to ask:

» Is my organisation entrepreneurial?

» Do corporate entrepreneurs feel at home?

This checklist has been designed to achieve this. It comprises a set of 32 statements in 6 categories. The more you find yourself in agreement with the statements, the more welcoming your organisation is to the entrepreneur and the would-be corporate entrepreneur.

If you cannot answer at least 20 of the questions positively, your organisation will exhibit something of a hostile environment for the corporate entrepreneur. The target should be higher than 20, of course.

Read the 32 questions carefully, think about what they imply, and then decide whether you agree or disagree that they describe your organisation. There is a table for your answers on page 261.

The organisation

1. My organisation is imaginative, it is not rigid about the way things have to be done.
2. There is clear evidence of proactive changes as well as an ability to react swiftly when the unexpected happens.
3. We react to opportunities as well as threats.

Organisation structure

All organisations have producers ('doers'), organisers (junior and some middle managers and administrators), integrators (middle and certainly senior managers) and entrepreneurs (agents of change).

In my organisation...

4. Producers are given the opportunity and encouragement to put forward ideas about their work.
5. Organisers focus on exploiting people's strengths rather than worrying too much about their weaknesses. The work is moulded to the people rather than the other way round.
6. Integrators ensure knowledge is shared around the organisation.
7. Entrepreneurs are allowed a prominent role all the time, not just when reactive change is essential.

Ideas

8. My organisation has proper systems and channels for people to put forward ideas.
9. There is no rigid belief that all the good ideas always come from the senior people.
10. People are given time to work on new ideas and projects.
11. When someone puts forward a good idea it is easy to see how it is taken forward. There are proper mechanisms for developing and commercialising good ideas and opportunities.
12. Not only are there mechanisms, capital can be made available.
13. If the person who has the idea is the wrong person to take it forward – for whatever reason – this is not a hurdle.
14. People are told why their ideas can't or won't be taken forward – there is no feeling of being ignored and rejected.

Objectives

15. The organisation has a clear direction, which is articulated and which people understand and support.
16. People know which rules and regulations are important and they comply with them. However, they don't feel that their hands are tied so that they have no individual freedom.
17. People individually know what is expected of them. They know they are being stretched but, at the same time, supported.
18. People's personal objectives don't work against the organisation.

People

19. We could describe our people generally as enterprising and energised.
20. It is normal to encourage people to break out of their comfort zones from time to time.
21. We help people to learn from their mistakes so they are unlikely to repeat the same ones. They may make others, of course!
22. People know they can use their initiative to act on triggers – for example, if they see something happening inside the organisation or a trusted contact tells them something significant.

Communications

23. Information gets shared in our organisation. In particular it reaches the people – the decision-makers – for whom it could be useful.
24. Contacts and channels are informal as well as formal.
25. Communications are effective both vertically and horizontally. People talk and share regularly with others on their level in other parts of the business, and with their managers and subordinates. Organisational position is not a barrier.
26. Various people are in regular contact with our major customers and suppliers.
27. We are aware of what our competitors are up to.

Recognition and reward

28. People would say that our reward system is open and fair.
29. We are able to track individual contributions and reward those who deserve it. High contributors are rewarded. In fact, our entrepreneurs are treated as heroes!
30. Employees would not automatically say it is a question of who you know.
31. When people make mistakes they are not covered up. However, people are not sanctioned such that they avoid taking any further risks.
32. Poor performers are not simply allowed to get away with it. They can find support to help them improve, and they know they must improve.

	Question	'I agree'	'I disagree'
The organisation	1		
	2		
	3		
Organisation structure	4		
	5		
	6		
	7		
Ideas	8		
	9		
	10		
	11		
	12		
	13		
	14		
Objectives	15		
	16		
	17		
	18		
People	19		
	20		
	21		
	22		
Communications	23		
	24		
	25		
	26		
	27		
Recognition and reward	28		
	29		
	30		
	31		
	32		
		Total agree	Total disagree

What about you?

In this chapter, if not earlier, you will have formed a view as to your potential as an entrepreneur.

But you will only achieve your potential if you do something about it. Why not list three steps that you need to take to make it happen and put a target and an actual date alongside for when it does happen?

Step 1: target date:	actual date:
Step 2: target date:	actual date:
Step 3: target date:	actual date:

One step might be to take that redundancy package. Another might be to find a partner to provide some entrepreneurial facets where you are not so strong. Another might be linked with an opportunity.

If your scores showed that you were not an entrepreneur, then perhaps you are an entrepreneur enabler who can help other entrepreneurs along the way or an enterprising person who can contribute to the entrepreneurial process.

Whichever is the case you can still identify the three steps you need to take to be a more effective entrepreneur enabler or enterprising person.

»» How did your business or project opportunity score against the health check?
»» What does that tell you about your next steps?
»» If you work in a large organisation what did the corporate health check tell you?

You can draw up a similar three steps target list if you are a potential corporate entrepreneur.

The title of this book includes the phrase 'Achieve your Potential' – we all have a potential within us that needs to be freed up and released. Talents are there to be used, opportunities are there to be taken, skills are around that need to be acquired – this applies to all of us, whatever our role, but in this book we have focused on the entrepreneur.

We hope that as you have read through you have been able to discover whether there is an entrepreneur within trying to get free, and that you will take specific steps to do something about it.

Above all, we hope that, entrepreneur or not, you will do all you can to meet what we see is the real challenge of the twenty-first century: **the release of the entrepreneurial potential in our midst**.

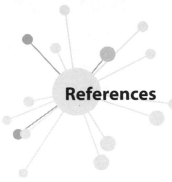

References

Here you will find details of the books and articles that we have used as source material.

Chapter 1

Crainer, S. (2001), *Business The Jack Welch Way*, Capstone
Larson, J.K. and E.M.Rogers (1986), *Silicon Valley Fever*, Unwin Counterpoint
Schumpeter, J. (1949), *The Theory of Economic Development*, Harvard University Press
Say, J.B. – see J.K.Galbraith (1991), *A History of Economics*, Penguin Books
re Philip Green – The *Times*, 16 January 2002

Chapter 2

re 'Charles' – Bygrave, B. (1998), Building an entrepreneurial economy: lessons from the United States, *Business Strategy Review*, 9 (2), 11–18

Chapter 5

Bolton, W.K. and J.L.Thompson (2000), *Entrepreneurs – Talent, Temperament, Technique*, Butterworth Heinemann

Chapter 6

Roddick, A. (2000), *Business as Unusual*, Thorsons, HarperCollins
Steiner, R. (1998), *My First Break*, News International
Dell, M. and C.Fredman (1999), *Direct from Dell*, HarperCollins Business

Chapter 7

Lowe, J. (1998), *Jack Welch Speaks*, John Wiley
Roddick, A. (2000), *Business as Unusual*, Thorsons, HarperCollins
Goleman, D. (1996), *Emotional Intelligence*, Bloomsbury
Sculley, J. (1987), *Odyssey: Pepsi to Apple*, Collins
Williams, S. (1993), *Breakout: Life beyond the Corporation*, Penguin
Best, G. (2001), *Blessed*, Ebury Press, Random House

re Linus Torvalds – *San Jose Mercury News*, September 1999
The Nature–Nurture model was included in Bolton, W.K. and
    J.L. Thompson (2000), *Entrepreneurs – Talent, Temperament, Technique,*
    Butterworth Heinemann

Chapter 8

Wallace, J. and J. Erickson (1993), *Hard Drive,* John Wiley
Wakelin (1997), *J. Arthur Rank,* Lion Publishing
Woolmar (1999), *Stagecoach,* Orion Business Books
Whybrow, P.C. (1999), *A Mood Apart*, Picador

Chapter 9

Gilder, G. (1986), *The Spirit of Enterprise*, Penguin
Woolmar (1999), *Stagecoach,* Orion Business Books
Steiner, R. (1998), *My First Break,* News International
Morita, A. (1994), *Made in Japan,* HarperCollins Business
Wakelin (1997), *J. Arthur Rank,* Lion Publishing
Welch, J. (2001), *Jack,* Headline
Roddick, A. (2000), *Business as Unusual,* Thorsons, HarperCollins

Chapter 10

De Architectum, *Vitruvius Pollio*, 1st century BC
re Stephen Hawking – The *Independent*, 12 January 2002
Kaplan, J. (1997), *Start Up,* Warner Books
Pais, A. (1982), '*Subtle is the Lord': The Science and Life of Albert Einstein,*
    Oxford University Press
Dyson, J. (1997), *Against the Odds,* Orion Business Books
Branson, R. (1998), *Richard Branson: Losing My Virginity,* Virgin
    Publishing
re Eric McKellar Watt – obituary in The *Times*, July 2001
Pendergast, M. (1996), *For God, Country and Coca-Cola*, Phoenix Paperback
Woolmar (1999), *Stagecoach,* Orion Business Books
Davies (2001), *The Eddie Stobart Story,* HarperCollins
Hammer, H. (1988), *Hammer: Witness to History*, Coronet edn, Hodder
    and Stoughton

Chapter 11

Davies (2001), *The Eddie Stobart Story,* HarperCollins
Wallace, J. and J. Erickson (1993), *Hard Drive,* John Wiley

Welch, J. (2001), *Jack*, Headline
Wakelin (1997), *J. Arthur Rank*, Lion Publishing
Forte, C. (1997), *Forte*, Pan Books
Folley (2001), *A Time to Jump*, HarperCollins
Law, A. (1998), *Open Minds*, Orion Business Books
Sculley, J. (1987), *Odyssey: Pepsi to Apple*, Collins

Chapter 12

Crainer, S. (2001), *Business The Jack Welch Way*, Capstone
Davies (2001), *The Eddie Stobart Story*, HarperCollins
Larson, J.K. and E.M.Rogers (1986), *Silicon Valley Fever*, Unwin
 Counterpoint
Welch, J. (2001), *Jack*, Headline
Forte, C. (1997), *Forte*, Pan Books
The Body Shop Charter
re bank manager advert – *Financial Times*, 2001

Chapter 13

Kennedy (2000), *Business Pioneers*, Random House
In the Field, Autumn 2001
re Brian Souter – *Scotland on Sunday*, December 1991
Forte, C. (1997), *Forte*, Pan Books
Fukuyama, F. (1995), *Trust*, Hamish Hamilton
Wakelin (1997), *J. Arthur Rank*, Lion Publishing
Roddick, A. (2000), *Business as Unusual*, Thorsons, HarperCollins
Dinnen (1996), *Rescue Shop*, Christian Focus Publications
— (2000), *Rescue Shop 2*, Christian Focus Publications

Chapter 15

Richard Branson: quotations extracted from various websites
Ken Morrison: material taken from articles in the *Yorkshire Post*
Alan Sugar: main source of quotations: interview in *Management Today*,
 April 2001
Brent Hoberman: main source of quotations: interview in *Management
Today*, January 2001
Mike Tamaki: public presentation in New Zealand, April 2002
Jack Welch: various websites and:
 Crainer, S. (2001), *Business The Jack Welch Way*, Capstone
 Lowe, J. (1998), *Jack Welch Speaks*, John Wiley

Samson, A. (1996), *Company Man*, HarperCollins

Welch, J. (2001), *Jack*, Headline

Eric McKellar Watt: based on an obituary in The *Times*, July 2001

Chapter 16

Davidson (2002), *Smart Luck*, Prentice Hall

Gidoomal, R. (1996), *UK Maharajahs*, Nicholas Brealey

Hanson, D. (1982), *The New Alchemists*, Little, Brown

Larson, J.K. and E.M.Rogers (1986), *Silicon Valley Fever*, Unwin Counterpoint

Wilson, J.W. (1986), *The New Venturers*, Addison-Wesley

Chapter 17

Aghion et al. (2002), *Competition and Innovation – An Inverted U Relationship*, DTI Working Paper

Davidson, A. (1999), Interview with John Browne, *Management Today*, December

Financial Times (2001), 'The World's Most Respected Companies', 17 December

Fradette, M. and S.Michaud (1998), *The Power of Corporate Kinetics – Create the self-adapting, self-renewing, instant action enterprise*, Simon and Schuster

Hamel, G. (1999), 'Bringing Silicon Valley Inside', *Harvard Business Review*, September–October

Lundin, S., H.Paul, and J.Christensen (2000), *Fish!*, Hodder and Stoughton

Morgan, G. (1993), *Imaginization*, Sage

Pinchot, G. III (1985), *Intrapreneuring*, Harper and Row

Terazano, E. (1999), 'Fresh impetus from the need to innovate', *Financial Times*, 25 June

The material on leader styles is summarised from: Thompson, J.L. (2001), *Strategic Management – 4th edition*, Thomson

Chapter 18

The action points material was first published in: Thompson, J.L. (1998), 'Will The Real Entrepreneur Please Stand Up!', Professorial Inaugural Lecture, University of Huddersfield, 6 October. ISBN 1 86218 018 0

A version of the entrepreneur process diagram appeared in Bolton, W.K. and J.L.Thompson (2000), *Entrepreneurs – Talent, Temperament, Technique*, Butterworth Heinemann

Index